Antonio Candido

ON LITERATURE AND SOCIETY

Antonio Candido

ON LITERATURE AND SOCIETY

*Translated, edited, and introduced
by Howard S. Becker*

PRINCETON UNIVERSITY PRESS

PRINCETON, NEW JERSEY

Library of Congress Cataloging-in-Publication Data

Cândido, Antônio, 1918–
[Essays. English. Selections]
On literature and society / Antonio Candido; translated, edited,
and introduced by Howard S. Becker
p. cm.
Includes bibliographical references and index.
Contents: On vengeance—Catastrophe and survival—Four
waitings—Repression's truth—Dialectic of malandroism—
An outline of Machado de Assis—Literature and
underdevelopment—Criticism and sociology : an attempt
at clarification—Teresina and her friends.
ISBN 0-691-03629-2 (alk. paper). — ISBN 0-691-03630-6
(pbk. : alk. paper)
1. Literature and society. 2. Literature and society—Brazil.
I. Becker, Howard Saul, 1928– . II. Title.
PN51.C32913 1995   809'.93355--dc20   94-32403   CIP

This book has been composed in Galliard

Princeton University Press books are printed on acid-free paper and meet the
guidelines for permanence and durability of the Committee of Production
Guidelines for Book Longevity of the Council on Library Resources

Printed in the United States of America

1   3   5   7   9   10   8   6   4   2

1   3   5   7   9   10   8   6   4   2
(Pbk.)

CONTENTS

Preface   vii

Introduction by Howard S. Becker   ix

CHAPTER ONE
On Vengeance   3

CHAPTER TWO
Catastrophe and Survival   22

CHAPTER THREE
Four Waitings   45

CHAPTER FOUR
Repression's Truth   75

CHAPTER FIVE
Dialectic of Malandroism   79

CHAPTER SIX
An Outline of Machado de Assis   104

CHAPTER SEVEN
Literature and Underdevelopment   119

CHAPTER EIGHT
Criticism and Sociology (An Attempt at Clarification)   142

CHAPTER NINE
Teresina and Her Friends   152

Index   195

PREFACE

IN SELECTING ESSAYS for this volume, from the large and varied body of Antonio Candido's work, I have tried to exemplify both the unity and the variety of that work, always looking for the essays that best embody his solutions to the literature-and-society problem.

So, first of all, I included essays on Western literature—on the theme of vengeance in Dumas's *The Count of Monte Cristo* and the themes of catastrophe and survival in the novels of Joseph Conrad, as well as the extended analysis in "Four Waitings" of four major works dealing with the situation of the worn-out society seeking, in conflict with the out-side, cultural and spiritual renewal.

I have also selected studies of Brazilian literature. Here the problem is complicated, because few people will have the patience to read lengthy analyses of works totally unfamiliar to them, as most Brazilian literature is to English-speaking readers. And yet to avoid these topics would only contribute to the problem. Here I chose a middle ground, with an essay on the Brazilian writer most well known outside Brazil, Machado de Assis, an essay designed to introduce Machado's work (much of it avail-able in English) to non-Brazilians, and a longer essay, which fully exem-plifies both Candido's analytic method and his gift for critical paraphrase and summary, on the nineteenth-century novel of the malandro, *Memórias de um sargento de milícias.*

Political themes are integral to Candido's work, and so I chose the short essay on the role of police and the long memoir about Teresina and her friends, in which political thought is dealt with explicitly and directly.

Finally, in addition to his gifts as an analyst of literary works, Antonio Candido is (despite his insistence otherwise) a first-rate sociological the-orist, and so I have included essays on criticism and sociology and on the situation of literature and writers in the developing world.

There are two major omissions. One of Candido's most important works is *Formacão de literatura brasileira: Momentos decisivos* (The de-velopment of Brazilian literature: Decisive moments) (São Paulo: Mar-tins, 1959). For the reasons already suggested, his description of a liter-ature almost all of which would be totally unfamiliar to readers of this volume weighed against including any of this work. I regret even more not using any of the short essays from *Na sala de aula* (In the class-room) (São Paulo: Ática, 1985), which deal with Brazilian poetry. The difficulties of translating poetry are well known, and, in this case, the problem would be doubly difficult, even were it within my powers, since his analyses make so much use of the sounds and rhythms of the Portuguese language, most of whose subtleties are integral to the effects he analyzes.

With these provisos, I believe that these essays give readers a good understanding of the breadth and scope of Candido's work and of the solutions he has provided and modeled for the perennial problem of art and society.

ACKNOWLEDGMENTS

Alan Sica, then editor of *Sociological Theory*, published the first of these translations, and without that encouragement I would probably not have dared a whole volume. Marcia Bandeira, Camillo Penna, and Gilberto Velho gave me useful advice on problems of translation, and Professor Candido went over the whole manuscript with care, found many errors, and made many invaluable suggestions. Dianne Hagaman read everything and asked tough but important questions. Mary Murrell saw merit in the project where others didn't and helped see it through to completion.

INTRODUCTION

Howard S. Becker

THE OPPOSITION of art and society is one of the great commonplaces of social theory: on the one hand, works of art (often, perhaps usually, literature, but encompassing music, visual art, drama, dance, and the rest) with all their internal complexities, mysteries, and aesthetic qualities; on the other, the society in which these works came into existence and in which people read and respond to them.[1] Only extreme formalists expect to understand works of art fully without referring to the organized social context they exist in. Only extreme sociologizers expect to understand those works completely by analyzing the conditions of their existence.

But: how to combine a full aesthetic appreciation, ordinarily provided by critics, of the works themselves with a sociological sense of the complex worlds in which artists create works and audiences respond to them?

Sociologists have considered these problems since the beginning of the discipline. The great names of the field—from Durkheim, Weber, and others of the founders to Pierre Bourdieu—have all weighed in with theories and research. Literary theorists from Taine, through the Frankfurt School, to the wide variety of critical theorists writing today have contributed their solutions. Many such discussions deal only with large-scale relations between the two realms of art and society considered in the abstract, not attempting the analysis of specific works of art. The ensuing heated, complex, arcane discussions have seldom produced much light: writers are usually more interested in proving that "their variable" is the important one than in understanding the works in context, or they get so involved in the detailed analysis of specific works that they lose sight of the general connections.[2]

Antonio Candido (pronounced KHAN-dji-du), for many years one of Brazil's leading men of letters, has, in books and essays published over the last fifty years, proposed effective ways of dealing with this classical problem and has provided exemplars of those methods at work. He combines detailed literary analysis with profoundly sociological insights. His writing has a quality, a profundity, a grace, and a penetration that, combined with the originality of his thought, ought long ago to have led to his recognition in the world outside Brazil. But, since Antonio Candido writes in Portuguese, and his work has never appeared in English or French or German (and in Spanish only in 1991),[3] it has never been read by the people who would recognize its worth had they seen it. The essays presented here will make his contribution more widely available.

This brief introduction discusses the problem of "literature and society"; describes Candido's perspective on it and especially the way he combines the analysis of works of literature with an understanding of the nature of society; tells something about Brazil and about Antonio Candido's life and work; and, finally, takes up the question of his Brazilianness, how being a writer and thinker in a developing country appears in his writing.

The Art-Society Problem

We can see the strength of Candido's approach by comparing it to common practice among those sociologists of art and culture and those literary critics and analysts who are interested in the idea that art is influenced by or connected to the society it is produced in.[4] Such analysts typically assert such a connection, then demonstrate it by pointing to congruences between specific works of art, specific aspects of those works, and specific aspects of the society in which the works were made.

The tricky part of all such formulations is the verb used to describe the connection, the term that specifies how the society actually does something to the work or how the work incorporates whatever it gets from the society. If we ask how the congruences between society and work have come about, the usual answer is that the latter reflects the former. "Reflection" envisions the literary work as a mirror, whose surface picks up and sends back whatever is placed before it. But this vague metaphor simply asserts that there *is* a connection, leaving the specific mechanisms unexplored.

Analysts, recognizing this weakness, have proposed many ingenious substitutes for "reflect": "influence," or "be congruent with," or "resonate with," among others. The connection is often asserted visually, by drawing arrows between the words "art" and "society," the arrows serving as a still more vacuous description of what is going on.[5] Neither the verbs nor the pictures do the job. Each evades a detailed analysis of the process by which the world shows up in the work, and each is just a way (in this reproducing a common fault of scholarly writing) of alluding to something without taking the intellectual responsibility for making an assertion so concrete that investigation could prove it wrong. The vague conceptions of reflection, influence, and congruence reveal the simplicity and inadequacy of the sociology.

Some writers in this mode spend most of their time on the work itself.

Their kit of analytic tricks makes possible subtle analyses of the contents of literary works, the excavation of social references and influences in the details of plot, characterization, and literary style. But these writers seldom have a similarly detailed understanding of the social context of the work, nor an adequately detailed theoretical framework for creating such an understanding. They have a sophisticated literary theory, but a crude, homemade sociology.

Practitioners in this style, having alleged that such a nonspecific connection as a "reflection" exists, then make an analysis that, I have suggested, is no more than an ingenious searching out of congruences between social phenomena and details or elements in the work under analysis, a demonstration, for instance, that the work of literature being analyzed deals with themes characteristic of the period and place in which it was written. The congruences do not demonstrate any actual connection, only similarities, and their number is limited only by the analyst's cleverness.

Another version of this "art and society" approach, favored by sociologists who want to make use of the insights into and information about society to be found in fiction, treats the work as a kind of reportage. The work reflects society as a journalist's account does. Since many authors have had just such intentions, many literary works lend themselves to being taken as such reportage—the kind of work sociologists would do, if only they wrote that well and were as imaginative. Social analysis in fictional form also allows the introduction of the detail of case studies in a way that seems more difficult in social science texts (although it has been done, e.g., in W. Lloyd Warner's Yankee City books,[6] as well as in the detailed accounts of such ethnographies as *Street Corner Society*[7] and *Tally's Corner*).[8]

So: Stendhal's *The Red and the Black* becomes a report on social class and mobility in France of the period, James Farrell's *Studs Lonigan* a report on the Irish community of Chicago in the twenties, and so on. This becomes more interesting, but simultaneously far more speculative, when, say, Kafka's *The Trial* is read as another version of Max Weber's description of the "iron cage" of modern bureaucratized societies. In either case, the interest of the literature depends on the knowledge of social reality that went into the work's construction and on the ingenuity of the fictionalization. Like reportage, the more detailed the description, as in Farrell's description of Chicago's Irish community, the greater the necessity for point-for-point accuracy in the translation to fiction. Unlike reportage, such works can evoke a generalized mood that need not be accurate in the details, as Kafka's book is not an accurate description of a specific bureaucracy, only of the essence of the phenomenon.[9]

For many sociologists and sociologically minded literary historians, the alternative to a search for congruences between the work and the society has been to see an artwork as the product of networks of cooperation among all the people whose actions are necessary to the final product taking the form it eventually does and to see further how being made in such a network shapes a work.[10] Hennion calls this a "repeopling" of the worlds of art, a bringing back of all the intermediaries involved in the making of artworks, and notes that this repeopling leads the analyst to apply all the conceptual resources of a sociology of work and institutions to worlds of artistic activity.[11]

The strategy is exemplified in Sutherland's analysis of the way writing for serial publication led, in Victorian England, to the episodic plots of Thackeray and the early Dickens—authors did not bother to develop complex plots in the early chapters of novels they would not finish if sales were insufficient—and a wordy style, predictable if you are paid by the word.[12]

Leading to a complex understanding of how literary works acquire their characteristic features, this social network is an order of fact to which Antonio Candido often appeals (as in certain aspects of his analysis of Dumas's *Count of Monte Cristo*). Such social analyses are usually not accompanied by any deep analysis of the literary text itself.[13] Sociologists usually lack the command of languages and the breadth of literary and artistic experience needed to do justice to works of fiction and, if they have those, usually do not have the tools of literary analysis. So we learn from them about the conditions of production but not much about the way authors work with available materials under those conditions to produce specific works. The results are long on general features of the work: we learn that authors write lengthy, wordy novels in three volumes because fiction at the time was mainly distributed through lending libraries that relied on books so composed to maximize rental income. But such analyses are typically short on analysis of the details that give works their distinction and unique qualities. Why did Emile Zola emphasize stairways so much in his accounts of working-class Parisian life? And here is where Antonio Candido provides what is generally missing: because the image of the stairway allowed Zola to use a new fact of urban France, the presence of tall tenements in which workers lived, to embody the precariousness of social ascent and descent characteristic of workers' lives.[14]

This example exemplifies the distinctive analytic stance Candido brings to the debate, his insistence on the importance of the details of the work's structure as well as the details of the structure of society for understanding the relations between the two. For Candido, literature and sociology are not two different fields of study. The chief thread in his scholarly life has been "the search for an open and integrative mode [of analysis or criticism] that rises above [conventional academic divisions between social science and the humanities] in order to arrive at a more coherent point of view."[15] He remarks further, "Academic sociology and Marxism accentuated my tendency to study the social and ideological aspects of literature, and I created some mixtures that constituted my way of attempting the greatest possible amplitude and avoiding dogmatisms, without losing my guideline. I found this guideline above all in the notion of structure, linked to those of process and of montage, as terms of an integrated vision."[16]

So, he is alert to the infrastructure of literature: the numbers and distribution of readers, and the results for the productive apparatus of publishing, as in his essay (in this volume) on literature and underdevelopment. But he is equally alert to the more subtle relations between social practice and literary work, as when he remarks ironically, of *The Count of Monte Cristo*, that the bourgeoisie could have nourished their children with massive doses of the book, "Not as furtive or marginal readings, soon transformed into a pretext for playing; but rather, and above all, as assigned readings, analyzed by the teacher, as a major part of the school program, to the end of transfusing them into the thought and action of every hour."[17]

What Candido writes, then, is not just critical analysis, not just sociology, and not just general speculations on the connections between abstractions, but a combination that finds the operation of society in the way the work is put together, a combination heavily influenced by social science but focused (in the anthropological rather than the sociological style) on specific cases.

> The anthropological idea of culture, implying the ideas of totality and organicity, influenced my way of analyzing literary works. . . . one cannot, for example, do a comparative literary analysis by taking (let's say) the function of money in Machado de Assis, in Dostoyevsky, and in Balzac, and making a comparison pure and simple. It is necessary to consider the work of Machado as a whole to see how money functions in it. It will certainly function differently than in Dostoyevsky and Balzac, seen as totalities in which it is inserted. . . . I believe that anthropology attracted me to the degree that it had links with the literary attitude and allowed me to better satisfy my taste for the concrete. The anthropologist relies more on intuition, on empathy, on personal experience and can do individualized case studies.[18]

To sum up Candido's approach in a formula (dangerous in the case of so subtle a thinker), we might say that authors use the material of social observation and analysis as the basis of the *structure* of a work more than of its content. The most successful works, artistically, are those in which the form exemplifies the nature of the social phenomenon that furnishes the matter of the fiction. Not reflection or congruence, but the active effort of an author to create a *form* that successfully embodies a social analysis or understanding. Not judgments based on a fiction's success in reporting facts that support an author's social theories, but judgments of how well the author has created a form that augments and complements our understanding of the subject matter. Candido gives a memorable example in his analysis of the fragmented narrative technique of Conrad's *Lord Jim*: "the effectiveness of Conrad's art is not due to the simple proposal of an attitude of life, but to the fact of translating that attitude into a method of narration, which becomes an indissoluble part of what the novelist means since, in the end, it is what he effectively says."

Another example. In his analysis of the *Memórias de um sargento de milícias*, an early-nineteenth-century Brazilian novel,[19] he identifies the duplicity of Brazilian society of the time with the constant movement of the book's characters from high to low. That movement, which *is* the structure of the book, emphasizes the interdependence of upper and lower strata of a stratified society, of the respectably moral and the disreputably poor and deviant, of the highest human aspirations and the lowest conduct. (This will recall, for those acquainted with the so-called Chicago School of sociology, Everett Hughes's discussions of the dependence of "good" people on others who will do their dirty work,[20] a theme Candido takes up in several essays in this volume, especially "Repression's Truth" and the essays on Dumas and Conrad.)

Brazil and Its Intellectual Tradition in the Human Disciplines

Antonio Candido, having made his career in Brazil, writes and thinks in a way that embodies much that is Brazilian, so a little background is in order for those not familiar with that country. Brazil is larger than most North Americans and Europeans realize. Covering more than three million square miles, it has a population of about 140 million, according to 1991 estimates, and is as large as the rest of South America combined. But it is less known elsewhere than countries like Mexico or Argentina, almost surely because its national language is Portuguese rather than, as in the rest of South America, Spanish.

Spanish, like French, German, and English, is one of the several languages that can be called a world language, one that is understood beyond the borders of its home country. Scholars who work in such a language address each other in it and expect (sometimes quite unrealistically) scholars everywhere else to be able to read their work. Portuguese, on the other hand, like Dutch or Danish, is not a world language. Scholars who work in such languages may write for each other in them, but when they address the world they do so in one of the world languages; they know that "no one" reads their native tongue. Being relatively small, countries such as Denmark or the Netherlands cannot support a large scholarly output in their own language. But Brazil, a very large country, has an educated class large enough to support publication and diffusion of knowledge in the national language, and so, though Brazilian scholars are typically at home in at least French and English, they do not produce their major works in those languages. Scholars in the major world languages seldom read Portuguese, so a vicious circle creates an ignorance elsewhere of Brazil's sizable, varied, and interesting intellectual output. (My speculation about the reasons for this situation may be arguable, but the fact is not.)

As a result, Brazilian scholarship, while fully cognizant of and embedded in the traditions of Western thought, maintained, at least until the 1930s, a strong tradition of scholarship in the humanities and social sciences as "letters."As Candido explains:

> The powerful magnet of literature interfered with the sociological tendency, giving birth to that mixed genre of essay, constructed in the confluence of history with economics, philosophy, or art, which is the most Brazilian form of investigation and discovery in Brazil. . . . It is no exaggeration to say that this kind of essay—which combines more or less felicitously imagination and observation, science and art—constitutes the most characteristic and original feature of our thought.[21]

When we look back at the early stages of modern, professional American sociology, we see works of sociological research: *The Polish Peasant in Europe and America* and the classic monographs produced at the University of Chicago under the influence of Robert E. Park. When Brazilian scholars look back, they see works whose virtues are as much literary as scholarly and scientific, exemplified (to mention books known outside Brazil) by Gilberto Freire's massive trilogy on Brazilian social history[22] and Euclides da Cunha's *Rebellion in the Backlands*,[23] or (to take an example not known abroad) Sérgio Buarque de Holanda's *Raízes do Brasil.*[24]

While academic disciplinary lines exist in Brazil, they are fuzzier and more permeable than North Americans and Europeans are accustomed to. The history of the social science disciplines and their relations to government and academic institutions are different, as are Brazilian traditions of intellectual life and production.[25] Writers respond to the specific constraints of Brazilian intellectual and academic life and draw on its unique traditions. As a result, literary ideas and standards permeate Brazilian social science in a way no longer imaginable in American sociology.

Antonio Candido's work, resisting the contemporary move toward disciplinary specialization in Brazil, belongs to this tradition and continues to mix, as Candido says of this tradition, "Imagination and observation, science and art."[26] It cannot, thus, be read as if it were a sociology of literature or literary theory or any of the specialized genres that now characterize Western scholarship in these fields. Candido does not construct arguments, in the modern professional style; he explores a work, seizes on its details, places the work in the context of the readers and literary world of its day, all to the end of achieving a deeper understanding of the mutual connections of work and setting.

SOME BIOGRAPHICAL NOTES

Antonio Candido is a man of letters in an older, inclusive sense, not only a critic of specific literary works and a writer on more general literary matters, but someone who writes analytically about his society and others, about historical and political questions, often basing his social analyses on literary materials.

His childhood gave him some incredible gifts for a writer on social and literary topics.

> I am the child of a studious physician, dedicated to his profession, but with strong interests in philosophy, history, and literature, and of a mother who had only the brief instruction in the nuns' schools of that time, but who was very intelligent and cultivated. . . . It was a house full of books, many with beautiful bindings, and I grew up among them. . . . One nice day, when I was about nine years old, my middle brother seven, and my youngest brother six, my father gave us a two-volume *Larousse universel*, saying: "Play with this." And we began to play, to look at the colored plates with maps, uniforms, mammals, reptiles, butterflies, fish, etc. Since I wanted to understand, I exerted myself, questioning my mother and gaining a growing understanding, between mistakes and lucky guesses. After spending a year coloring the wigs of historical characters, putting mustaches on Roman emperors, a goatee on Louis XIV, and similar things, we had acquired some familiarity with the entries and learned a little French, reinforced by mother's Berlitz lessons. . . .
>
> I have always been an indiscriminate devourer of books, from the age of nine until my sixties, and I believe that I thus accumulated much information, not least because I read compendia, dictionaries, and encyclopedias.[27]

But Candido didn't go to school, at least not for very long; instead, his mother tutored the children at home. When he was eleven, his parents took him to Paris for "a year that was decisive for my cultural development." The children's French teacher, in addition to giving them lessons at home, took them on Saturdays to "museums, churches, institutions or, sometimes, to the Comédie Française, explaining the plays to

us beforehand, in a way that was accessible to children of our age. . . .
With this strong saturation and our stay in France, I became more or less
bilingual."[28]

Back home, they were taught English and introduced to English literature by a teacher trained in a North American institution in Brazil.
They were also in close touch with an Italian friend of their mother, who
spoke Italian and sang opera with them, and who introduced Candido
to the ideas of socialism.

He was trained as a scholar when the "French mission," a group of
French scholars (of whom Claude Lévi-Strauss is the most well known,
but others of whom—especially Roger Bastide and Jean Maugüé—had
a greater influence on him), was organizing the curriculum and teaching
the first classes at the then almost new University of São Paulo. Brazil
had traditionally turned to Paris as a cultural center, and modern universities, when they were finally created in the thirties, got a jump start from
the sizable number of French scholars who were sent to bring French
civilization to such outposts. Candido was part of the first generation of
professionally trained social scientists in Brazil, among whom the out-
standing name in sociology is Florestan Fernandes.

The classic British anthropology of Malinowski, Radcliffe-Brown,
Evans-Pritchard, and others always inspired Candido more than sociology. Mariza Peirano, an anthropologist who has written about Antonio
Candido's work in social science, comments that "American sociology,
for example, seemed to him totally *uninspiring* [English in the original]:
'Social surveys, the atrophied sociology of American universities.'" In
the end, Candido found sociology boring: "If I study a primitive culture, I end up preoccupied with the human problem of the person who
is before me. How he walks, how he sings, how he dances, how he sees
the world. At the other extreme, that of sociology, I don't see any person at all. I see that 7,283 people use Kolynos toothpaste."[29]

So he changed fields, teaching sociology for almost fifteen years but
eventually becoming a professor of comparative literature. He now in-
sists that he is not a sociologist—"If you were to ask me what I am,
principally, I would say, italicizing it, 'teacher'"[30]—but is known still for
his dissertation, a major sociological investigation of a rural community
in the state of São Paulo.[31] During his years as an academic sociologist,
he always wrote literary criticism, as well as publishing his classic work,
The Development of Brazilian Literature:[32] "I taught sociology without
being a sociologist, I had no training in literature and taught literature,
I had a close call with medicine, I studied law without using what I
learned, I read a little of everything with no method. You can understand why I consider myself someone with irregular and heterodox
training, but, modesty aside, productive."[33]

Though Candido is serious about his renunciation of sociology as an academic field, we can't ignore the connections to sociology, broadly conceived, in his work. His sociological thoughts are not the truisms so often uttered by humanists with only a vague understanding of the social sciences, but deeply sociologically insights into social organizations, processes, and practices, as we see in a comment on the situation of Latin American writers:

> the problem of publics presents distinctive features in Latin America, since it is the only group of underdeveloped countries whose people speak European languages (with the exception, already noted, of the indigenous groups) and have their origins in countries that today still have underdeveloped areas themselves (Spain and Portugal). In these ancient mother countries literature was, and continues to be, a good of restricted consumption, in comparison with the fully developed countries, where publics can be classified according to the kind of reading they do, such a classification permitting comparisons with the stratification of the entire society. But, as much in Spain and Portugal as in our own countries, there is a basic negative condition, the number of literates, that is, those who could eventually constitute the readers of works. This circumstance brings the Latin American countries nearer to the actual conditions of their mother countries than are, in relation to theirs, the underdeveloped countries of Africa and Asia, which speak different languages than those of the colonizers and confront the grave problem of choosing the language in which to display literary creation. African writers in European languages (French, like Léopold Sendar Senghor, or English, like Chinua Achebe) are doubly separated from their potential publics; and are tied either to metropolitan publics, distant in every sense, or to an incredibly reduced local public.[34]

In this analysis, Candido combines several fundamental social facts to outline the situation of Latin American writers. They live and work in underdeveloped countries. But they write in the language of a mother country, a country in which literature is, as it is where they live, a good of restricted consumption, relatively low rates of literacy leading to small, class-restricted audiences. Embedded in this network of class, linguistic, and national connections, their problem of finding readers, topics, and language differs from that of their counterparts in Africa and Asia.

Throughout his long career as teacher and writer, Candido has also been an active participant in the political and cultural life of his country. A lifelong socialist, he has been concerned with political and social issues. The concern has been practical, as in his active participation in the founding of the Partido dos Trabalhadores, the Brazilian Workers Party.

He was a "bad" militant, he says, because he had no taste for politics, but was nevertheless very active, in his youth, in the former Socialist Party, working in election campaigns and giving workers' classes.

> Marxism was always a strong influence for me, and I believe that the dialectic march is visible in my critical work. Nevertheless, I was not a Marxist properly speaking. . . .
> Marxism is a totalizing philosophy, and to be a Marxist is more or less like being a Catholic: you have to pass all the reality of the world, of being, of action, through the sieve of doctrine. Now beyond the general suggestion of method . . . Marxism was important for me above all in the field of politics. I think, for example, that without concepts like the class struggle one cannot understand social reality correctly. But I was soon convinced that it was not a closed doctrine, but rather an instrument of great analytic and practical power, which must always be adjusted in the light of new knowledge.[35]

His political concerns also led him to investigations of political thought and action, nowhere better illustrated than in the long memoir "Teresina and Her Friends," in which he describes the political life of the woman who taught him and his brothers Italian and opera, to whom circumstances gave no opportunity for meaningful political action but who nevertheless embodied for him a "socialist way of being." Deeply sociological, the analysis of Teresina's life separates the problem of political orientation from that of political action and shows how the latter depends on what the situation makes available to the actor.

The deceptively simple conclusion of this essay—in which Candido shows how a seeming correlation between political moderation and anti-fascism in the Italian community of São Paulo is, after all, historically contingent and not to be taken as indicating a general relationship—embodies a profound understanding of a classical sociological phenomenon, the shaping of social action by contingency.

Candido's style will come through to the English-speaking reader only imperfectly in these translations. It is (he attributes this to his French training)[36] characteristically lucid, clear, free of jargon, aimed at a discerning reader who will take the time to follow the line of thought.

> While I was teaching sociology, I was against rebarbative language, precisely because this language is at times just a conventional dressing up of banalities. I always thought that, since sociology is a humanistic discipline, it would be a good idea to use, by preference, common language, adopting only those technical terms that are indispensable, which anyway soon become clear, like mobility, stratification, acculturation, etc. . . .

I always acted in the field of literary studies as I had previously in sociology, preferring also common language and using indispensable technical
terms parsimoniously.[37]

This style's naturalness, avoidance of pompous constructions and os-
tentatious displays of scholarship, and easy exploration of bypaths recalls
conversation. He pays close attention to details, using them to reach
fundamental characteristics of the work in question, as in his discussion
in "Four Waitings" (in this volume) of the national origins of the names
of characters in Dino Buzzatti's *The Tartar Steppe*. We find ourselves
sharing the experience of a careful, subtle reader.[38]

Candido constructs an argument deliberately, without the para-
phernalia of scientific "hypotheses," preparing the ground carefully before presenting a conclusion that you have not foreseen but that nevertheless follows clearly, even obviously, from what you have already
learned. Thus, the minutely detailed stories of Teresina's Italian socialist
friends lead inevitably, though not foreseeably, to his conclusion:
though it might seem obvious that milder and more tentative socialists
would have resisted the appeal of Mussolini's Fascism where the more
aggressive radical socialists could not, in fact these connections are historically contingent and could have easily turned out otherwise.

A WORLD WRITER

Despite what I have said about his Brazilianness, it would be a mistake
to think of Candido as representing a South American or Brazilian or
Latin American point of view, or to think that his most important or
most characteristic work is that which deals with literature from that part
of the world or with the problems of Third World development.

We can think of the intellectual life of the Western tradition as a conversation to which people from all over the world contribute their
thoughts and discoveries—in literature, in philosophy, in criticism, in
social analysis. Candido certainly participates in this conversation as
someone fully rooted in his time and place, Brazil in the mid–twentieth
century, personally involved in the development of a Brazilian literary
modernity, helping to shape its concerns through his critical practice
and historical and analytic writing. He has wanted to see Brazilian literature develop in a way that would entitle it to stand alongside work from
the major centers of Europe and North America and has devoted himself
to establishing literary studies in Brazil on a firm footing.

Thus rooted in his country's literary history and life, he is nevertheless
fully involved in the literary conversation of the contemporary world.
He writes about world literature, especially that of the Western tradition

(Europe and the Americas, but also including the literature of former colonies in the languages of the metropole). He writes about topics of world interest, such universal topics as vengeance or catastrophe, as well as the common topics of contemporary critical writing: class, social change, political engagement.

He draws deeply from the world's resources. His substantial knowledge of world languages and literature is today uncommon; he is at home not only in Portuguese, but in Spanish, French, Italian, and English as well. And not only in the languages, but in the literature and history associated with them, so that he draws examples from all those societies, bringing to the conversation a breadth of comparison seldom available to contemporary critics. And not just literature, but film, drama, and the other arts as well.

The last writer in English who commanded such a wealth of intellectual resources and had such a breadth of interest was the North American critic Edmund Wilson. Oddly enough, Wilson, the literary writer, did more direct reporting on society, in his wonderfully detailed and researched pieces of reportage that amounted to a kind of anthropology or sociology,[39] than does Candido, trained in sociology, whose *Os parceiros do Rio Bonito*, while masterful, is his only work in that genre. But Candido differs from Wilson, who was in so many ways a nineteenth-century anachronism, in being rooted in the twentieth century, at home with its problems instead of resenting them as a reminder of the lost privileges of class. And Candido is a more generous spirit, with greater human warmth than the egomaniacal Wilson.

Though Candido takes so much from the world of literature, that world has had little chance to accept the important return of those gifts he offers. Being Brazilian, his language is Portuguese, and he did not, as others with his knowledge, interests, and desire to participate might have done, as Brazilian intellectuals so often did in earlier times, move to Paris (or, later, New York) and undertake a career in those central places on the literary map. He stayed in Brazil, wrote in its language, and devoted much of his effort to its literature, unfamiliar (with a few exceptions) to non-Portuguese-speaking readers. And so his work is almost unknown elsewhere. His remarks on Machado de Assis, the great Brazilian novelist of the late nineteenth and early twentieth centuries, and on the problems of Latin American writers generally speak of the difficulties and opportunities contained in his own situation:

> at the deepest levels of creative elaboration (those that involve the choice of expressive instruments), we always recognize our inevitable dependence as natural. Besides, seen thus, it is no longer dependency, but a way of participating in a cultural universe to which we belong, which crosses the

boundaries of nations and continents, allowing the exchange of experiences and the circulation of values. And when we in turn influence the Europeans through the works we do (not through the thematic suggestions our continent presents to them to elaborate in their own forms of exoticism), at such moments what we give back are not inventions but a refining of received instruments.[40]

Candido brings to the world conversation a point of view that, rooted in the experience of his country, in its literature, its history, and its social problems, provides new perspectives on literature and its relation to society. He does not just apply the already developed perspectives of the Western intellectual community to some new material, or show that Latin Americans too can master these methods. Rather, like Jorge Luis Borges, whose literary inventions altered twentieth-century literature, he introduces something new, something the rest of that community can now take up and use, something that enriches the common conceptual stock, that arises from his unique mixing of a knowledge of the world's literature and the situation of a country that is the intellectual descendant, as he says, of a poor relation of contemporary European thought.

A fundamental stage in overcoming dependency is the capacity to produce works of the first order, influenced by previous national examples, not by immediate foreign models. This signifies the establishment of what could be called, a little mechanically, an internal causality, which makes the borrowings from other cultures more fruitful. . . . We know, then, that we are part of a broader culture, in which we participate as a cultural variant.[41]

Notes

1. Vera Zolberg's *Constructing a Sociology of the Arts* (Cambridge: Cambridge University Press, 1990) is organized around this opposition. Antoine Hennion's *La passion musicale: Une sociologie de la médiation* (Paris: Métailié, 1993) summarizes the current state of the debate by focusing on the idea of "mediators" in worlds of art.

2. As Hennion argues, *op. cit.*

3. Antonio Candido, *Crítica radical*, ed. and trans. Márgara Russotto (Caracas: Biblioteca Ayacucho, 1991).

4. A full analysis of the literature on this topic can be found in Hennion, *op. cit.*

5. See Michael Lynch, "Pictures of Nothing? Visual Construals in Social Theory," *Sociological Theory* 9 (Spring, 1991), 1–21.

6. E.g., W. Lloyd Warner and Paul Lunt, *The Social Life of a Modern Community* (New Haven: Yale University Press, 1941).

7. William Foote Whyte, *Street Corner Society: The Social Structure of an Italian Slum*, third edition (Chicago: University of Chicago Press, 1981).

8. Elliot Liebow, *Tally's Corner: A Study of Negro Streetcorner Men* (Boston: Little Brown, 1967).

9. Since Weber's descriptions were "ideal types" rather than empirical reports, the comparison raises an interesting question about the connection between two such generalizing strategies.

10. I have elaborated this conception at length in *Art Worlds* (Berkeley: University of California Press, 1982).

11. Hennion, *op. cit.* There is a substantial overlap between this point of view and Bruno Latour's analyses of scientific activity as the operations of networks of a variety of actors, e.g. in his *Science in Action* (Cambridge: Harvard University Press, 1987).

12. John A. Sutherland, *Victorian Novelists and Publishers* (Chicago: University of Chicago Press, 1976).

13. This is the place to confess that I am a chief offender in this respect (see the analyses in *Art Worlds*).

14. Antonio Candido, "Degradacão do espaço," pp. 55–94 in his *O discurso e a cidade* (São Paulo: Livraria Duas Cidades, 1993).

15. "Os vários mundos de um humanista," interview with Antonio Candido conducted by Gilberto Velho and Yonne Leite, *Ciência Hoje* 16, no. 91 (June, 1993), 28.

16. Ibid., 38–39.

17. In "On Vengeance," in this volume.

18. "Os vários mundos," p. 34.

19. "Dialectic of Malandroism," in this volume.

20. Everett C. Hughes, "Good People and Dirty Work," pp. 87–97 in his *The Sociological Eye* (New Brunswick, N.J.: Transaction, 1984).

21. Antonio Candido, *Literature e sociedade: estudos de teoria e história literária* (São Paulo: Editora Nacional, 1965), p. 130.

22. Gilberto Freire, *The Masters and the Slaves: A Study in the Development of Brazilian Civilization; The Mansions and the Shanties: The Making of Modern Brazil; Order and Progress: Brazil from Monarchy to Republic* (Berkeley: University of California Press, 1986).

23. Euclides da Cunha, *Rebellion in the Backlands* (Chicago: University of Chicago Press, 1944).

24. Sergio Buarque de Holanda, *Raízes do Brasil* (Rio de Janeiro: José Olympio, 1956). See also Antonio Candido, "Raízes do Brasil," pp. 135–52 in his *Teresina etc.* (Rio de Janeiro: Paz e Terra, 1985).

25. I have provided a little more detail on these points in "Social Theory in Brazil," *Sociological Theory* 10 (Spring, 1992), 1–5.

26. Antonio Candido, *Literature e sociedade*, p. 130.

27. "Os vários mundos," pp. 30, 40.

28. Ibid., p. 30.

29. Mariza Peirano, "O pluralismo de Antonio de Candido," *Revista Brasileira de Ciências Sociais* 12 (February, 1990), 43.

30. "Os vários mundos," p. 38.

31. *Os parceiros do Rio Bonito: Estudo sobre o caipira paulista e a transformacão dos seus meios de vida* (Rio de Janeiro: José Olympio, 1964).

32. Antonio Candido, *Formação da literatura brasileira: Momentos decisivos* (São Paulo: Martins, 1959).

33. "Os vários mundos," p. 35.

34. From "Literature and Underdevelopment," in this volume.

35. "Os vários mundos," p. 40.

36. Ibid., p. 37.

37. Ibid., p. 38.

38. I have made use here of the thoughts of Davi Arrigucci Jr., "Movimentos de un leitor," pp. 181–204 in Maria Angela D'Incao and Eloísa Faria Scarabôtolo, editors, *Dentro de texto, dentro da vida: Ensaios sobre Antonio Candido* (São Paulo: Companhia das Letras: Instituto Moreira Salles, 1992).

39. See, for example, Wilson's *Europe without Baedeker: Sketches among the Ruins of Italy, Greece, and England, Together With Notes from a European Diary, 1963–1964* (New York: Farrar, Straus and Giroux, 1966); *Red, Black, Blond, and Olive; Studies in Four Civilizations: Zuni, Haiti, Soviet Russia, Israel* (New York: Oxford University Press, 1956); and *Apologies to the Iroquois: With a Study of the Mohawks in High Steel by Joseph Mitchell* (New York: Farrar, Straus and Cudahy, 1960).

40. From "Literature and Underdevelopment," in this volume.

41. Ibid.

Antonio Candido

ON LITERATURE AND SOCIETY

Chapter 1

ON VENGEANCE

When all is told
We cannot beg for pardon.
—Louis MacNeice

THE SUN had nearly reached the meridian, and his scorching rays fell full on the rocks, which seemed themselves sensible of the heat. Thousands of grasshoppers, hidden in the bushes, chirped with a monotonous and dull note; the leaves of the myrtle and olive-trees waved and rustled in the wind. At every step that Edmond took he disturbed the lizards glittering with the hues of the emerald; afar off he saw the wild goats bounding from crag to crag. In a word, the isle was inhabited, yet Edmond felt himself alone, guided by the hand of God. . . . He then looked at the objects near him. He saw himself on the highest point of the isle, a statue on this vast pedestal of granite, nothing human appearing in sight, whilst the blue ocean beat against the base of the island, and covered it with a fringe of foam.

Not long before, this man had fled from the dungeon where he had lived through fourteen years, a day at a time. A skillful sailor, an exemplary employee, he was nineteen when an anonymous denunciation sent him, without his knowing why, into solitary confinement in a fortress situated on another island. He hoped, he despaired, then resolved to starve himself to death. But chance put him in contact with a neighbor in the prison, a learned priest who opened the world to him through the cultivation of his spirit, analyzed the causes of his imprisonment, taught him science and wisdom, and gave him a map leading to an incalculable fortune, buried on the island where he now stood. The priest died and was about to be buried; Dantès took his place and was thrown into the sea from the heights of the fortress, a cannonball fastened to his feet. Thanks to luck, to his energy, and to a variety of skills, he succeeded in being saved, arrived at the island after some time, and somehow managed to remain there alone; now it is the decisive moment in which he will learn if the treasure really exists.

It does exist and it is beneath his feet. From there, he will gradually find the hidden entrance, which lacks nothing to fit the finest stereotypes of this kind of literature: a stone hiding a large iron ring, a flagstone to be removed, stairs, a cave, two buried chests. Simple, eternal, and always the same. He will take possession of the riches that have waited for him for almost three and a half centuries, he will be omnipotent, he will do everything he desires. With the disgrace and the imprisonment, there gradually rose out of the ingenuous sailor a new man, to whose changes we are witness. But the final realization, the man who is really *other*, we will only unexpectedly see, some chapters later, in the midst of the revelry of the Roman carnival. In this instant, when he is on the peak of the island, we find him still only halfway there, because it is still a few minutes until he will begin to come gradually into possession of the resources permitting him the final development of his being.

It is the halfway point of his destiny, between two poles of the human imagination: the mountain, from which one sees the world and has the sensation of power; the cave, where the mysteries that give power are hidden. The pinnacle that enlarges, the recess that concentrates. The immensity where the imagination flies, the egg in which it germinates. He is two minutes from the cave, looking at the world from the top of the hill; when he emerges from the entrance of the cliff and contemplates it anew, he will already be in possession of the hidden riches and everything will look different. He will be anxious to leave and begin his new career, giving scope to the projects he had sketched in prison. "It was no longer a question now of spending his time contemplating this gold and these diamonds, and remaining at Monte-Cristo like a dragon watching over useless treasures. Now it was necessary to return to life among men, and to seize the worldly rank, influence, and power in society given him by this riches, the foremost and greatest force of which human beings can dispose."

From the heights of his island, he contemplates the world, before and after. Proust intended to write an essay on the role played by altitude in the novels of Stendhal. In fact, many decisive events in those novels take place at elevated points, though the battle of Waterloo occurs on the plain: the tower of Father Blanès, in which the little Fabrício learns and reflects; the Torre Farnese, in which he is imprisoned and loves Clelia Conti; the mount of the Delphinian Alps, in which Julien retires to think and to take decisions with the good Fouqué, or the tower of the jail, in which he vacillates between his two women and awaits the guillotine. But it would be necessary to go further and evaluate the role, in human decisions, of the heights transformed in literary image, in symbol, in myth, in unconsciously selected fictional space. How many poems are called "In the Mountains," or occur at the summits of hills?

In Romanticism there are many, and the poets leave these heights only to climb further still. If, in a poem by Magalhães, the founder of Brazilian Romanticism, Napoleon crosses his arms atop his cliff, in order to contemplate in his imagination destroyed kingdoms, the liberator poet of Castro Alves takes an albatross's wings and flies over the slave ship. Tower, mountain, the island peak, the isolated cliff, the elevated castle, space itself, are favorite places of the Romantics, who situate the encounters of men with their dreams of liberty or power in them. Turning away from the burial of old Goriot, Rastignac hurls his famous challenge to Paris, from the heights of Montmartre: "Now it is between the two of us!" The city that lies before his feet is the World, the kingdoms of earth, and within him is a demon who incites him—Jacques Collin, or Vautrin, or Trompe la Morte, the future Father Herrera. These Romantic heroes do not reject the tempter, not even when they are toughened by deprivations in the wilderness of men, like Edmond in prison. They accept the challenge. The heights show the universe, as they did in the dream of Faust, who, from the heights of his Sunday hill, wanted to be a bird accompanying the sun, in a world without twilight.

But the effort of Romanticism was to add to the world seen from above a world seen from below, associating Mephistopheles with Faust, the witches' recipe with his desired transformation to youth, Walpurgis Night with the love of Marguerite. From below come the roots, the humus, the compost of foliage. Victor Hugo shows life from the heights of Notre Dame, the convulsive universe of Cláudio Frollo, his dream of power and lust. But he shows too the Hall of Miracles, a kind of vast underground of society, which sends its filaments into every part. Then everything is subverted, mixed, and it is the freak, Quasimodo, who defends the purity from the tower's heights. In another book Hugo shows the sewers of Paris, from which Jean Valjean comes forth on his work of salvation, as in life he redeems himself and redeems others, starting from the moral subsoil of the galley and social infamy.

Here the planes begin to cross, the atmosphere of the heights is mixed with the emanations from below, and we see that the imagination of the heights is fed by energy acquired in the depths; that the vigor unveiled on the mountain is able to act thanks to the temptations hidden in the cave; that the clear and luminous dominion practiced on the heights has a dark underside. This occurs exactly at the moment when Edmond sees the world, standing on a summit that has for its depths a cave from which will issue the conditions of his strength. And he knows quite well what this implies, to judge by what he will say later in a conversation in which he defines his being and his aim:

> I too, as happens to every man once in his life, have been taken by Satan to the highest mountain in the earth, and when there he showed me all the kingdoms of the earth, and as he said before to Christ, so he said to me: "Child of earth, what wouldst thou have to make thee adore me?" I re-

flected long, for a gnawing ambition had long preyed upon me, and then I replied, "Listen,—I have always heard tell of Providence, and yet I have never seen it, nor anything that resembles it or which can make me believe that it exists. I wish to be Providence myself, for I feel that the most beautiful, noblest, most sublime thing in the world is to recompense and punish." Satan bowed his head and groaned. "You mistake," he said; "Providence does exist, only you have never seen him because the child of God is as invisible as the parent. You have seen nothing that resembles him, because he works by secret springs and moves by hidden ways. All I can do for you is to make you one of the agents of that Providence." The bargain was concluded. I may sacrifice my soul, but what matters it? If the thing were to do again, I would again do it.

One cannot express it better, with such Romantic (and even sub-Romantic) phrasing, this new avatar of an old theme. Romantically, the devil confers a substitute divinity on the initiate, who will have in consequence a double nature, divine and infernal. All this is at work in Edmond at this moment in which we see him at the highest point of his island, the island that is both peak and cave, sun and darkness, whose name he is going to take, dissolving himself in it, adopting its two planes. He is alone, as a Romantic hero must be. The lizards teem from the cracks in the rocks like premonitory emeralds. The sun, on high, will rise again in the metal hidden in the chests, as in the sonnet of Cláudio Manuel,

> As the fertile flames spring up in gold.

Edmond contemplates the sea, which is the world. For the world, he himself will rise like a pinnacle, when he is merged with his island. But, like his island, he will have in his innermost being another world, which will develop, take form, which will make up the final design of both his open and his secret being—placed on high, nourished from below. He is going to begin the Romantic battle against society, the battle that began, perhaps, with Schiller's Karl Moor, that was refined in the melodramatic characters of Byron, and that will be the principal crystallization of the myth of rebellion, until the passing of events permits other forms of subverting the heights with strength coming from other caves.

II

The Count of Monte Cristo was written by Alexandre Dumas with the collaboration of Auguste Maquet and orders itself around three principal fulcrums, geographically distributed, which Dumas himself designated as Marseille, Rome, Paris.[1] Accepting this division, we can say that the Marseille part is good, the Italian part (done entirely by Dumas) excellent, the Parisian part—which comprises most of the book, of which it occupies around two-thirds—mediocre.

The mediocrity comes not only from the content and the journalistic tone, but principally from the prolixity, the redundancies, the dialogues padded without the least shame in order to make the material "pay." While these defects are worst in the Parisian part, they exist throughout the work, least in the Roman section, which has a lightness of touch and a charm that recall Stendhal. The stories of the bandits, the mixture of religion, love, and blood, the settings of the palaces and ruins have something of the air of an "Italian chronicle," though Dumas revealed a certain French philistinism toward the customs, the furnishings, and the food. Beyle would have rejected all this, but he would certainly have approved of the nocturnal adventure of Albert de Morcerf, who sleeps tranquilly while his life is at stake and while the captain of the bandits who imprisoned him in the catacombs reads Caesar's *Commentaries* with attention.

In other parts, above all the third, Balzac comes to mind, in the overly elegant description of elegant settings, in the preoccupation with financial operations, the political maneuvers, the rise of the middle classes. We remember him, too, in certain glimpses of prison and of wrongdoers. But above all in the case of Mlle. Danglars and her friend Mlle. d'Armilly, who run away together; Mlle. Danglars, brunette and strong, dresses like a man, though men as such do not interest her, and their looks ricochet off her as "on the shield of Minerva, which some philosophers assert sometimes protected the breast of Sappho." At other times we think of Balzac through the affinity of certain silly things that clash in the solid fabric of the *Comédie humaine*, but fit comfortably in the loose stuffing of the good Dumas, seldom galvanized by the rush of imagination and the felicity of the phrasing. The passage below seems to have come from a Balzacian pastiche by Proust, who was extremely skilled in seeing the ridiculous traits of the great novelist:

> Mercedes asked for six months, to wait and lament for Edmond.
> "In fact," said the priest with a bitter smile, "this would add up to eighteen months. What more could the most adored of lovers ask for?"
> And he murmured the words of the English poet: *Frailty, thy name is woman!*

But if we recall the names of these two great writers when we read this minor contemporary, the author who impregnates the entire book, perhaps more than Dumas himself saw, is Byron. The Count is a Byronic hero par excellence, the Byronic hero constituting the simplest and most widespread formulation of the pattern of the romantic hero—as it appears in the novel of terror, the fantastic tale, the sentimental and macabre melodrama, and narrative poetry.

"Franz could not see him, this true hero of Byron [the Count], or so much as think of him, without imagining this gloomy face on the shoulders of a Manfred or beneath the cap of a Lara."

"I would see in him one of those men of Byron, who disgrace marked with a fatal stamp; a Manfred, a Lara, a Werner."

One of the characters, the Countess G., is the actual Teresa Guiccioli, the last of the English poet's mistresses; she mentions him [Byron], and, terrorized by Monte Cristo's bloodless and sombre aspect, she likens him to the vampire Lord Ruthwen, whom she says she has known personally.[2]

But, leaving aside the almost anonymous Byronism of the times in which the novel was written (the Byronism of the fatal, dark hero, who was only one manifestation of a character ideally established in the Romantic consciousness), leaving aside, then, what had become public property, there is the orientalism, which appears here in tonalities and themes that are clearly Byronic. Monte Cristo possessed seraglios in Egypt, in Asia, and in Constantinople, he lives part of his life in the Orient, traffics with Muslim princes, has for his slave a beauty who, exactly like the enchanting heroine of *Don Juan*, is Greek, is called Haydée, and is the daughter of an old man. One of the important moments of the plot is the denunciation she makes, which demoralizes and finally brings to his death Count de Morcerf, the onetime fisherman who betrayed Edmond and took his bride. The denunciation consists of revealing that he betrayed the Pasha of Janina, his protector and benefactor, to the Sultan. For Europeans, Ali Pasha was linked to the battle of the Greeks against the Turkish Empire, and Morcerf possessed the Order of the Savior, which showed that he had fought in the Greek war of independence, in which Byron died. Byron, on the occasion of his first voyage to the Orient, was also in Janina and was well received by Ali Pasha, whom he celebrated in Canto II and the notes related to it of *Childe Harold*:

> *Ali* reclined, a man of war and woes:
> Yet in his lineaments you cannot trace,
> While gentleness her milder radiance throws
> Along that aged venerable face,
> The deeds that lurk beneath, and stain him with disgrace.

Finally, we note an ultimate Byronic feature: the symbolic incest, exactly in the untimely love of the Count for the daughter of Ali Pasha, the Haydée already referred to, whom he buys at the age of eight from a

Turkish trader to use as an instrument of vengeance and raises lovingly as a daughter.

Thus, there is a clear link with the universe, the themes, the experiences, and the legend of Byron; and with respect to the already mentioned analogies with Stendhal and Balzac, these show how *The Count of Monte Cristo* is linked to a certain type of fiction and psychological ideal of its time, without reckoning with its kinship to its still more modest brothers—the novels of Fréderic Soulié or Eugène Sue.

For the adult reader of today, the central of the book's defects is the prolixity I have already referred to—because the others become merits, when we accept the journalistic convention and fortify ourselves with a sense of humor . . . The longer the book goes on, the harder it is to read, despite the unfailing invention of incidents. It is as if the originality of tone had dried up rapidly, the style losing its bite and the psychology its verisimilitude, the author going astray in the interminable dialogues, the surfeit of descriptions and considerations, in the boring emphasis on moral features—in a spreading corruption of uselessness. But even here there are spirited and thrilling sections, good strokes of expression, which sustain the fat of the padding.

The themes ordered around the Count and his singular destiny continue, however, to interest us. Seen thus, this diffuse book has a coherence and organization, if we consider the principles, not the development of the narrative. And, instead of losing ourselves in the events alone (as we do in childhood), we interest ourselves in this perfect example of a certain Romantic theme—having to do with egotism, satanism, the will to power, solitude, stewed together around the dialectic of good and evil, crowned by the synthesis of a somewhat disrespectfully manipulated Providence, palpably embodied in the Count, in order to circulate among men.

In fact, the Count's great idea, which justifies and animates him, as we saw at the beginning of this essay, is that he has been constituted as a conscious instrument of Providence. This establishes a first contradiction in him and in the book, because it collides with the orientalism he professes, which assumes the blindness of fate's game. In a crucial moment, when Mercedes begs him not to kill her son in a duel, and he, to serve her, accepts the eventual sacrifice of his own life, it seems to him to interrupt his voluntary course of vengeful action, what he calls Providence, and he exclaims to himself: "This burden, almost as heavy as a world, which I had raised, and had thought to carry to the end, was too great for my strength, and I was compelled to lay it down in the middle of my career. Oh, shall I then become a fatalist, whom fourteen years of despair and then of hope had rendered a believer in Providence?"

We see that the idea of Providence enters subtly into his personality as

a rationalization, permitting him to develop his will's plans methodically, attributing them to the fulfilling of the divine will, to which he
thus transfers responsibility. But it is clear, throughout the book, that
the homage the Count gives to God is what the English call "lip service." For him, as for the majority of the Romantics, divinity is an explanatory resource and a vague sentiment, perhaps a mere projection of
individual problems and a convenient alibi.

Which the Count needs, because all of his Byronism, his "lionism,"
his use of hashish, his fame as a vampire, his infallibility (as if he were an
initiate), his dominion over the heights and depths of society, converges
toward an emotion and a dominant form of behavior to which he desires
to attribute this providential character: vengeance.

Just as group vengeance dissolves the avenger in the collective interest
(whether it be the honor of the Greek Kings in the *Iliad*, or the tranquillity of the Portugese landowners in the poem *The Arab's Vow* of
Gonçalves de Crespo), personal vengeance distinguishes him, indicates
his prominence and his superiority to others. The man who avenges
himself openly has a powerful belief in himself and considers other people's violations of his integrity as just so many assaults on the equilibrium of the universe. He sees himself as does a big industrialist, who
justifies the unleashing of a war if it will help his business.

For this reason, instead of giving their children stories full of sentimental stoicism—in order to show them, sugarcoated, the tenacity that
great feelings must inculcate in them—the bourgeoisie might better
have nourished them with massive doses of *The Count of Monte Cristo*.
Not as furtive or marginal readings, soon transformed into a pretext for
playing; but rather, and above all, as assigned readings, analyzed by the
teacher, as a major part of the school program, to the end of transfusing
them into the thought and action of every hour . . . Nor, it should be
clear, do I mean this as a joke, since *The Count of Monte Cristo* is a complete portrait of personal vengeance; personal vengeance is the quintes-
sence of individualism; individualism was and, in a way, still is the axis of
bourgeois conduct.

Taken as a compendium of morality, the book would have taught
children and youth, who read it for amusement, to take to their ultimate
consequences the principles of competition and the apotheosis of individual success, new forms of the right of the strongest, and the ethical
foundations of the capitalist era. Edmond Dantès (an arriviste like Rastignac and a Bonapartist like Julien Sorel) is one of the many young men
Romantic literature took, in the nineteenth century, to illustrate the new
phase of the conquest of social position through selection by talent and
ability. At bottom, it is the same glorification of initiative and firm determination we see in Stendhal and Balzac.

III

Accepting *The Count of Monte Cristo* as a Treatise on Vengeance, we might develop what was suggested above by saying that, in this respect, it is a Romantic novel par excellence or, better, a novel that best expresses certain fundamental characteristics of Romanticism.

In the study of Tristão de Athayde (Alceu Amoroso Lima) on Afonso Arinos, there is a quotation from Saintsbury, with respect to "minor writers, who give the key of a literature much more surely than the greater ones." This is not true of minor writers in general, but perhaps it is true of Alexandre Dumas in particular, in whom are found the tumultuous aspects of the Romantic soul.

Among classic works, only the really great encompass the characteristics that a literary tendency proposes for its pattern. In Classicism, in effect, the ideal patterns that guide the creative act almost always involve the victory of order and moderation over excess and the aberrant. Now order and moderation, from a certain level on, are found almost exclusively in authors of the first rank. In the vacillating hands of lesser authors, classical beauty tends to the dry and the frigid.

In Romanticism, however, the characteristic element is not uncommonly confounded with the corresponding disequilibrium, thanks to an aesthetic based on movement, on the incessant dislocation of planes. Thus disequilibrium authentically represents the Romantic ideal, which does not fear the immoderate and is inclined, at the limit, to the subversion of discourse. From this comes the pertinence with which writers of the second rank, like Alexandre Dumas, represent and embody essential aspects of the school. Among these aspects, vengeance is extremely important.

Literary movements select, from the natural and social world, the themes most suited to the necessities of their expression. Some themes are so rooted in the human experience that all schools make use of them, try to recreate them in their own way. This is the case with vengeance, which, though as old in literature as literature itself, received in Romanticism some special touches. It would not be excessive to recall that it then became a resource of literary composition, of psychological investigation, of sociological analysis, and of a vision of the world.

We note, to begin with, that the perfect conjunction of vengeance with Romanticism could be achieved thanks to the literary form of the novel, in which it is much more eventful and complete than in drama, for example, which is a species of romanticized tragedy. The perfect vision of vengeance is not realized in one moment; it requires the successive linking of events, which carry the initial motive to the final retaliation. It requires duration, so as not to reduce itself to a parable and to appear, as in truth it is, a complex mode of human activity, inserted fundamentally in time. The Romantic novel, on its side, needed movement and events, in order to satisfy the serialized voracity of the literary sections of newspaper and magazines. While revenge, as a theme, permits and even presupposes an ample supply of incidents, serialized fiction, as a genre, requires the multiplication of incidents. From which arises the fruitful alliance referred to, which attends to the necessities of composition created by the expectations of the author, the editor, and the reader, all three interested directly in the story being as long as possible; the first for the remuneration, the second for the sales, the third for the prolonging of the emotion. The aesthetic tendencies of Romanticism, eager for movement, converged in this case with the economic conditions of the literary profession and the psychological necessities of the new public, interested in a sensationalism that propitiated strong emotions.

But, though vengeance corresponds to the characteristic constant motion of the Romantic aesthetic, it is above all to the Romantic conception of man and society that it offers itself as a theme. The Romantic actor—dramatic, immoderate, bloody—found there the atmosphere of contradiction and surprise which permeates his psychology. It served not rarely as an amplifier; the gesture became immense, the energies titanic. The contradictions also served as precipitants: the avenger emerges from the meek, the assassin saves the fragile child by risking his own life. In a word, the antithesis is born of the conditions created by vengeance.

With reference to society, it is convenient to observe that one of the greatest contributions of Romanticism was what could be called the *sense of capillarity*: the notion that, just as the strata of the spirit communicate with one another mysteriously, the higher interpenetrating the lower until the distinction between good and evil is obliterated, the same occurs between the strata of society.

The society of Romantic novels (prolonging and bringing to term the society sketched in the novels of the eighteenth century) is diversified in the extreme, stratifying itself minutely and communicating from segment to segment. And vengeance in the grand style resembles a hunt on horseback, that is, a varied peregrination passing through many places, searching for many people. One can understand in this way one of the reasons why vengeance could, in Romanticism, perform a function more or less analogous to the voyage in the picaresque novel or the later novels inspired by the picaresque tradition: the voyage provided the possibility of proving the unity of the man in a diversity of places; vengeance was one way of verifying the complexity of man and society, permitting him to circulate from high to low in the social scale. Vengeance was closely linked to the hunt and to the mysterious—which could, besides, in themselves, perform the same investigative function. We remember the long persecution that is the life of Jean Valjean, or the mystery that surrounds the personality of Vautrin—occasions for the analysis of the society and the man. In Victor Hugo, in Balzac, in Eugène Sue, in Dumas, vengeance is the passport with which the novelist circulates freely through society, linking strata and unmasking obscure connections.

The avenger needs, generally, partners, informants, people to carry out the work. The duchess approaches the beggar and the criminal can enter the orbit of a respectable citizen. Alongside the "coeur mis à nu," which constituted a fundamental aspect of Romanticism, was a laying bare of society, showing how the illegitimate son of the procurator of the Crown, buried alive by his father, becomes a bandit who can demolish the father's situation (*The Count of Monte Cristo*); or how the impeccable lion of fashion lives on the hooliganish extortions of an old convict (Balzac's *A Harlot High and Low*); or, further, how the dominant men of the time can base their prestige on the fact of being, at the same time, members of a powerful secret society, side by side with criminals (Balzac's *The Story of Thirteen*). This problem of the real foundations of a social situation so preoccupies the entire century that, even in the English novel, much less daring than the French from this point of view, we can see the clear interpenetration of social strata, as in *Great Expectations*, notwithstanding the dilutions by means of which Dickens softens the problem.

With this in mind, one can evaluate the importance of social and journalistic novels, in which the rubbing of shoulders motivated by vengeance levels high society to the *bas-fond*, turning over, like a ghostly plow, consciences and social levels as it goes.

IV

In *The Count of Monte Cristo* Vengeance is, in a way, the chief character. As we saw, we begin with an honest youth, a good professional, a good employee, a good son, a good fiancé, a good friend—a situation of equilibrium so repugnant to Romantic art that the writer hurries to provide a triple felony that will destroy it and open the way for the incessant agitation of incident. Then follow the years in the dungeon, the meeting with the wise priest, the clarification of his imprisonment, the acquisition of science. Then, liberty, riches, the exercise of power, and the largest experience of life. Some years of mystery are necessary for the Count to emerge from the sailor, and vengeance from the Count. Then the exercise of this revenge, with method and proficiency, through the remainder of the book. At the end, remorse, that most Romantic of endings.

In Romanticism there are various poems of vengeance; but *The Count of Monte Cristo* is its Treatise par excellence. For the first time in literature, the long intellectual, moral, and technical preparation, enthroned as the ideal of modern conduct by the victory of bourgeoisie, appears related to the primitive and simple act of revenge. Constructing the character to the measure of the society in which he will act, Dumas submits him to a delicate and exhaustive preparation. The Chateau d'If symbolizes the phase of retirement from the world bourgeois education presupposes in adolescence: a drastic retirement in which the weapons of the spirit are forged and refined before being used in the world. There, the old Father Faria not only gives Dantès the key to the treasure of Cardinal Spada but also suggests the fundamental maxim that clarifies the past for him and that will guide him in the future: everything that we are and have in a way deprives others of what they would wish to be or have. Above all, he initiates him into learning, which will be the basic weapon of his vengeance—learning based on knowledge condensed, reduced to principles, ready for application, which can be amplified indefinitely:

> "Alas! my child," said he, "human knowledge is confined within very narrow limits; and when I have taught you mathematics, physics, history, and the three or four modern languages with which I am acquainted, you will know as much as I do myself. Now, it will scarcely require two years for me to communicate to you the stock of learning I possess."
>
> "Two years!" exclaimed Dantès; "do you really believe I can acquire all these things in so short a time?"
>
> "Not their application, certainly, but their principles you may; to learn is not to know; there are the knowledgeable and the learned. Memory makes the one, philosophy the other."

In Balzac's *The Girl with the Golden Eyes*, Henri de Marsay is prepared for the world, as a boy and an adolescent, by a cynical and affectionate priest, who, unlike Faria in relation to Dantès, initiates him into the ways of corruption, making of him a scoundrel adapted to the society, so that he can triumph by means of the usual methods. The position of Dantès is much more *romantic*, in the conventional sense, just as Dumas is much more *romantic* than Balzac. He guides himself by a clear distinction between virtue and vice and assumes a capacity in the Self to confront and overcome the world.

The old priest dead, Dantès flees and finds himself effectively furnished with knowledge, an ethic, and an immeasurable material power. Like a captain of industry at the beginning of a great enterprise, he can exact from society what his will to power judges is due him. Note that from here on the fortuitous will not interfere in his life, until the moment when his life begins to falter. It unfolds as a product of will, as the realization of a plan derived from initial premises, from the three bases that he implicitly equates with action: knowledge, will, and power. His own power, moved by his inflexible intention, is nourished by his knowledge, which is also a kind of science of good and evil, acquired in the purgatory of the Chateau d'If and signifying the loss of innocence, of his juvenile and honest paradise.

He is transformed, then, into a scientific avenger; he acquires the means of creating definitive loyalties, of linking himself to forces that can be useful to him, of enriching his own experience with infinite variety. When he appears to the other characters, he is the paradigm of the man who controls all the resources of his times: to us, he looks like one of the most characteristic types of the great Romantic hero. Once a sailor, prisoner, and smuggler, he is now learned, a millionaire, aristocratic. He has the sense of a mission to be accomplished and puts into his accomplishment of it the fervor of one who embodies a rebellion. Against society, which unjustly condemned him, he develops that capacity for negation which is the very essence of Romantic satanism. But he engages in strange practices, lives in the midst of strange things, with the correct demeanor of an Alfred de Vigny in the clutches of his frustrations, or of a Baudelaire in his aggressive eccentricities. He is handsome and extremely elegant; he is agile and herculean; he is eccentric and mysterious; he is melancholy and visionary, but at the same time precise and infallible. Capable of rendering himself unrecognizable through multiple disguises, he shows himself in the guise of three or four personalities; he sets in motion at a given moment an event slowly prepared for; he receives the homage of highwaymen and smugglers; he has a right to the gratitude of Pope and Kings; he arrives from Cadiz exactly on the stroke of the clock for a luncheon appointment made long before in Paris. With all this, he is supremely unhappy, and, as he develops the vengeful act, he increasingly substitutes himself for God in the work of manipulating destiny. In this so Romantic identification, he relives, as he himself finally recognizes, the myth of the first Romantic, who was Lucifer.

But he possessed, over Lucifer, a modern superiority of planning, of action rationalized and submitted to a plan. In contrast to the commonplace avenger, whose principal characteristic is the blindness of passion (like Vasco, in *O Monge de Cister*, by Alexandre Herculano), he put the precision of the plan and the coherence of the instruments first. When circumstances led him, for the first time, to hesitate in the prosecution of his intention, the principal feeling that manifested itself was that he was interrupting a well-made project: "what I lament is the ruin of my projects so slowly elaborated, constructed with so much work." For this reason, he uses the new possibilities to amplify, satanically, the influence of the Self on (and, principally, against) the World, using the semaphoric telegraph to deal a financial blow to Danglars, mobilizing, in order to destroy Villefort's family through his wife, a profound knowledge of chemistry and medicine. According to Lord Wilmore, one of his pseudonyms, "he is a skilled chemist and no less competent a physicist," having invented a new kind of telegraph.

Nowadays constrained by or accommodated to modern credit and industrialization, vengeance, the old ancestral pull, appears here integrated in a new vision of existence. Thanks to it, Monte Cristo puts into play a human capacity (much increased in his time) to act more freely and powerfully on nature and fellow humans, liberating himself from the coercion of the one, taking maximum advantage of the productivity of the other. His life as a scientific avenger realizes a modern dream: the advent of a new rhythm of life, through which space is compressed and time amplified, by mechanized mobility on the one hand, and the economy of gesture on the other. Master of consciousnesses, knower of secrets, infallible calculator of feelings and acts, he can be everywhere thanks to his agents, automated like machines, to his speedy ships of sail and steam, to the relays of horses he disperses around the highways.

Nevertheless, the Romantic soul (in consonance with the transitory moment that conditions it) lives by contradictions and not uncommonly glories in them. The mentality of the Count was no exception and is nourished at the same time by this modern audacity and by the most antiquated concepts. Thus, human relations seemed to him to have deviated from old patterns they ought to have continued being guided by, because they were carriers of moral and social truth. Faithful to the orientalism of Byron's heros, for him the men of the Levant "are the only ones who know how to live." Women must be slaves and men must be capable of being enslaved. Regarding economic life, his position as a nabob lolling in treasure rests on a retrograde conception, which would horrify any "progressive" character of Balzac's—as in the case of the classification of fortunes he explains to Danglars, in which he deprecates economic initiative and gives value to assured incomes and property.

This way of seeing is coherent with the contradictory presence of Spada's treasure. Torn out of the bowels of the earth, it brings to the book the presence of myth and archetype, corresponding in the imagination to riches acquired magically or by chance. On the plane of literary verisimilitude, it was how the novelist enriched his hero, without the necessity of slow acquisition. Symbolically, however, Dantès carried out a long apprenticeship of fourteen years in solitary confinement, an almost initiatory testing through which he became worthy of obtaining the treasure. However gained, the treasure contrasts with the normal growth of other fortunes, above all with speculation, which has in the book an almost Balzacian presence; and it is curious to see how the treasure serves purposes that are at the same time retrograde, and thus compatible with it (like the oriental display of luxury or the purchase of consciences), and advanced, and thus incompatible with it (like the intervention in economic life, and the acquisition of the machinery that corresponds to the modern mentality).

There thus coexist in the Count a hard-hearted Levantine and an adept of the new types of rational action. This contradiction not only demonstrates the Romantic mixing of past and present, legend and reality, but also the contradiction of the arriviste, who climbs by virtue of his capacity to adapt to the new world and nevertheless preserves all the backwardness of his origins.

The Count is an arriviste in all the good and bad meanings of the word. Despite, for example, the impeccable elegance of manners the novelist has given him, he shows himself off and boasts with a wonderful indiscretion. He praises his own cigars; he focuses the conversation, at a banquet he hosts, on the rarity (and therefore the price) of the delicacies; he boasts of the immensity of his fortune; he asserts the breadth of his knowledge, all with a lack of tact and courtesy, another contradiction in the book and in his personality.

But this is part of the paranoia of the Romantic hero, thanks to which he places himself, quasi-ingenuously, above other men, And he incarnates the superhumanity of the paradigm with such precision that Albert de Morcerf observes to his friends: "When I look at we others, elegant Parisians . . . and I recall this man, it seems to me that we are not of the same species." And Villefort, after a visit in which the Count, exhibiting wisdom and mistreating his visitor, describes his theory of life and affirms his character as a missionary of Providence: "I was unaware that I should meet with a person whose knowledge and understandng so far surpass the usual knowledge and understanding of men."[3]

In order to elevate himself to such a height, from which it is possible to maneuver feelings and destinies freely, Monte Cristo starts from a psychological simplification and a sociological verification. Psychologically, his strength comes from the circumstance that he divides men, without nuance or refinement, into good and bad, without appeal, having as a point of reference the role of those who caused his disgrace in his youth: Danglars, Morcerf, and Villefort. Sociologically, his strength comes from the knowledge that the society of his time, in the midst of structural reconstruction, was composed in good part of adventurers and arrivistes who have climbed, as he himself has, and that therefore the links of the highest spheres with the dregs of misery or crime were still fresh, palpable, and manipulatable.

The progress of the vengeance will permit him to enrich his psychological vision, going beyond his initial scheme. When the disasters he has prepared scientifically begin to accumulate, there arises the problem of the innocents who are linked to the guilty, and of guilt itself, the Count finally sparing the life of the principal author of his imprisonment, Danglars, after, to be sure, having cast him into shame and poverty. Having achieved the maximum of revenge, doubting himself and what he has done, he loses the mighty energy that has made it possible for him to act without remorse. His extreme individualism, after developing freely, unveils its vacuity and casts him, again, into the necessity of support and communion. Monte Cristo disappears into the future after having provided for the happiness of those he considers just, leaving behind a declaration of humility and relativism. He asks that they pray "for a man who, like Satan, thought himself, for an instant, equal to God. . . . Perhaps those prayers may soften the remorse he feels in his heart. . . . There is neither happiness nor misery in the world; there is only the comparison of one state with another."

V

And thus we have our Count, come to the end of his mission, discovering that everything is illusion. In effect, the unlimited development of the will to power tends to isolate its agent, once it places him too far above other men. The tribute paid by the master is the isolation implicit in all elevation. The great capitalist (who beat his wings freely in the Count's time) pays, in isolation and dehumanization, all that he has extracted of the humanity of others through the exploitation of alienated labor. The profound melancholy that assaults Citizen Kane, at the pinnacle of his victory, is related in this respect to that of the genius Romantically conceived, and is expressed better than in any other symbol by the Moses of Alfred de Vigny:

> Hélas! je suis, Seigneur, puissant et solitaire,
> Laissez-moi m'endormir du sommeil de la terre!

This is in part the drama of the Count of Monte Cristo, child of the century, patriarch of *self-made men* [English in the original], who ignores solidarity and equality, understanding only subordination and dependence, required also by his extraordinary sadism. He is a Romantic hero through his cold and mysterious appearance, which disguises indomitable passions; by the infinity of his desires, his eccentricity, his love of "artificial paradises," his orientalism—but also by his taste for blood and the macabre and his refined sense of moral torture, which makes of his revenge a work of art as well as a work of science. His pallor, his cold hands, give some the idea that he is one who has come from the tomb, a vampire who feasts on the blood of others. This vampirism, at least symbolically, is without doubt present in his mode of being, giving a peculiar sense to the expression "thirsty for vengeance," which we associate with him. An expert in weapons and tortures, he watches them with the most suspect pleasure: "At every stroke a jet of blood sprang from the condemned man's neck. This time Franz could no longer control himself, but pulled himself back and sank, half fainting, into a seat. Albert, with his eyes closed, remained standing, but only by gripping the window curtains tightly. The count was erect and triumphant, like the Avenging Angel!"

His theory of the gradation of vengeance corresponded to a monstrous desire to extend the suffering to the maximum, and he applied it meticulously, adding moral tortures to death until he was sated and hesitant. Even when he intends to help, he causes suffering, as in the case of Valentine de Villefort. He decides to save her for her beloved Maximilian, but the idea he carries out so carefully could only pass through the brain of an executioner: he lets Maximilian think for months that she is dead . . . in order to improve him morally! Beneath an impeccable correctness of appearance and manners, Monte Cristo manifests certain aspects of demonic, bloodthirsty rage, which come close to the characters created by the "frenetic" current of Romanticism.[4]

This fury shows us that Providence is only an allegorical projection of his intentions, which combine with social factors to define the Count's will to power and to explain the vacillation that suddenly assaults him, when he sees himself on the heights, "puissant et solitaire." The immoderate affirmation of the self widened the silence and solitude around him, until he felt the final vertigo of individualism and drew back from his work of revenge. He drew back late, probably, because in such cases it is almost never possible to turn back. When we give ourselves, as he did, to the exercise of our personal whims at the expense of of our fellow man (the exercise of personal whims is almost always to the detriment, not the benefit, of others), we cannot avoid others turning away from us, because to the degree that we exalt ourselves as individuals, we dehumanize ourselves by the loss of human contact. And when we succeed in imposing on others everything we insist on saying, doing, and shaping, we do not have the right to insist, above all, that they carry the weight of our burden. From the heights of his monumental vengeance, Monte

Cristo feels this curse, implicit in individualistic morality and economic careerism, and tries to rehumanize himself by some acts of disavowal of his omnipotent will.

This recovery of ethical normality cannot fail to be half deceptive, after such a great effort of excepting oneself from the rule. Everything is going to revolve around axes, and the bourgeois can give this book to the children with ease. . . . Its end, without erasing the prior movement (that is, the right to impose one's self violently, this always leading to spiritual or material growth), pays the tribute owed to the common denominator of civic virtues, the guaranty of every society. . . . The drawing back of Monte Cristo, being the logical imperative of all individualistic hypertrophy, is also a renunciation of the dangers of creative Romanticism. The Count tires, like every worker; he files away the passion of fire and ice that had moved him for more than twenty years, seeing dimly, in a first impulse of senility, comfort in the sweet arms of the young Haydée. "Wait and hope," he advises then. But will there be a place for those who survive their mission, constructive or destructive?

> When all is told
> We cannot beg for pardon.

NOTE

The basic elements of the plot of *The Count of Monte Cristo* were extracted by Dumas from a police report, narrated under the title "Le diamant de la vengeance," in J. Peuchet, *Mémoires tirés des archives de la police de Paris depuis Louis XVI jusqu'à nos jours*, 1838. In his *Causeries* (1857), Dumas relates the genesis of the book. He intended to write a descriptive work on the city of Paris; the publisher, however, insisted on a novel, in which the descriptive elements could serve as a framework. Dumas resolved to develop the "Diamant de la vengeance." Since one visit to the island of Monte Cristo had fascinated him with the place and the name, he began the narrative in Italy, with the experience of Franz d'Epinay in the island's magical cave, and wrote, in the first person, all of the Italian part (the present chapters 31–39, which make up a fourth of the book). A mysterious character, the Count, would meet the young narrator and his friend in Rome and then would go to Paris on the pretext of knowing them, but in truth in order to avenge himself, according to the line of the police case—as Dumas, in fact, wrote. At this point Maquet suggested that he develop the Marseille part, with the prison and its antecedents, and made a complete outline of the final Parisian part. Dumas accepted this and they both went to work.

See Alexandre Dumas, *Le Comte de Monte Cristo*, avec introduction, bibliographie, notes et variants par Jacques-Henri Bornecque, 2 vols. (Paris: Garnier, 1956), which has in the introduction Maquet's till then unpublished plan and, in the appendix, the section of the *Causeries* alluded to above and Peuchet's narrative. Also see Henri Clouard, *Alexandre Dumas* (Paris: Éditions Albin Michel, 1955); chapter 7: "Le Comte de Monte-Cristo et autres romans de moeurs," pp. 297–307; André Maurois, *Les Trois Dumas* (Paris: Hachette, 1957), sixth part: "Monte Cristo," pp. 218–26.

NOTES

First published as "Da vingança," in *Tese e antítese* (São Paulo: Companhia Editora Nacional, 1964), pp. 3–28.

1. See the note at the end of this essay.

2. In 1819 appeared with great success *The Vampire*, a novel that carried, fraudulently, the name of Byron as author but in fact was written by his doctor, Polidori, and that developed a narrative invented by Byron in conversation. The work appeared in the same year in a French translation, and this inspired Cyprien Bérard to write *Lord Ruthwen ou Les Vampires* (using the same name for the protagonist), which Charles Nodier published. Soon afterward, Nodier collaborated in extracting a melodrama, *Les Vampires*, from the work. See Mario Praz, *La carne, la morte e il diavolo nella letteratura romantica*, 3rd ed. (Florence: Sansoni, 1949), pp. 81–83; and Pierre Georges Castex, *Le conte fantastique en France de Nodier à Maupassant* (Paris: José Corti, 1951), pp. 130 and 136.

3. Referring exactly to the two chapters from which these quotations are taken, Gramsci says that they contain a theory of the Superman—which joins the argument developed here. For this Marxist thinker, it is probable that the French journalistic literature had contributed to Nietzsche's ideas on this topic; and, in an evident allusion to Mussolini, he remarks, "In whatever way, it seems to be possible to affirm that the much alleged Nietzchean *superhumanity* has as its unique origin and model of doctrine not Zarathustra but *The Count of Monte Cristo*." Antonio Gramsci, *Letteratura e vita nazionale* (Turin: Einaudi 1950), third part, "Letteratura Popolare," pp. 122 and 123. This entire part, which studies the function of the journalistic novel, with frequent reference to Dumas's book, is very suggestive.

4. On this Romantic tendency see Mario Praz, chap. 2, "Le metamorfosi di Satana," and 3, "All'insegna del divin Marchese"; Pierre-George Castex, "Frénesie romantique," in *Les petits romantiques français* (Les Cahiers du Sud, 1949), pp. 29–38. Alexander Dumas cultivated the genre of the macabre and the vampiresque in the tales in his book *Les milles-et-un fantômes*. See Albert-Marie Schmidt, "Alexandre Dumas Père et ses fantômes," in the same work, *Les petits romantiques français*, pp. 206–11.

Chapter 2

CATASTROPHE AND SURVIVAL

Para a catástrofe, em busca
Da sobrevivéncia, nascemos

[Toward catastrophe, searching for
survival, we are born.]
—Murilo Mendes

JOSEPH CONRAD paid for his popularity. When he arrived, it was thanks to the exotic character of his first books, to the breath of marine incident and poetry (which he reintroduced in the works of his last phase). But, though he was a sailor, he did not feel himself to be a "writer of the sea," nor did he wish to be considered an author of adventure books—since his preoccupation was always, and increasingly, to present a dramatic vision of man, independent of the circumstances of place. "The picture of life, there as here, is drawn with the same elaboration of detail, coloured with the same tints" ("Author's Note" to *Almayer's Folly*).

Modern criticism, conscious of this much more important feature, adopted and developed his point of view, diminishing as much as possible the significance of the exotic element. It was necessary at all costs to save him from the dangerous company of people like Karl May.

Nevertheless, adventure and the picturesque are fundamental elements of his art, as important as the ethical preoccupation, the dramatic feeling, and the pompous style. The sea, the remote outposts, the setting of the episode in exoticism, constitute one of the frameworks of his philosophy. Nor could it be otherwise, in a writer who insisted on his respect for his own experience as a source of the imagination, and who in this way succeeded in communicating to the reader with unequaled power the enchantment of a foreign landscape, the atmosphere of the sea and of tropical nature, and the mystery of the elements, for those who try to decipher them.

If we take as an example the description of the landscape, we see that in his work it plays, beyond the normal function of providing a setting, a decisive role in psychological characterization and in the composition itself. This is already true in the first books, disparaged by critics, showing that from the beginning it included some of his most typical resources of construction and of his conception of life. Part IV of *An*

Outcast of the Islands might serve as an example, with the impressionist elaboration of the long, decisive night, the shadow and light in the house of the scheming Babalatchi, the dawn, the sky cloudy during the discussion, the rain soaking the earth, illuminating the leaves—and Willems abandoned, forsaken, exhausted, symbolically fighting the mud in the sloping courtyard.

This descriptive treatment does not result in detailed objectivity, but in a kind of broad suggestiveness, involving things and people. In the same book, the scene of Lingard's blow (fragmented, in a quiet room of impressions in themselves disconnected, its general significance as an act needing to be recomposed in the reader's mind) demonstrates that gestures become meaningful by the creation of an atmosphere appropriate to the moment in which they occur, in which their workings are altered, making them seem much more powerful, thanks to a complex interplay of magnifying lenses. The opposite of reportage, it is suggestion at its most powerful. One could say, in the manner of Conrad's most beloved authorial voice, Marlow, that "to him the meaning of an episode was not inside like a kernel but outside, enveloping the tale which brought it out only as a glow brings out haze, in the likeness of one of those misty halos that sometimes are made visible by the spectral illumination of moonshine" ("Heart of Darkness").

There is without doubt in all this a certain complacency of composition: an abuse of ornamental images, an analytic excess, a sometimes indiscreet search for the anthologizable passage. But a good part of Conrad's art rests on this stylistic effort, on his capacity to elaborate revelatory metaphors. At times these present a certain blandness of facile allegory, like the house of cards Lingard builds for the little girl, while he tells Almayer his fantasy of treasure (*An Outcast of the Islands*). But they correspond to an artistic and human universe that included, among other things, a tenacious belief in the adjective and in opulent description, as much as in the existence of basic principles of honor; and a noble persistence in the style and the morality, aiming at unity, integrity, and the capacity to choose with conviction. To choose from an established point of view, in the midst of things that dissolve in the transience of impressions; to choose from a moral position, in relation to a character that dissolves in the twists and turns of conduct.

II

Still, analyzing himself and other men, Conrad felt the limits of the unity to which he aspired and that obliterated itself at every step in a "line of shadow." In his most significant works certain factors (among them exoticism and adventure) act, revealing subtle and painful elements, creating a milieu conducive to the formation and emergence of some of his most revealing themes: *isolation, occasion*, and *man surprised*, arranged around the fundamental preoccupation with the *act*, in which, for him, man is really reflected.[1]

Isolation, not only physical, but moral as well—the

> solitude of the bull in the field,
> . . . solitude of the man in the street,

of which the poet speaks—impregnates his work and is admirably expressed by the circumstances in which the narratives of the sea and the tropics are developed, utilized to establish what is almost a myth of the man surrounded, encircled. Seen this way, there is in his work a *feeling of the island* that functions with metaphoric and allegoric value. Beyond the actual island (the one in *Victory*, for example) there is the ship, a kind of floating island (*The Nigger of the Narcissus*, "Typhoon," "Youth," "The Shadow Line," "The End of the Tether," "The Secret Sharer"); and there are tropical outposts on riverbanks, isolated from the world (*Almayer's Folly, An Outcast of the Islands*, "Heart of Darkness," "An Outpost of Progress").

From this comes the feeling of being trapped in a situation whose limits press in on one, forcing man to a critical confrontation with his fellows or himself. From this point of view, the most eloquent and, so to speak, symbolic passage is perhaps the one in *Nostromo*, the description of the boat in which Decoud transports the silver treasure (to an *island*, where he will risk his destiny), which sinks in a darkness more compact and oppressive than ever before created in literature; an absolute darkness, which cuts man off in the opacity of the world.

In his work, however, the metaphor of being on an island is not the end of the matter; it is the preamble to the decisive problem, the act, whose mechanism it sets to work, as is verified in an exemplary fashion in *Victory*, perhaps his masterwork.

The Swede Heyst concludes that action is a diabolic thing, responsible for the evil in society. To act wounds essentially: me, because the act, always imperfect, jeopardizes at every step my purest substance, my ideal reality, which cannot manifest itself in an impure vehicle; the other, because my act amounts to limiting, then crippling, his possible actions. As a result, Heyst resolves to abstain from any action whatsoever and, putting his theory into strict practice, departs for a small island in the Pacific—a symbol of his misanthropy—where he is the only white man. But the illusory solitude opens the way to the common shocks of life, resulting from love, from avarice, from hate. Heyst helps a young woman who has been abandoned; a troublemaker directs toward his refuge the ambition of three criminals, who force him to fight inside this small world. So arises the irony of the situation: having refused to act, he has isolated himself; his sudden interest in the girl leads him to violate this rule of conduct and to do something that, by giving him company, thoroughly revolutionizes his original intent. This consequence could, on the other hand, give him completeness, creating the possibility of dialogue and closing off forever the necessity of another act. Heyst's development of his self would be completed through the mediation of the woman, produced in his solitude by his need for companionship, a little in the manner of the myth of Eve, and it is he himself who says: "There must be a lot of the original Adam in me, after all."[2] That act is revealed, moreover, as the beginning of a series of acts that reinstall him in the normal conditions of life, obliging him to observe, to calculate, to fight, or to succumb. The world had been hunting him on the island, teaching, as in others of Conrad's books, that to refuse the action required by the moment is to bring into being other actions more wounding to the self's integrity.

From this arises the importance of the second theme—that of the *occasion*, of the opportunity that, Sophocles said, "directs the enterprises of men," often emerging from the folds of fortune, as it is put so beautifully in "Freya of the Seven Isles": "And this possibility had come about without any planning, one could almost say naturally, as if events had mysteriously shaped themselves to fit the purposes of a dark passion." The occasion is the origin of the event, and this, despite its relative discrediting in contemporary literature, is the foundation of the novel, constituting one of the manifestations par excellence of the human situation.

A large part of the good fiction of this century exalts psychological *durée*, the internal law of the character, as a reaction to the exaggeration of incidents made into banal, exterior solutions. Some novelists subject events to an elaboration that, as it increases, gains its own reality and relegates the event to a secondary plane, at times to no more than a vague pretext. Already, in such precursors of the contemporary novel as Dostoyevsky, everything is arranged around dramatic conjunctures, necessary and brutal acts, which change the course of the narrative and define the characters. Nevertheless, each conjuncture is so enveloped in a dialectic torrent, examined so abundantly, that it finishes by seeming, not the determining circumstance, but a component of a human process that invests and transcends it. When it emerges, like a bursting forth of concentrated passions, we have already anticipated it more or less confusedly—whether it is the intervention of old Karamazov in the meeting with the *Starets*; the invasion of Dmitri in the inn where Grushenka has met the Poles; or, in *The Devils*, that of Lebyadkin in the salon of Varvara Petrovna; or, in *The Idiot*, that of Rogojin and his gang in that of

Nastasia Filipovna. In these novelists—of whom Proust is the pattern and Joyce could be considered the extreme case—the event disappears beneath what precedes, accompanies, and follows it.

In the work of Conrad, there is something similar, but only in part. Even though extraordinarily purified and contained, the event retains its nature as something that has happened, its nature as a fact in relation to which actions are defined, and that will be linked in concatenation with other events. In Conrad, the event is not an absolute law of the narrative, as in the novel published in serial form, but it is one of its supports. Yet it is never a sovereign and independent factor, changing the destiny of characters who would not exist without it. Characters have a predisposition for a certain kind of event that, when it emerges, is really the occasion, almost the opportunity, that determines their fate. Therefore, events and incidents have their own reality; but they have meaning as long as they are occasions for the character to define himself. In Conrad's work, the external occurrence and the interior vision join with great balance, situating the work at an equal distance from Alexander Dumas and Marcel Proust, permitting the involvement of reality through suggestive poetry.

Having said this, we understand the degree to which the destiny of characters, without violating their own internal law, is often dictated by an external element, which brusquely stimulates the capacity to decide, condemning or redeeming.

Lord Jim, who "saved" himself, avoiding involvement in vulgar activities in order to preserve his state of virginity for a brilliant, pure deed, untouched by the detritus of everyday life, fails precisely by refusing to recognize that impure, imperfect circumstance is what reality offers us and that it is incumbent on us to confront it. As Unamuno said, "Lo más urgente es lo de ahora y de aqui; en el momento que pasa y el reducido lugar que ocupamos están nuestra eternidad y nuestra infinitud" [What is most urgent is the here and now; our eternity and our infinitude are in the passing moment and the restricted place we occupy.] (*Vida de Don Quijote y Sancho*). There is no ideal moment to act, appearing with prior notice for our triumph, at hours that are neutral, static, without responsibility; the exceptional moment is born every moment, and every moment imposes a corresponding action. For this reason, everyone who continues to wait for the ideal moment either ignores the urgency of the present and condemns himself to inaction, or acts precipitately, without any restraint, and risks destruction. Willems thought he could leave the right road for an instant, imagining that the quotidian does not constrain capable men, aware of their perspicacity, and that it is always possible to treat as nothing the small shocks to which it subjects us: he was destroyed by the irregular act and became "the outcast of the islands."

When action is rejected (whether to aspire to a kind of contemplative immobility, like Heyst; or to have, like Lord Jim, the illusion of awaiting a glorious moment), it returns by other paths, compelling unforeseen attitudes that bloom at the touch of opportunity. The agent does not recognize himself then; he is surprised by what he does, not identifying himself with what has been done. Lord Jim does not recognize his desertion of his post as legitimately his, nor Willems his financial transgression, nor Heyst the rape of Lena, nor Razumov the accusation of Haldin (*Under Western Eyes*). It is as if consciousness, taken by surprise, were to produce an unknown, extra Self, which projects itself along a different path than the one habit assigns to consciousness. In all these cases, the third theme selected here to investigate Conrad's complex art appears: that of the man surprised by the *occasion*, who surprises himself by his own act, sensing the formation of a duality of self.

The man surprised acts without apparent motive, in a kind of impetuous and inexplicable discharge, an act formally gratuitous, from which flows, however, a second stage, since he is obliged to remake himself, should he aim at reacquiring his inner equilibrium. Lord Jim, who was not a coward, impetuously jumped over the rail, abandoning his post, fleeing his duty, and is punished by expulsion from the merchant marine. Following that, he painfully reconstructs his self-respect in a long life of danger, struggle, and dedication. Heyst suddenly resolves to kidnap Lena—and then acts methodically and deliberately, elaborating the plan in order to confront the bandits. Razumov denounces Haldin in a fury; much later, he consecrates his life to rehabilitating himself, together with the dead man's mother and sister.

Still, on closer analysis, we see that in Conrad these sudden actions seem pure and gratuitous only because they precipitate themselves; in truth, behind them lies a slow-moving past that explains them and, in fact, almost requires them. We have already seen that in *Lord Jim* there is the problem of reserve, the supervaluation of the Self, which leads Jim to avoid commitment and live in the paralysis of the conditional; when opportunity, inflexible, presents itself it produces panic. In the case of Heyst, his absolute reserve drives him almost to the loss of his own consciousness, resulting in a self-negation that calls for a compensatory act of reequilibration. He "suffered from failure in a subtle way unknown to men accustomed to grapple with the realities of common human enterprise. It was like the gnawing pain of useless apostasy."

And thus we arrive at the limits of the process: abstention corrodes, definitively, more than imperfect contact with others. A man isolates himself and refuses to act; but the isolation gives rise to more decisive actions than any other situation; the occasion unleashes the avoided, or unforeseen, behavior, and the man is surprised by what it reveals in him:

good, as in "Youth" or "The Shadow Line"; evil, as in *An Outcast of the Islands* or *Lord Jim*. Even when apparently gratuitous, however, the act composes itself in a profound germination, which eventually explodes on the pretext of the occasional circumstance. For this reason, the exotic, remote, different situation, as well as the adventure and the incident, constitute fundamental elements of Conrad's art. They allow the favorable configuration of isolation, of occasion, and of the man surprised, which explain one of the main directions of his conception of life.

III

To understand the position of these themes in the whole of Conrad's work, some reference, however brief, to that conception or, better, to his vision of man and of coexistence in society is necessary. For him the man surprised is a self in crisis, submitted to a decisive test of individuality. The crisis derives, in general, from conflict with a group, or with group norms: whoever has a foundation overcomes it and remakes himself; whoever does not is dissolved in things or, what for Conrad amounts to the same thing, in the banality of social conformism. Because, for this man so respectful of values, attachment to them is only valid when it represents a kind of conscious acceptance, a profound choice. Mere acceptance is equivalent to its absence.

In some of his stories the tropics are what is Evil, fascinating, dizzying, and, at the same time, a kind of test, because they threaten the integrity of the good man—the *gentleman*, a human type whom Conrad's own deracinated condition led him to overestimate, and who would have the function of embodying, through his divided consciousness, perplexed in a universe of shaky values, a kind of steadying rock.

In the first phase of his work the feeling of struggle between the white man and the tropics is more vivid and schematic, although he soon reaches the admirable symbol of "Heart of Darkness," to arrive finally at the creation of Heyst, in which the picturesque is only a pretext for dramas of the soul.

In "An Outpost of Progress" we see that initial position, of the white man in the tropics, reflected in the personalities of two mediocrities, whose resistance is broken with relative ease and whose mediocrity is expressed in their passive integration into the social patterns of their origin. The novelist says that the group sustains the individual in such a way that his incapacity is not apparent, nor does it create grave problems as long as he lives in the herd. But, confronted with the primitive conditions imposed by exotic countries, the civilized person is thrown back on himself and, if he does not possess sufficient interior power, crumbles, because of the absence of group support. The social, which levels people, appears as something contemptible, which makes possible the survival of the inept and which the true man does not accept. The characters of "An Outpost of Progress" make the title a tragic irony: "They were two perfectly insignificant and incapable individuals, whose existence is only rendered possible through the high organization of civilized crowds. Few men realize that their life, the very essence of their character, their capabilities and their audacities, are only the expression of their belief in the safety of their surroundings."

This novella expresses a constant in Conrad's work, whether in convictions openly expressed, or in the drama of a white man disorganized by the inability to deal with the conditions of colonial life. It affirms the idea that for him human values, which society tries to inculcate, can express automatism as much as moral grandeur, according to whether they represent a profound attachment, leading to sacrifice and to heroism, or do not go beyond conformity to the median of virtue. And this redeems in part his admiration for the British *gentleman*, which at times seems a little foolish.

We can now go further, and say that his preferred kind of humanity is organized around two ideal types, which fascinated him successively or simultaneously, forming the poles, or the two halves, of his psychology: the man of noble sentiments, whose conduct is nobly right and whole, whose actions derive from the integrity of his humanity and from his harmonious adjustment to values; and the man mysteriously assaulted by forces which divide him, who acts, in consequence, on the basis of obscure impulses and impetuous decisions, due to a combination of circumstances which act so as to extract from him acts and attitudes which leave him perplexed.

IV

Two tales in Conrad's work embody these poles with maximum purity: "Prince Roman" and "The Secret Sharer," the first no more than a story of good quality, the latter a masterpiece, showing that the best part of what he wrote is what is structured around the second pole, which this essay tries to characterize.

We know from his autobiogaphy that Prince Roman (Sanguzko) was a hero of the Polish insurrection, a friend of his grandfather, and was exiled for many years in Siberia. In the story, he is the paradigm of the first type (which, by the way, enters into the formula of the majority of Conradian heros who respect themselves); and we realize that the novelist feels at home in the character's rectitude. "A man who was eminently a man, among all men capable of feeling profoundly, believing firmly, and loving ardently," qualities that seemed to Conrad the highest and least accessible to modern man, hyperanalytic, seeker after antidotes to greatness, incapable of accepting people and things without having doubts. "A certain magnitude of soul is necessary to interpret patriotism justly; or, rather, a sincerity of sentiment denied to the vulgar refinements of modern thought, which cannot comprehend the august simplicity of a feeling which originates in the very nature of things and of man."

Conrad sees this *nature* of man (which to us seems the fruit of history and convention) as a primary datum, an immediate reality that manifests itself to those capable of perceiving it, because they are mentally and morally equipped for such things. According to him, this is the case of the true *gentleman*, nourished by sound values, treading on a firm ground of convictions and attitudes. To live out of values in this way is denied only to those who are incapable of it. From this comes his disenchantment with the contemporary world and his attachment to the universe of honor and duty, symbolized in the navy; from this comes his distrust of the ferment of skepticism and of analytic crudeness. "Everything is vacuity only for vacant men and everything is a joke only for those who have never been honest with themselves."

But this is, as we have said, only a part of Conrad. And, be that as it may, for us, men of a century that sees itself in the fragmentation of Joyce and Picasso, in the absurdity of Kafka, in the going against the grain of serial music—for us his strength does not lie in this unitary conception.

Indicating that the basic problem of his most characteristic works is that of evil, one critic noted:

> The nature of this complex "undefinable" evil can be better expressed by stating what is opposed to it. In a famous sentence in his Preface to *A Personal Record*, Conrad wrote: "Those who read me know my conviction that the world, the temporal world, rests on a few very simple ideas: so simple that they must be as old as the hills. It rests, notably, among others, on the idea of Fidelity." Douglas Hewitt has shown in his *Conrad: A Reassessment* that as a clue to Conrad these words are not to be taken precisely at their face value. Fidelity is the barrier man erects against nothingness, against corruption, against evil which is all about him, insidious, waiting to engulf him, and which is, in some sense, within him unacknowledged. But what happens to a man when the barrier breaks down, when the evil without is acknowledged by the evil within, and fidelity is submerged? This, rather than fidelity itself, this is Conrad's theme at his greatest.[3]

Which is, put differently, what I am trying to say. This is why his most interesting man is of the second type mentioned, the one surprised by himself, including by the negation of values apparently anchored in his conception of life—like Lord Jim.

The type appears clearly and, in a way, symbolically, in "The Secret Sharer ." The young captain-narrator, who has the experience of his first command in a ship whose crew is mistrustful and hostile, is surrounded, par excellence, on this moving island. His weapon is the routine of duty that he learned, perhaps, superficially and did not incorporate into his deepest life experiences. And then there occurs the occasion, the fruit of circumstances fortuitously connected: his decision to take the dawn watch, the rope side-ladder inexplicably not hauled in from the rail, the swimmer who climbs it. It is a murderer, Leggatt, a fugitive from the *Sephora*, anchored nearby; against the code of honor and professional duty, he hides Leggatt for days in the tiny cabin, risking at every instant his career and his own integrity. Something profound and inexplicable ties him to this companion, this nocturnal partner outside the law, whose soul he understands and with whose action he feels himself mysteriously sympathetic.

This story "provides the perfect psychological case—the hidden self 'exactly the same' as the other, but guilty, and always of necessity concealed from the eyes of the world; dressed in a sleeping suit, the garb of the unconscious life, appearing and disappearing out of, and into, the infinite sea."[4] There is in it "a unique artistic use of the divided man, that modern fission of personality inexorably foreshadowed during the last century by Hoffman, Poe, Stevenson, and Dostoyevsky."[5] Effectively, this gives substance to a latent tendency in the best of Conrad's work, linking it to one of the most characteristic developments of the contemporary novel, that which, even when it does not appear explicitly in the working out of the story, comes from the "black novel," the grotesque novellas of Gogol, from *The Double* of Dostoyevsky, enriching itself at the fringes of surrealism, from which Julien Gracq drew *The Opposing Shore*, a masterpiece dealing with the isolated individual, surprised by circumstances.

According to this tendency, man is eminently a self who does not know himself, who resembles at times a colony of selves dominated by the conventional synthesis that education has elaborated on the basis of our precepts, but that can escape in unanticipated ways, in which the Self feels itself Other. Pirandello said, in *Each in His Own Way*, "Illegitimate thoughts are every bit as real as illegitimate children," and that "outside the honest confines of wedlock, outside the framework of the conscious mind" we permit ourselves numerous illicit relations with ideas and fancies, hurriedly relegated to the basement of the spirit. The case of Conrad's character is one of those in which we see these unwelcome guests climb to the top of the stairs. But (and here enters his profound comprehension of the dynamism of psychic life) in this story such an invasion is accepted, understood, and comes to constitute the basis for a strengthening of the self and a rectification of conduct. On this point, he distinguishes himself from writers who descend to the deepest part of the spirit and leave us perplexed, paralyzed, gone astray, from the weight of these dangerous examinations. M. D. Zabel reminds us that for Conrad the best solution for a psychological crisis is the more harmonious integration of the individual with social values; and thus his books transform themselves from personal investigations into studies of the way people confront these values. "The divided man—the face and its mask, the soul and its shadow—is never, in Conrad, an individual and nothing more. He becomes—especially in novels of historical scope or parabolic implications like *Nostromo, Under Western Eyes,* and *Victory*— a metaphor of society and of humanity."[6]

"The Secret Sharer" utilizes a symbolic method of projection, in fact making of the fugitive the *double,* the other half of the narrator (the "duplicate," Mario de Andrade would say). "My double," "my own grey ghost," "my other self," "my second self," "myself" are the expressions he uses, showing the clarity with which he feels, in the presence of the stranger, the reality of this unfolding of his soul. From this arises an immediate complicity, woven of whispers, maneuvers to hide what is happening, fascinated interest, and affective identification. He hides the other in the cabin as if he were hiding himself; which allows the other to say that he acts as if he had expected his arrival. The reason is that the narrator feels himself "almost as much a stranger on board as himself." Before the hostile and mistrustful veterans, he experienced an insecurity that drew him out of himself, leading him to deviate from routine (which is *of* others, which is *the* others), and to reach out to the unanticipated, to adventure. At this point the fugitive rose from the sea, as if he had emerged from the captain's own consciousness, and the captain felt more connection to him than to the norms of the service. The fugitive only gives reality to the division of the captain's self, which he feels "more dual than ever." We see thus how the occasion, rising out of the mystery of the propitious oriental waters, surrounding the man isolated morally or physically, calls forth these surprising revelations of the depth of the spirit. We cite again the American critic who sensed so well some of the problems dealt with here, who refers to an "enemy" latent in Conrad's men, " 'our common enemy," "leaping from unknown coverts, sometimes from the hiding places that fate has prepared, but more often and seriously . . . from the unfathomed depths of our secret natures, our ignorance, our unconscious and untested selves."[7]

But this presence of the hidden self opposing the apparent self does not inevitably end, in Conrad (as it does in Graciliano Ramos), in an ethical or psychological atomism, in a relativism that dissolves personal integrity. For him, integrity is formed, on the contrary, beginning with the experience of the Other, of the Double who lives in us. After Leggatt leaves the ship, swimming toward the unknown, the narrator feels himself, finally, exorcised, master of the situation, conscious of his total personality. The frank acceptance of experience, of its at times dangerous suggestions, allowed him this decisive encounter. "But before Leggatt finally disappears, the captain has come to know the secret soul he lives with. His life is changed. A new vision of humanity has broken in upon the masked and impersonal regimen of his days."[8]

Thus, for him, above duty and coherence, suggested by education and society, there is a risk that man must assume, though it may discredit him in the light of the usual norms. This risk is an act of courage and challenge, which expresses something profound: a release of energies that carry the self and the actor abruptly down a certain road, whose validity will only be calculable by the actor himself. The narrator resolved to break the rules and conceal the murderer, to make of him a kind of hidden partner, in the complicity of this profound link; the reason for this act will only be establishable by the conscience itself, and it is only to it, as to a court, that he owes an accounting. When he attains this interior strength, the dangerous phase is overcome and man is man; the ship, having sailed audaciously near the cliffs, so that Leggatt can be gotten off, allowing him to escape, maneuvers, symbolically, almost to the point of breaking up on the rocks, then finds the favorable current and catches in its sails the wind it needs to free itself from the stagnation of the Gulf of Siam. Disregarding human respect, confronting the profound realities of the soul, the narrator finds himself mature, master of the situation, overcoming the initial indecision that diminished him as an interloper in the (also symbolic) eyes of the crew, who are the others. "Perhaps nothing more could affect him, after he had survived the attack of the dark powers" (*Lord Jim*).

When it is all over, the integrated man, mentioned earlier, can reconstitute himself, or return surreptitiously, to take up the tensions and risks of the divided man, not as one who flees from himself, but as one who, having accepted the attractions of the interior abyss, overcomes them and is now ready for the higher spheres of humanity. In this case, the man surprised by his own image, which comes to frighten him with the shock of the occasion, conquers integrity, not in relation to a duty mechanically learned and painfully maintained (like the captain of the *Sephora*, a pale and impeccable automaton who comes looking for Leggatt on the narrator's ship); but aware of his self, against what is petty in our norms. There thus exists in Conrad (as he often affirmed) a belief in permanent values to which each person's ethics can be reduced, but of which the supreme judge is the individual himself confronted by conscience, far from an automatic conventionalism, the only support of those poor Belgians destroyed in "An Outpost of Progress." A free conception of responsibility is manifested in this encounter of man with himself; and this encounter is the ideal limit of those inexplicable acts, those unforeseen passions that come to destroy a life but can permit its reconstruction in terms of authentic nobility. Far from the good youth who virtuously follows the road of duty, Conrad's man must go through dubious experiences in order to test his fiber, ending in one of the ways it is possible to end: defeated, like Willems; dead in the ecstasy of totally interior triumph, like Heyst; literally dehumanized, like Kurtz, in the solitude of the heart of darkness; finally made whole at the hour of death, like Jim; master of himself, like the narrator of "The Secret Sharer." "Who does not know the regions of evil does not understand much of this world; the stoic perhaps ignores them, but the saint knows them well," said Jacques Maritain, responding to a letter of conversion from Jean Cocteau. Evil, perhaps; certainly the abysses of the world and of the spirit, sounded by the more meaningful characters of Conrad as an initiation into true humanity.

V

The novelists of complexity frequently leave the impression that the complex is an *event*, something exceptional and curious. Even for their great master, Dostoyevsky, the contradictory plurality of the soul appears most of the time associated with a certain moral abnormality or, at the least, a certain personal instability. In Conrad this latent naturalism does not occur. The strength and the novelty of his work reside in the fact that this division or plurality appears as the norm, not a deviation. In many of his novels and stories it is human nature itself that is represented, implicitly or explicitly, as a multiplicity of potential selves, who reveal themselves, or not, depending on circumstances.

From this point of view *Lord Jim* is very significant, because in it such problems appear linked to the play of the three elements already pointed out—isolation, occasion, and the man surprised—above all by virtue of the narrative technique, which communicates in its structure the vision of man fragmented and the search for unity, in such a way that what has to this point been analyzed as *content* will now appear confirmed at the level of *form*. And only then will we be able to see that the effectiveness of Conrad's art is not due to the simple proposal of an attitude of life, but to the fact of translating that attitude into a method of narration, which becomes an indissoluble part of what the novelist means since, in the end, it is what he effectively says. In *Victory* we meet in a manner perhaps still purer the play of the three factors; but we do not find the technique of "splintering." In *Chance* this technique of fragmentation

appears in a more refined way than in *Lord Jim*; but the propitious constellation of factors does not occur.

Lord Jim tells the story of an officer of the merchant marine who
abandons his post in a moment of danger. Tried, he loses his certifica-
tion and lives a precarious life, fleeing as soon as he is recognized, until
he seeks refuge in Patusan, a forgotten place in the interior of Malay-
sia.There, where his past is ignored, he becomes a kind of good and
strong adviser, seen by the natives from an angle that redeems him. A
group of European adventurers attack the settlement; Jim (who is
strangely fascinated and intimidated by their chief, Brown), after neu-
tralizing them, agrees to let them leave free. On the way, they kill the
son of the indigenous chief with whom Jim is allied as a counselor and
friend. Expiating his final sin, he allows himself to be killed by the old
man.

The kernel of Jim's problem (which will be discussed here only in
relation to the first part of the book, before the departure for Patusan)
was already suggested in the previous pages. It is that of the man normally worthy, thirsty for adventure, bright, waiting for the ideal moment that will take his measure; and who nevertheless fails when put to
the test, without knowing exactly why.

He was first mate of a rusty old steamboat, the *Patna*, commanded by
a German scoundrel with three white machinists and a native crew,
which was taking eight hundred pilgrims to Mecca. One night a muffled
thud is heard. Investigating what happened, Jim sees through a doorway
that the iron bulkhead, weak and corroded by rust, had given way under
some impact and water had gotten in. The pilgrims were sleeping, scattered around the quarterdeck; there weren't enough lifeboats; the sink-
ing was probably so rapid that there was no time to lower them. Seeing
the situation, the commander and the machinists, unknown to Jim, try
to escape by freeing one of the boats for themselves. But the boat's pul-
ley is jammed, so that he arrives in time to witness their grotesque efforts
to lower it, without himself taking part, with no definite intention to do
anything, refusing to help the others, paralyzed by the perplexity of the
situation. One of the men dies of emotion; the others, who have already
succeeded in lowering the boat, don't realize it and call him repeatedly.
But it is Jim who, in an impetuous decision, vaults the rail and falls into
the boat; the boat separates from the ship and the others have the impression that the ship will sink any minute since, in addition to the water
and the mist, the angle of the heeled-over ship hides the light of the
watch from the fugitives. The following day they are picked up by a ship,
and Jim, after some time, learns that the *Patna* did not sink but was
towed to safety by a French gunboat. Thus ensues the shame, the pro-

fessional crime, the trial, the finished career, his own country forbidden to him by the embarrassment he would feel should he meet relatives and friends.

Being the only honest man among the whites on the *Patna*, the youth was morally isolated on board by the impossibility of establishing contact with the others, as well as being physically isolated in the immensity of the Indian Ocean—"still, without a stir, without a ripple, without a wrinkle—viscous, stagnant, dead." When the unexpected situation arises, it does not present itself as a conjuncture favorable to brilliant heroism. It has none of those characteristics that surround such feats, in the exemplary narratives of books of great actions. It is only the moment, like any other, that he does not foresee (as obscure moments are not foreseen), but that is decisive, that imposes the choice of life or death. And in this moment, which was not the ideal he had prepared himself so long and confidently for, an unexpected Jim, who will surprise him and torment him the rest of his life, shows up and acts like the scoundrels who flee their duty, abandoning to their fates the ship, the crew, the eight hundred Muslim pilgrims.

Why? asks Jim, and so do we. This question without an answer takes almost half of the novel and is pursued through a very complex combination of points of view, or narrative foci, involving dramatic scenes, dialogues, and descriptions, subordinated to an extraordinary technique of slow motion and unforeseen conclusions, which precede by fourteen years the analyses of Proust, and which perhaps had developed, at least in part, under the influence of the explanatory discussions of Dostoyevsky.[9]

From the formal point of view, the problem is that of the correspondence between a vision of man and the technical means used to express it. How to transmit in a lively way, not on the less convincing plane of exposition pure and simple, the division of the self, the abysses, and the fragmentation that transform each of us into a precarious unity, always ready to break into pieces? Conrad rejected introspection, which could here function as a kind of elastic panacea. If one had recourse to that, one of two things would happen: either Jim would be able to explain himself, in which case there would be no problem, transforming the novel into a clear-sighted confession; or he would not be capable of interpreting himself, which in this case would only incessantly recreate the problem. The novelist put resolutely to one side, therefore, the subjective angle (which was never to his liking) and chose the objective, that is, those which focused on the subject from the outside looking in, even when they were identified ideally with his personality. Thanks to them he could, in compensation, reinstall a maximum of subjectivity, which largely uncovered Jim, but not in a direct manner. The angle is objective and indirect: the protagonist talks to Marlow, who tells his friends what Jim has said and what others have said about him. This always leaves the possibility that what has been narrated may be in part Marlow's personal vision, not a pure manifestation of Jim. And all this part of the book is a world of quotation marks within quotation marks, from the beginning in which the omniscient narrator speaks.[10]

If we look at the order of the narrative, we see how this technique rests on an extremely complex temporal game, which one can get a clear idea of through the alphabetical representation of J. W. Beach. Imagining the normal sequence of an account as a series of steps ordered alphabetically, from A to Z, the sequence of *Lord Jim* is the following (each comma marks a chapter):

KLMP, WA, E, B, E, E, H, GD, HJ, FE, E, E, F, F, F, FK,
I, I, R, I, KL, MN, N, QM QPO, OP, P, QP, P, P, P, Q, P,
Q, Q, Q, R, ZV, YX, S, S, S, TY, U, U, U, WXY.[11]

Thanks to this game, we have the tangible display of an interior reality that is fragmented and complex, that we come to understand only with difficulty, and that is completed by an equally multiplex exterior reality, which we approach in an intricate and discontinuous manner.

We are in the first part of the book. In the beginning, the omniscient narrator speaks, entering directly into the presentation of Jim, in the phase that (we will learn later by inference) follows his trial and judgment and precedes the departure for the backlands of Patusan. This Jim, an active representative for shipping agents, had the peculiarity of moving farther on whenever something that bothered him came to light. And, with an allusion to his withdrawing into the Malaysian jungle, the narrator turns to his origins and development, relating a fact that contains the germ of his entire future tragedy: his hesitation in coming to the assistance of a lifeboat in an emergency, during his naval apprenticeship. Then comes the voyage to the Orient; a disaster that leaves him hospitalized for some time; the engagement as first mate of the *Patna*. The narrator then describes the voyage bound for Arabia, up to the night of the accident, which occurred at the moment when the commander was going to replace him for the dawn watch. Here a temporal jump occurs and we are taken to the inquiry room, where we see him respond to some requests for clarification after the occurrence. His eyes meet those of a spectator, the chapter ends, the omniscient narrator disappears and the narrative is now told by this spectator, Marlow. In a few words, Marlow tells how he saw the strange group of men of the *Patna* for the first time and some episodes that followed. He returns to the inquiry, recounts the violent reaction of one of the commission's members, Captain Brierly, recounts what the mate Jones told him about

Brierly's death, returns again to the inquiry, recounts his meeting with Jim, and gives a long account of him, interrupted from time to time by commentary. We now learn how Jim saw the doorway inundated and what occurred up to the flight in the boat. Then follows the account, heard much later and more casually, of a French lieutenant who gives the final elements of the case (one of the most admirable scenes in the book and in all of Conrad's work). The conversation with the young man ends and Marlow tells how he arranged a job for Jim, which led to his life as a shipping agent, referred to in the opening lines of the book. With this the initial part of the book is concluded, and the second and final part begins, with the life in Patusan, where there will intervene a still greater complication of indirect narratives, letters, etc.

As has been seen, it is a discontinuous chronological zigzag, with interrupted episodes embedded in one another, seen through diverse narrative mediations. An event begun comes to be clarified much later, the end appears before the beginning, the focus varies while time is extended sequentially or in jumps, the premonitions and anticipations give the story that quivering of which Conrad is the master. If the people and the events are mysterious, the road to understanding them is equally complex and strange, made of pieces found in the four corners of the world—from India to Indonesia, from Indonesia to Australia, from Australia to Indochina.

The reason for Jim's act is broken up in a series of long conversations, with explanatory digressions, and the answer is not given. It remains hidden between the lines, clearly enough that we can see that it is a matter of one of those invasions of hidden subjectivity, one of those unexpected visits of the Other, which materialized in "The Secret Sharer." If the self is multiple, not something we can apprehend, the best narrative approximation will be not only to attack it from various sides but, further, to show its similarity to other selves (two ways of testing and investigating the fragments we are able to learn). For this reason, only some of the facts are seen by the omniscient observer, who has the privilege of revealing what Jim feels but can only use this privilege to give detailed descriptions of scenes that, in the end, could be known and described by any one: his childhood, a brief summary of his growing up, the night of the *Patna*, the collision, the investigation of the accident, the hearing of the commission of inquiry. Here, this narrator of limited omniscience stops, returning only briefly in the second part; but even in that beginning he is not stationary, and his angle varies. In the *Patna*, he seems to be an ideal observer who hovers over the ship and later descends in order to present what occurred there; in the hearing room he is only a more knowledgeable spectator, who nevertheless understands nothing and is just there. With respect to decisive moments and sequences, Marlow takes over, and it is from his subjective angle that reality unfolds, with no guaranty of objectivity. Actions are shown and commented on according to the judgment of a witness, either that of Marlow himself, or that of Jim through him. This functions as a kind of distancing from certainty, which in an odd way reinforces the verisimilitude of the narrative. Jim does not know the reason and seeks it until he finds some formulas, which could well be rationalizations. Marlow, insofar as he hears, makes an effort to understand, which could also be distorting; and we get the two distortions, constructing out of them our own understanding and our own judgment. Reality appears, as it in fact is, a source of possible, but not certain, understanding, upon which we build our character and our conduct.

In order to clarify the act under discussion, the novelist unfolds the narrative on two levels, the second functioning (as we see) as a replica, or approximate reproduction, that echoes the first. On the first level is Jim, who narrates minutely, prolonging for pages and pages the few minutes the action on the *Patna* lasted—according to a time that seems to slow up, subdivided into endless moments. Thanks to this it is possible to decompose the action into instants that cannot be measured, only lived, and that memory later organizes in its own way. Just as these moments were everything in Jim's life (for they decided his life once and forever), in the novel they are extended as if they had lasted for years, as if each infinitesimal portion, given its significance, had transformed itself into a space abounding in events and feelings. That is why the narrative is not continuous. Marlow intermingles commentaries with his narration, establishes the connections of marginal events, and leaves Jim in order to bring in the testimony of others: the officer of the French gunboat, who furnishes the missing pieces that complete the sequence of events, and the mate Jones, who tells the story of Captain Brierly.

VI

This Brierly constitutes, so to speak, the second level, the level of the narrative's resonance, and his presence is fundamental not only for the vision of man divided, but also for the divided technique that corresponds to it. His function is to be a mysterious confirmation of Jim, being in a certain way his negative, in the photographic sense. When he first appears, we don't know who he might be; from Jim's angle, told us by the narrator, he is only one of the experts who, with the magistrate, make up the commission of inquiry into the case of the *Patna*. For the time being, he is just a "a heavy, scornful man, thrown back in his seat, his left arm extended full length, [who] drummed delicately with his finger-tips on a blotting pad." Later on, Marlow's narrative furnishes his identity, telling us that he is Big Brierly, captain of the best ship of the Blue Star Line, handsome, strong, serene, competent, brave, covered with honors and rewards, envied by all. Through his conversations with Marlow, we come to know his "wrong" side and witness his uneasiness with the inquiry, which he considers dangerous, shameful, and compromising for the profession; he wants to convince the young man to flee, with money he, Brierly, will give him. We see that he feels himself exposed by Jim's case, all his honor at risk, possessed by a strange feeling of inquietude, which shakes his disdainful superiority, his perfect standard of conduct. And then comes the shock, in the course of the narrative in which Marlow is characterizing him: "The sting of life could do no more to his complacent soul than the scratch of a pin to the smooth face of a rock. This was enviable. As I looked at him, flanking on one side the unassuming pale-faced magistrate who presided at the inquiry, his self-satisfaction presented to me and to the world a surface as hard as granite. He committed suicide very soon after."

In effect, after taking the measures required by duty, the brilliant Brierly also jumps the rail, like Jim—but for death. Without motive, without justification, without any explanation, reminding us of the no less imposing Richard Cory, in the poem of Edward Arlington Robinson. The uneasiness that agitates him during the inquiry opens the way, still, for an interpretation that is more in line with Conrad's methods, and that has not escaped the critics.[12] Like Leggatt for the young captain in "The Secret Sharer," Jim represents for Brierly the Other, the enigmatic and terrible *duplicate* in which is displayed the self, and which opportunity brings to the surface of consciousness. Without the least necessity of commentary, we feel that his integrity has been shaken to its foundations by contact with a troubling reality (Jim's action), awakenng in him God knows what parallels and forebodings. There is a mysterious sympathy between these selves, which multiplies the interior divisions without end.

As a matter of fact, we are not only intimately divided, despite the unity imposed by social norms, but we feel in other people fragments of an affinity that reveal us to ourselves, as if all others were, in some part of their being, our doubles. Jim's major horror, for example, resides in the fear of being made the equal of those lamentable scoundrels of the *Patna*, who had fled the inquiry, leaving him to bear the weight of the action that was theirs before it was his, the action he nevertheless joined in, bringing himself down to their level. For this reason he suspects that he has in him something in common with these men: the fat and greasy captain; the chief mechanic, eaten away by drunkenness; the second mechanic, shaking with cowardice. At the end of the book, in Patusan, the same feeling of an excusable and inevitable solidarity weakens him in the confrontation with the arrogant Brown, who asks him if his conscience is clean to the point of allowing him to judge others; and who alludes insidiously to the inevitable community of men. "Being likewise a social outcast and a leader, Brown bears a grotesque resemblance to Jim; and their meeting may be compared with the lifeboat scene on the *Patna*, as the second notable example in the book of Conrad's dramatic and visual rendering of a psychological issue. Brown's trickery succeeds because Jim, a fallible human and not the supernatural being of his legend, cannot destroy his past even in a land without a past."[13]

Brierly's suicide, following the violent and unexpected moral reaction, furnishes a decisive link in the chain of echoes and resonances, which establishes a profound solidarity among all men, however diverse their apparent conduct may be. Under the stability of these standards of conduct there is a gradation of moral nuances that brings us close to one another. Thus, at an extreme, there are the scoundrels of the *Patna*; later, there is the honest Jim, who at one moment acts like them; there is Brierly, who never violated, so far as we know, his standard of behavior, but who kills himself because of his contact with Jim's action; there is Marlow, who resisted, but comments to his friends at every step that Jim "was one of us," a man of good, recalling that many were exposed to similar acts in their youth. Marlow associates himself with Jim, protects him, and understands him, even though he feels the gravity of what Jim did, because he has a vague sense of dark interior possibilities—and also a curiosity about the other that seems to be a projection and that leads him to leave appearances to one side, in order to search for the essential in each one. "Nothing more awful than to watch a man who has been found out, not in a crime but in a more than criminal weakness. The commonest sort of fortitude prevents us from becoming criminals in a legal sense; it is from weakness unknown, but perhaps suspected, as in some parts of the world you may suspect a deadly snake in every bush—from weakness that may lie hidden, watched or unwatched, prayed against or manfully scorned, repressed or maybe ignored more than half a lifetime, not one of us is safe." "Was it for my own sake that I wished to find some shadow of an excuse for that young fellow whom I had never seen before, but whose appearance alone added a touch of personal concern to the thoughts suggested by the knowledge of his weakness—made it a thing of mystery and terror—like a hint of a destructive fate ready for us all whose youth—in its day—had resembled his youth?" "He was one of us." "He was one of us," says the author himself, speaking of his character and concluding the preface of his book with these words. In that way, Conrad himself is included in the chain of resonances and affinities, bringing us to include ourselves also, to make Jim's action into a chapter of our own potential. All the studies have repeated that phrase, in turn, as a key phrase, which nevertheless does not signify only that "He was at bottom a man of good, of the same class, resembling what we are by profession and convictions." According to the interpretation proposed in this essay it signifies above all: "We are all, also, made of a stuff that may bring us to similar actions."

This deep linkage exposes the theory implicit in Conrad, already set forth above: that the troubling complexity of the self, which leads us to surprise ourselves by an unforeseen action, is normal, not unusual. It expresses itself in the constellation of characters who bear witness, one after another, and determines the use of a multiple angle of vision. Conception and technique are intimately mixed; psychological fragmentation is translated into fragmented time, the fragmented narrative, a multiplicity of points of view, which envelop reality, dissociating it in order to recompose it. Reality is always seen *through* someone, without the novelist revealing himself directly at decisive moments, and the final intermediary is death, which completes and realizes the character, giving to his life a meaning it had not had before. It is not only the final datum for understanding, but the running out of time for the self. In death, there are no more incidents, no more sequences of events, no more actions of he who is dead. Heyst, Razumov, Decoud, Almayer, Kurtz, Jim. Only death explains them, above all when life becomes an unconscious preparation for it. Jim avoided it on the *Patna*; and so it became his involuntary goal, and he was only free of the Other and reconciled with himself when he met it, after a long purification, accepting it as a conscious sacrifice. He dies paying for a new mistake; but a mistake of magnanimity and renunciation, which redeems the catastrophe through moral survival.

NOTES

First published as "Catástrofe e sobrevivência," in *Tese e antítese* (São Paulo: Companhia Editora Nacional, 1964), pp. 57–93.

1. "Conrad's sense of the crisis of moral isolation and recognition in which the individual meets his first full test of character is repeatedly emphasized in his novels." Morton Dauwen Zabel, "Editor's Introduction," in *The Portable Conrad* (New York: Viking Press, 1947), p. 25.

2. "In spite of the accurate local color, *Victory* has a pervasive allegorical quality. Heyst and Lena are Adam and Eve in their island paradise, until her innocent transgression brings evil and death in the guise of the mysterious Mr. Jones, who is depicted in the traditional satanic terms." Lionel Stevenson, *The English Novel: A Panorama* (London: Constable, 1961), pp. 452–53.

The allegorical aspect of Conrad's work, especially in the biblical sense, is the basis of Paul Wiley's book, *Conrad's Measure of Man* (Madison: University of Wisconsin Press, 1954), where we read: "The allegory in *Victory* has wider universal significance than the single conflict of good and evil in the individual, for which reason the background myth of lost Eden is more clearly defined than in any other work after *An Outcast*" (p. 150).

3. Walter Allen, *The English Novel* (New York: Penguin Books, 1958), p. 304.

4. M. C. Bradbrook, *Joseph Conrad: Poland's English Genius* (Cambridge: Cambridge University Press, 1941), pp. 36–37.

5. Vernon Young, "Joseph Conrad: Outline for a Reconsideration," *Hudson Review*, 2 (1949), 6.

6. Zabel, *op cit.*, p. 29.

7. Zabel, *op. cit.*, p. 19.

8. Zabel, *op. cit.*, p. 30.

9. This is the second time I have alluded to Dostoyevsky's influence on Conrad, who denied such a thing tenaciously and considered Dostoyevsky a paradigm of what was repellent in the "Russian soul" for him, a Pole, child of a victim of czarism. Nevertheless it is evident, and many critics have recognized it. This is the case of Joseph Warren Beach, in whose excellent *The Twentieth-Century Novel* (New York: Appleton-Century-Crofts, 1932), chapter 29, "Impressionism: Conrad," p. 340, we read: "Again, he may have disliked in Dosteovski the specifically religious cast of his 'mysticism.' And then, is it not possible that he was affected unconsciously by the very natural desire to make little of an artist by whom he had been so greatly, if so unknowingly, influenced?" Reconsidering some of Beach's statements and developing the theme in the ideological field above all, Irving Howe gives the theme a decisive treatment in *Politics and the Novel* (New York: Horizon Press, 1957), chapter 4: "Conrad: Order and Anarchy." This influence is also recognized by Albert Guerard, perhaps his best contemporary critic: *Conrad the Novelist* (Cambridge: Harvard University Press, 1958), *passim*.

10. Marlow appears as the intermediary of the narrative in a number of other works by Conrad. F. R. Leavis analyzes astutely some of the defects imputable to this practice of the author, but in general he tends to underestimate its function (*The Great Tradition* [London: Chatto and Windus, 1948], Chapter 4, "Joseph Conrad," pp. 173–226). The defense is made convincingly by W. Y. Tindall, who not only shows the function of "aesthetic distancing," usually alluded to, but that of the reinforcement of the realism as well ("Apology for Marlow," in Robert C. Rathburn and Martin Steinmann Jr., editors, *From Jane Austen to Joseph Conrad* [Minneopolis: University of Minnesota Press, 1958], pp. 274–85).

11. J. W. Beach, *op. cit.*, p. 363.

12. This is the problem of moral resonance, explained admirably in the already cited book by Albert Guerard, pp. 147–51, where it is summarized in these words: "Dramatically as well as theoretically, *Lord Jim* is a story of sympathies, projections, empathies . . . and loyalties. The central relation is that of Marlow and Jim. . . . He is loyal to Jim as one must be to another or potential self, to the criminally weak self that may still exist. . . . Marlow is not fatally paralyzed or immobilized by this young 'double.' But Big Brierly is. . . . He has recognized in Jim an unsuspected potential self; he had looked into himself for

the first time." In the novel, Marlow himself refers to Jim as "my youngest brother," imagining that people back home will ask for stories of him. In another passage: "I don't know why he seems to me symbolic (of youth). Perhaps this is the real cause of my interest in his destiny."

13. Paul L. Wiley, *op. cit.*, p. 59. Albert Guerard says, commenting on Brierly's suicide: "The episode's chief function is to prepare us to understand (or at least accept) Jim's paralyzing identification with *Gentleman* Brown, and suicidal refusal to fight with him" (*op cit.*, p. 149). In the confrontation with Brown, there emerge "echoes, as it were, of a small voice within him. . . . Bound to Brown by a shared guilt, Jim brings ruin on Patusan, and is killed himself by the villagers." Walter Allen, *op. cit.*, p. 307.

Chapter 3

FOUR WAITINGS

FIRST: IN THE CITY

WAITING FOR THE BARBARIANS

What are we waiting for, assembled in the forum?

    The barbarians are due here today.

Why isn't anything happening in the senate?
Why do the senators sit there without legislating?

    Because the barbarians are coming today.
    What laws can the senators make now?
    Once the barbarians are here, they'll do the legislating.

Why did our emperor get up so early,
and why is he sitting at the city's main gate
on his throne, in state, wearing the crown?

    Because the barbarians are coming today
    and the emperor is waiting to receive their leader.
    He has even prepared a scroll to give him,
    replete with titles, with imposing names.

Why have our two consuls and praetors come out today
wearing their embroidered, their scarlet togas?
Why have they put on bracelets with so many amethysts,
and rings sparkling with magnificent emeralds?
Why are they carrying elegant canes
beautifully worked in silver and gold?

    Because the barbarians are coming today
    and things like that dazzle the barbarians.

Why don't our distinguished orators come forward as usual
to make their speeches, say what they have to say?

    Because the barbarians are coming today
    and they're bored by rhetoric and public speaking.

Why this sudden restlessness, this confusion?
(How serious people's faces have become.)
Why are the streets and squares emptying so rapidly,
everyone going home so lost in thought?

    Because night has fallen and the barbarians have not come.
    And some who have just returned from the border say
    there are no barbarians any longer.

And now, what's going to happen to us without barbarians?
They were, those people, a kind of solution.[1]

This poem by Constantine Cavafy, written in the first years of the twentieth century, is dry and precise, without any emphasis, not even a flash of emotion. It manifests a repressed longing for catastrophe, expressing the contradictory anguish that can assault consciousnesses and civilizations, an anguish with roots, perhaps, in the Romantic period, when the division of personality, sadomasochism, and the taste for death on the individual plane increased so much in literature; as did, on the social plane, the vertigo of ruin and the certainty that nations, like individuals, die.

The setting of the poem must be somewhere in the Hellenistic world, perhaps some part of the Near East, steeped in Greek culture since the conquest of Alexander the Great, but now in a later phase, because the text alludes to signs of a Roman presence. This historical moment is favored in the poetry of Cavafy, a Greek from Alexandria in Egypt and, as much in the poems that speak of Egypt as in those about ancient Greece or Christianized Imperial Rome, there predominates a disenchanted vision of man and society, as if both were victims of an irremediable fraud that poisons situations and undermines heroism. It is well known that many of Cavafy's poems (this one included) focus on the blind alleys countries may find themselves in at moments of excessive maturity, when their splendor has gone and their horizons have closed in on them.

These situations are more impressive still if we think of his historical poems as a kind of game with marked cards. Since they generally refer to identifiable moments or situations, they make us see that premonition foretells disaster, that the impending downfall will occur without any possible escape. In "The God Forsakes Antony," for example, we know that Antony will soon be beaten at the battle of Actium, that he will lose Cleopatra, and that he will kill himself. "Nero's Term" simply reviews the antecedents of the fall and death of this emperor and his replacement by Galba. The courtesan-poet of "Darius" does not know, but we do, that his king Mithradates will be destroyed by the Romans, and that the doubt of the poem is the certainty of history. The king of Syria in the poem "Demetrius Soter, 162–150 B.C." suspects, but we know, despite the appearance of grandeur that remains, that the days are numbered until the Romans appear—and so on. Cavafy shows us present actions filled with presentiment, many of which have culminated in a destructive reality.

"Waiting for the Barbarians" makes no reference to a concrete, historical event, as do the poems just cited. It deals with a generic situation, valuable because more exemplary, hinting perhaps at the destructive impact on the Hellenized, overly civilized states of the Near East that did not resist the more energetic or primitive peoples who attacked them.

Arnold Toynbee's philosophy of history defines the so-called barbarians as an "external proletariat," originating in less refined cultures and coveting the riches of civilization. If when an "external proletariat" exerts pressure from the outside, a simultaneous pressure is exercised from within by an "internal proletariat" (the oppressed lower classes), one of the factors that provokes a civilization's end has emerged.

In this poem the conjuncture of events is different. The internal pressure probably originates in weariness and disbelief, which create a loss of any raison d'être. As a result, the too-mature state does not know how to resolve its problems and, obscurely, fear mixed with hope, it hopes for the emergence of that external pressure, which will unleash the process of eventual destruction as an alternative to the blind alley. Cavafy's corrosive irony lies in the paradoxical disappointment caused by the news that the city is saved. Thus, as José Paulo Paes says so well, "The fall was not ready to happen, but it has happened already."[2] And he comments: "The subtle atmosphere of dissolution that pervades 'Waiting for the Barbarians' is related to symbolist decadence, with its taste for twilight moments of the end of the race, of resignation before what is supposed to be inevitable."

In the same sense Bowra emphasizes that this "theme has had a certain popularity in our time," mentioning similar poems: Valery Briúsov's "The Arrival of the Huns" and Stefan George's "The Burning of the Temple." But he points out a feature that is important for an understanding of our text: while these poets share the sentiment that the time is ripe for catastrophe, and therefore situate themselves psychologically *within* the theme, Cavafy remains outside, without participating. It is not a matter of his own sentiments or desires, but of the dispassionate presentation of the sentiments of others. This gives the poem a touch of playful irony.[3]

The drama of mature civilizations at the twilight of extinction appears in a more general way in a earlier poem, whose title varies in the Spanish,

French, or English translations I know: "Finished," "End," and "Finalities." In it, the fatality of catastrophe is more general and more abstract,
completely separated from the references to institutions and customs
that abound in "Waiting for the Barbarians." In an undetermined place,
there appears a hint of a terrible danger that threatens everyone and that
everyone, in the midst of apprehension and disorientation, tries to
avoid. But it was only a false alarm, probably some misunderstood news.
What in fact happens is a quite different catastrophe, which no one even
imagined. And, as no one has prepared themselves to confront it, it destroys utterly.

There thus seem to be three levels in Cavafy's historical poetry: that
of unnamed forces acting in an unidentified space, which is the case of
"Finalities" (or whatever other name it might be given); that of destructive forces acting in the territory of a more or less well-defined civilization, as in "Waiting for the Barbarians"; and the case of an historically
identified catastrophe, as in "The God Forsakes Antony."

"Waiting for the Barbarians" concerns a rich, hierarchical state,
whose culture suggests the influence of Roman institutions in an atmosphere of Oriental luxury (like the Egypt of the Ptolemys or the Syria of
the Seleucidis). There is an emperor, a senate, consuls, praetors, hon-
orific titles, eloquent orators, all dressed in their togas, wearing precious
garments and carrying solemn staffs. The hovering threat of the invaders
brings everyone together in the plazas, making them feel that, confronted with the invaders, the state is worthless. The invaders are another race, with a culture that is probably primitive and ferocious, unin-
terested in laws or in thought, but sensitive to flattery and riches. In a
firm and progressive composition, the social panorama and the progress
of events reveal themselves with a despoiling precision, without variation or modulation. The data come to us as questions and answers given
in the same dispassionate tone, which does not alter even when the two
stages of the paradoxical outcome occur. The first stage: the waiting
proves useless, because messengers from the front announce that there
is no sign of barbarians and, therefore, no threat; the state is saved and
the fear of its destruction is erased. Then the second stage, unbelievable
in its unexpectedness: the news is terrible, because the barbarians would
have been a solution for an already eroded society.

Note that Cavafy neither explains nor comments on anything. He
only assembles the data by means of a dramatic method, expressed in a
kind of impersonalized chorus. A sort of fragment, the poem situates
itself between two absences of information, two "abyssal fractures," Ungaretti would say, "between which there arises 'the text as a sparkling.'"[4] In fact, the news about the decadence of this exhausted
state is implied first; afterward comes the pathetic frustration due to a

social life so empty that destruction would be a kind of tragic redemption. The anticipation of fear, coldly described by the poet, is mysteriously wedded to a profound longing for catastrophe. From this stems the ironic impartiality of the narrative voice, made more corrosive by the lack of information.

Cavafy's short, dense poem, with its ferocious crux, filled with implication, serves as a good introduction to the world of anguished waitings, of acts without logical sense, of blind aspiration for individual and social death, which constitute one of the most tragic threads of contemporary culture, and which will appear more fully developed in the texts to follow.

SECOND: AT THE WALL

"The Great Wall of China," a story written for the most part in 1917, consists of fragments Kafka left on this theme, some of which were eventually published. They have been given diverse titles and arrangements. To avoid doubt, let me make clear that I will base my commentary on two connected sequences that describe, first, the construction of the wall and, second, the message of the emperor. They are found in the volumes *La colonie pénitentiaire* (Paris: Egloff, 1946), the French translation by Jean Starobinski, and *The Great Wall of China* (New York: Shocken Books, 1946), English translation by Willa and Edwin Muir, but I have also read the more modern and varied arrangement, incorporating other fragments that multiply the ambiguities, in the edition of the complete works published in the Bibliothèque de la Pléiade, volume 2, 1980.

As in other texts of Kafka, this is a narrative *becoming* a theme, with detours and a lack of design. One cannot say that the narrative is intentionally disorganized, since what we have are the pieces of an unfinished story; but we should remember that all of Kafka's work, like that of Nietzsche in philosophy, has the spirit of a fragment. It proceeds in short, at times discontinuous, units; up to the last minute, the text of a book like *The Trial* continued to suffer alterations in the number and the order of its parts. I will not give great importance to this, but rather to another perspective on the fragment.

The narrator, who took part in the building of the wall and speaks about it as a work already done, gives us, in a half-capricious way, information on the building methods used, the reasons for the wall's construction, the recruitment and treatment of the workers, his own life, the top managers of the project, political power, and the Emperor of China.

The wall was planned to defend the country against the barbaric nomads of the north, but its defensive ability is doubtful. The construction began at two separated southern points, one in the southwest, the other in the southeast, the two sides being intended to meet in a certain place in the north, in such a way, it seems, as to create an immense angle. But the method chosen was to erect isolated pieces in each sector. The work groups had to recapitulate, in miniature, the general course of the work, to construct, working from the outside in, two pieces of five hundred meters each. When joined, they would extend a thousand meters. But the exhaustion and the satiation of the workers required the creation of a system of changes of locale, intended to revitalize them. Thus, having finished one piece of a thousand meters, they were transferred to another region and given parties and other rewards that renewed their vitality.

As a result, there were large open spaces between finished pieces of the wall, making defense precarious, since the nomads could easily go around the pieces and destroy the defenders. Further, these nomads, always on the move, had a much more complete vision of the whole, while the builders never knew, and never could know, if the wall was in fact finished, even after it was officially considered done. The reader concludes that the result must have have been a kind of dotted line, a series of fragments destined for eventual ruin, unable to fulfill their purpose.

But, in fact, no one knows if this is the case or if the wall was ever completed, just because the enterprise was largely useless, above all for the southern regions the narrator comes from, which the barbarians could never have reached, and where they functioned as simple bugaboos to frighten children. Some said the wall could be the base on which to erect a new Tower of Babel, this time capable of completion and realizing its aim, which, as we know from the Bible, was to reach heaven. But the narrator rejects this hypothesis, because the walls were incomplete, and because they did not have the necessary circular form. One way or another, the reader notes the idea of a vast human accomplishment, which might be supposed destined to reach toward the divine sphere.

What must be especially emphasized is the peculiarly fragmentary nature of the enterprise, which apparently was seen from the beginning as something never to be finished. So much so that the method gives the impression of having been based on a paradox: since men are incapable of the constant effort required by monotonous and tiring work, they must be transferred far away, so that the change of place will revitalize them. The reader concludes that the contradiction resides in the fact of planning a gigantic work, while simultaneously admitting the visceral incapacity of the builders, a principle that negates the project. It is possible, thus, that the acceptance of the fragment is reciprocally related to a conception of human nature and a vision of human weakness. The absurdity, then, would be a way of penetrating the lack of sense in life, in action, in the human project as well as of negating simplified visions.

To this point, we have been thinking of the wall and its fragmentary construction from the angle of the narrator and the reader. But it is necessary to complement this with another angle, which the narrator can only present in a very conjectural way: that of the higher powers who decide on the construction and the method and are called the "high command" in the English translation of Willa and Edwin Muir. The High Command is impersonal, unknown, eternal, arbitrarily sovereign. It must always have been decided to construct the wall, and the threat of the nomads could not have served as a pretext, since it was known that the fragmentary method of defense guaranteed nothing. Here is a suggestive quotation: "Far rather do I believe that the high command has existed from all eternity, and the decision to build the wall likewise. Unwitting peoples of the north, who imagined that they were the cause of it! Honest, unwitting Emperor, who imagined he decreed it! We builders of the wall know that it was not so and hold our tongues."

Now we are in the presence of mysterious beings who decide the destiny of people and societies. This unidentified High Command corresponds to the imponderable entities that rule destiny in Kafka's works: the unnamed and impalpable judges of *The Trial*, the invisible lord of *The Castle*. The protagonists of these novels try in vain to know why they are punished or submitted to a restriction. In this story all the citizens depend on an immense undertaking prescribed by agencies they know nothing about, in order to realize a nonexistent aim (since the alleged aim is simply a pretext). But if they don't obey they will lose the sense of life itself and even the consciousness of themselves. The reader comes to imagine that the unfinished wall was meant to be the impossible base of an imaginary tower, designed to reach some unattainable powers, which would be the High Command. This launches the entire country on an adventure whose only purpose is to keep life moving and to preserve its own intangibility.

Just as the Emperor knows nothing, he can do nothing and may not even exist, since the social and spatial separation between him and the people is great, so that we might think a particular emperor is reigning, even though he has already died, and another one reigns in his place. There is even uncertainty about the dynasties. The obvious proof of this lack of communication between the apparent ruler and the people is the impossibility of transmitting the message that the dying emperor addresses to each of his subjects. The messengers cannot so much as leave the palace, and, if they do leave, they cannot get beyond the limits of the imperial city.

It is easy to see that in this narrative time is suppressed: the news of one's destiny arrives with the delay of light moving through the universe; the identity of the governors is always uncertain because, owing to this delay, no one knows who is in power. Further, history itself is uncertain, since the Emperor orders nothing, knows nothing, and can do nothing. Knowledge seems to be the privilege of the High Command, and for this reason it is necessary to obey their directives blindly. But what is the High Command, and who composes it? It can't be known. There remains to human beings the consciousness of oneself alone, but only as a reflection of the pattern designed by the High Command, which weighs on them. Thus, the complicated organization of the empire, expressed through the immense effort of constructing the wall, rests on reasons that cannot be known, and life cannot be more than daily existence, limited to the narrow ambit of the neighborhood. Above this reigns a total irresponsibility, embodied in the cyclopic project meant to defend against invaders who are, at bottom, harmless to a civilization without purpose, by means of a wall full of holes, due to directives emanating from an unknown power. Beside the wall, people wait in vain for what will never happen, but their destiny is ruled by this inevitable waiting and, in Kafka's narrative one finds, between every line, allegories filled with cheerless satire. An uncharacteristic China seems to dissolve in the general society of men.

Amid all this, there appear contradictions that are augmented by the character of the narrative, fragmentary in the strict sense, since in it the major significance of the fragment is not so much the isolation of the unfinished texts, but the fact of using them to describe a method of construction by pieces. By the way, note this: Kafka did not hesitate to publish segments of incomplete works, which seems to show that in fact this type of composition is not just an accident of an unfinished writing, but a method he adopted in correspondence with his vision.

As with others of his writings, there are diverse interpretations of the eventual symbolism of this one. There is no lack of ingenious analysts, for example, Clement Greenberg,[5] who sees in the tale the presence of Judaic themes. I prefer to say that "The Great Wall of China" is perhaps part of the vast spirit of negativity that grew out of romanticism, manifesting itself here through a fragmentary process, itself a link in the chain Kafka forged to describe the absurdity and irrationality of our time. Going much farther than the disenchanted meditation of the Romantics, he did not limit himself to counterposing the contradictory rhythms of building and ruin through history. He described a process in which a building is erected as already a ruin, since each segment of the wall, isolated from the others and vulnerable to demolition by the no-mads, is a candidate for immediate destruction. Thus, in the script of Marcel Carné's film, *Quai des Brumes,* Jacques Prévert has the desperate painter say, "For me, a swimmer is someone already drowned."

THIRD: IN THE FORTRESS

The Tartar Steppe (1940), by Dino Buzzatti,[6] tells the story of a young officer, Giovanni Drogo, ordered to leave the Military School for the Bastiani Fortress, situated on the frontier of a kingdom to the north. Beyond the frontier there extends an immense plain, the Tartar Steppe, from which for centuries there has been no sign of life. So the military garrison seems useless, because there are no visible, or even probable, enemies. But there is an illusion of real and constant danger, which might cause a war and give officers and enlisted men the opportunity to show their valor. Because of this, they all live in a permanent state of anticipation, which is at the same time hope, the hope of one day being able to justify life and have an opportunity to shine.

The narrative is organized, on the surface, in thirty chapters, but its purpose, manifesting its deep structure, seems to express itself by a movement through four stages, creating four segments that we can call, according to their basic themes: incorporation into the fortress (chapters 1–10); the first match between hope and death (chapters 11–15); the attempt at disincorporation (chapters 16–22); the second match between hope and death (chapters 22–30).

Throughout the book there radiates a paradoxical and disenchanted vision, expressed in an economical and severe language that masks the melancholy pessimism of the plot. Buzzatti, a writer who in other works handles humor with such ingenuity, is here unafraid to assume a purely serious style, in order to dress in it the heroic austerity of the protago-nist, who is doomed to win his life at the hour of death, only after using it up on the fantastic doorstep of the Tartar Steppe. There time evapo-rated for him, in the enormous Fortress, stretched from hill to hill, clos-ing the world in a stopping place of stone surrounded by mountains and gorges, circled by steep rocks, succeeded by the steppes. And all this completely empty, completely separated, like a solitary stage where men possessed by an impossible dream of glory live in anxiety.

Incorporation into the Fortress

At the beginning of the book our attention is called to the way the fort is, so to speak, separated from the world. Drogo "did not even know exactly where it was, nor how far he had to go to reach it. Some people had said a day's ride, others less; no one whom he had asked had ever really been there." The friend who accompanies him for some kilometers, Francesco Vescovi, shows him the summit of a distant hill, which he knows because he has hunted there, saying that that is where the fort is. Thus, the ride will not be long. But not only does the hill disappear from Drogo's sight, shortly afterward a cart driver tells him that he has never heard anyone speak of a fort near there. At nightfall he arrives at a building that seems to him, but is not, his destination; it is an abandoned fort, and from it one can just make out, on the most remote line of hills, the profile of Bastiani, "solitary and almost inaccessible." Then the hill disappears from view and Giovanni sleeps under the stars. He sets out the following day in the company of Captain Ortiz, whom he had met on the road, who tells him that this was a secondary post in a forgotten sector of the frontier; it had never taken part in a war and seemed to be quite useless.

The first segment, dominated by Lt. Giovanni Drogo's entering and remaining in Fort Bastiani, thus begins with a strange journey, in search of a spot that is hidden and governed by ambiguities, the first being, as he learns having arrived there, that he was *sent* to a place to which one ordinarily went by *request* (the time of service at the Fort was counted double). Nevertheless, he does not like the place and decides to leave without delay. But, to make the formalities easier, and because of an inexpressible attraction, he agrees to wait four months, during which he is taken prisoner by the fascination that ties officers and soldiers alike to the monotonous work in the Fort. For this reason, at the moment of signing the petition for a transfer, he decides impetuously to stay for two years. The incorporation proceeds effectively, due as much to local conditions (the Fort attracts him mysteriously) as to his own deep impulses, but he still does not know that he is a prisoner in this place and will never be able to get loose of it. This produces a rupture with his earlier life, the symptoms of which appear slowly, as if the narrative were a field mined with them.

Even during the trip which brought him to the Fort for the first time, he began to feel disconnected from his previous existence, and now he seems to be entering into something strange. One sees this also in the symbolic difference between the gait of his horse and that of his friend Francesco Vescovi. We must keep this subterranean process in mind to understand why, at the moment when he could leave, before he has even begun his service, he accepts the doctor's suggestion to wait four months. Seeing a piece of crag through the window of the doctor's office, he felt that "A vague feeling to which he did not have the key was gradually penetrating into his inmost being—a stupid and absurd feeling, a baseless fancy." A little later he imagines that he perhaps sees something within himself, "an unknown force."

We see then that the Fort (perhaps an allegory of life) is a mode of being and living, which captures those who have Drogo's idealistic and uneasy nature, who interpret their situation as a long wait for a glorious and unique moment in which everything justifies itself and time is redeemed. From the Commanding Colonel, named Filimore, down to the Chief Tailor, Sergeant Prosdoscimo, everyone exhibits an ambiguity that leads them to say that they want to go away and, at the same time, to desire to stay in order to be at their posts when the long-awaited hour comes. Years pass, perhaps centuries, and nothing happens; it is even possible that the Tartars of the north have never existed.

Things like these shape the already mentioned rupture with the previous world. This is reinforced by means of the supreme law of the Fort, the routine of service mapped out by the regulations, which function as a suggestion of life, that is, as a model proposed as a norm of conduct. Routine organizes the time of each of them and every one in a uniform way, standardizing not only the acts, but also the sentiments, for which it seems to want to substitute. It is the "pitch of insanity" created by "the rigid laws of army life," creating a collective attitude that seems conditioned by imminent war. But since war never comes, the routine moves meaninglessly in the soothing void that has for centuries been life in the Fort, where the strictness of the sentinels, guard duty, and their signs and countersigns are all organized in relation to nothing. The routine of service is a paralysis of being, a freezing of conduct, contrasting with everyone's ideal: movement, variety, the surprises of war = adventure. This ideal and routine make a contradictory and ambiguous pair.

To organize time, the routine reduces it to an eternal present, always the same, while adventure is a way of opening it to a coveted future. For this reason life in the Fort is in part a drama of time, which seems to empty out of it, like water running out of a pipe, spending itself uselessly. Drogo feels time's "unrecoverable flight," since in the Fort the present is in fact a kind of prolongation of the past, the two being made equivalent by the routine that petrifies them. This produces anxiety about the future, which could make movement and transformation possible, through the adventure of war that, nevertheless, never comes. Individually, Drogo's problem could be defined as the substitution of pasts. He cannot return to his own past, that is, he cannot continue the kind of life he lived in the city, and now he leaves it behind forever. For this reason he feels that, since the beginning of his life in the garrison, a heavy gate has closed behind him. It only remains to him, then, to take on the past of the fort, renouncing his own and waiting for the future, which in turn is devoured by the never-changing routine of work, as if time did not exist. One nucleus of the book is defined in chapter 6, which in a certain way prefigures Drogo's destiny: an unawareness of himself in relation to the present, which pushes him toward the past of the Fort (to the end that the present is equal to what its own past was); and illusion with respect to the future. As the sole reality ends by being reduced entirely to the past, since the future never gives what is hoped for, disenchantment results. The Fort is the closed gate behind each person, which kills the present by reducing it to a past that is not that of the individual, but that is imposed, and by proposing a false future as the way out.

The officers then cling to this doubtful, only way out, under the prodding of hope, which becomes a kind of sickness. They all await a great event, victims of a common illusion fed by the vision of the coming of the imponderable Tartars.

Drogo sees all this and thinks hopefully that these illusions have nothing to do with him, since he is only staying four months. What he does not know is that he is already contaminated too, mysteriously imprisoned in the web. The old tailor's assistant reads this in his eyes and advises him to leave immediately. But he is on land that is already undermined, though he feels himself, ingenuously, free of the common illusion, which dominates the Fort and is expressed, among other places, in a section of chapter 7:

> It was from the northern steppe that their fortune would come, their adventure, the miraculous hour which once at least falls to each man's lot. Because of this remote possibility which seemed to become more and more uncertain as time went on, grown men lived their lives out pointlessly here in the Fort.
>
> They had not come to terms with ordinary life, with the joys of common people, with a mediocre destiny; they lived side by side, with the same hopes, never speaking of them because they were not aware of them or simply because they were soldiers who kept to themselves the intimacies of their hearts.

This combination of adventure and routine, conformism and aspiration, immobility and movement, ends up in the birth of a new being in Drogo. When the four months are over and the doctor is preparing the certificate that will free him, he feels himself imprisoned in the Fort, whose beauty suddenly appears to him in contrast with the city's grayness. Then he decides to stay. As powerful as the appeal of the possible adventure, the routine of daily life and all the acquired habits operate in him too. Adventure and routine are confounded in the very rhythm of military life, creating in Drogo a second nature, in accord with which the Fort is less a place than a state of spirit.

The First Match between Hope and Death

The action of the first segment of the novel lasts four months. The second begins two years later and lasts two years more. Drogo is really incorporated into the Fortress, not only in the military sense, but in the sense of having interiorized everything that characterizes its life: routine, leisure, the redefinition of time—turned toward hope, the anticipation of the great moment. From now on he is going to come in contact with another reality that complements the first, but remains hidden: death. The second movement of the novel is the match between hope and death, which now take on a concrete reality.

One night, when he is in command of the New Redoubt, an advanced post that overlooks the steppe, a lost horse appears. One of the sentinels, Private Lazzari (thinking it is his, escaped he doesn't know how), succeeds in evading the sentries at the moment of the changing of the guard, so that he can leave the redoubt and capture it. But the password having changed while he was gone, he cannot give the right response when he returns and, even though everyone recognizes him, and despite his anguished appeals, he is killed by one of his friends, a sentinel, who acts in obedience to the inflexible norm of the regulations.

Nevertheless, the horse must have run away from the troops of the neighboring country, since a few days later tiny remote contingents begin to march toward the Fort. This creates a bellicose excitement, everyone prepares themselves for a war which is at last possible, the commander is on the point of saying something about it to the officers who share a great emotional tension, when a messenger arrives from Headquarters, announcing that it is only a troop ordered to finish the long abandoned work of demarcating the frontier.

So the dream is dissipated and there remains only the attempt to be faster and more efficient in the placement of boundary markers. To do this, a detachment is sent to the crest of the hills, commanded by Captain Monti, an enormous and vulgar man, who has as his second in command the aristocratic and somewhat remote Lieutenant Angustina who, in addition to being fragile and sick, wears ordinary riding boots, instead of the climbing boots the others have on. The climb is thus an incredible sacrifice for him, aggravated by the cruelty of the Captain, who forces the march or looks for difficult paths in order to increase Angustina's torment. But he resists and does not fall behind, maintaining the rhythm and efficiency by an incredible effort of will. Arriving almost at the top, the detachment finds out that they have been anticipated by the foreigners, who have already planted markers, giving their country an advantage. Darkness comes, snow falls, it gets very cold, and the soldiers of the Fort, sheltered in a niche in the rock, prepare themselves for a bad night, made still worse by the scorn of the foreigners, settled down a little above them, at the crest of the hill, from whence, with jovial sarcasm, they offer help. Exposed to the weather, the two officers play cards in order to give the impression of good morale; but Captain Monti finally quits and takes shelter with the enlisted men, while Angustina, in the open air, beneath the snow, continues to play cards by himself and to announce the score, in order to give those above a spectacle of ease and strength. He does this until he freezes to death, under the astonished eyes of Monti, who finally understands the stoic grandeur of his sacrifice.

The cases of Private Lazzari and Lieutenant Angustina show the contrast between death as it is imagined and the reality of death. In dreams, above all in daydreams, the officers imagine (like Drogo) the din of battle, the unexpected situation resolved by heroism, the glorious wounds. When it is announced, for example, that the foreign contingent is approaching across the desert, the Commanding Colonel, still fighting the memory of past frustrations, finally believes that war is imminent and sees "Fortune approach in silver armor and with a blood-stained sword." In a room in the Fort there is an old picture representing the heroic end of Prince Sebastian, propped up against a tree, in shining armor and at his side the sword of battle. This is the ideal death, which justifies the waiting.

Real deaths are different. Accidental, obscure, they contrast with the splendor of dreams, but they have an important role in the economy of the book—Lazzari's death, because it embodies the limits of the tragedy that can occur through routine, that is, the law of the Fort; Angustina's death (which interests us more), because it will have a decisive function in the development of the book's final meaning. For this reason, it is carefully prepared, being preceded by a premonitory dream, in which Giovanni Drogo sees his colleague, still a child, kidnapped by a procession of goblins and fairies, a small corpse floating in space. The importance of Angustina's death lies in the contrast between it and the daydream of spectacular death, which shows that there can be greatness in an end like his, during an ineffectual peacetime expedition, without an heroic setting or an exceptional situation. Thus (a decisive piece of evidence for an understanding of the book), heroism depends on the person, not on circumstances, and great deeds can occur without the conventional signs of identification. As Major Ortiz says, commenting on Angustina's death: "After all, what we get is what we deserve." Why, in consequence, wait for the time that never comes? Ortiz advises Drogo to leave the Fort before it is too late, as it already is for him, who no longer intends to leave before retirement. Drogo then decides to go down to the city to ask for a transfer.

Attempt at Disincorporation

The third segment of the narrative is taken up with the attempt at disincorporation. The previous segment described failures that affected the entire garrison, frustrated in its hope of war and wounded in its integrity by the death of two members, the officer and the private. This segment will describe clearly the individual failures of Drogo, who, provided with a recommendation obtained through his mother, tries to get himself transferred. Just as the second segment contains two central sequences—the death of Lazzari and that of Angustina—this segment similarly has two basic sequences: a conversation with an old sweetheart, Maria Vescovi, and an interview with the General.

The encounter with Maria is a game of hesitation, repressed impulses, and smothered intentions, all in a kind of ambiguity with no way out. In the composed atmosphere of the sitting room, in a conversation ruled by etiquette, the two young people would like at bottom to declare their affection for each other, but they don't say anything. Both would like to make each other feel that they are dependent on the other's decision, but both contain themselves. They seem, the entire time, while the afternoon dribbles away, to await some movement of their companion that does not come. Thus, the opportunity disappears, the fault of both of them, without anyone wishing it and also without anyone wishing anything else. Drogo seems to be awkwardly tied up in an impossible game of speak-and-don't-speak, of wish-and-don't-wish. At the end they say good-bye with an "exaggerated cordiality." Then he goes, "walk[ing] toward the gate with a military step, and the gravel of the pathway crunched in the silence."

The interview with the Commander of the Division is a comedy of ambiguities, marked by the progressive chilling of the false cordiality the General, strutting behind his half-insolent monocle, assumed at the beginning. Drogo has spent four years in the Fort and this gives him, implicitly, the right to a transfer. But there has been a certain change in the regulations that he does not know about and according to which he should have made his request earlier, a fact his colleagues, interested in their own transfers, have kept from him. In addition, his file carries a "reprimand" because of the accidental death of Private Lazzari while under his command. And even though a considerable reduction in the size of the contingent may be anticipated, his request is not granted.

Feeling himself deceived by his colleagues and treated unjustly by the authorities, Drogo sinks in the deception.

Nevertheless, an attentive reading shows that it is not only this that causes his return to the Fort. As soon as he arrived in the city, he felt that he no longer belonged to that world of home, of family, of friends, where even his own mother had other interests. But, if everything seemed strange to him, it was because he was already captive in the Fort and unconsciously manipulated fate in order to stay there, under the convergent action of an external force, which ordered him to return, and another, internal one: the feeling of no longer belonging to his native world. The attempt at disincorporation thus ends by confirming his irremediable link to the Fort. Melancholy, he climbs the hills once more and goes home to a useless wait.

To this point four years of Drogo's life and about two-thirds of the book have gone by; from here to the end, that is, in a little less than a third of the book's pages, a generation will pass. The essential data have been put forth and it only remains to show their final combinations.

The Second Match between Hope and Death

The episodes of the third segment took up the short period of a leave. In the fourth, Drogo's life is described in sequences separated by long intervals, over a total of almost thirty years, during which waiting and death are intertwined more than ever with the rhythm of time, which goes now rapidly, now slowly, and at the end stops all at once.

The story begins with the departure of half the garrison, leaving the Fort, where only the forgotten appear to have stayed, semideserted. But one night Lieutenant Simeoni, who owns a powerful telescope, calls Drogo to show him some vague luminous points moving at the most remote limit of the desert, where one loses sight of things in a barrier of constant fog. And here begins for both of them a phase of burning anticipation, since Simeoni perceives it as the construction of a highway. The anxiety of the two young men, stretched on the parapet in order to probe the immensity, gives the narrative rhythm a sluggishness that correspondends to their greedy impatience. But the Commander, fingers burned by the false alarm two years earlier, prohibits the use of powerful field glasses, and Simeoni stops looking out at the desert, leaving only Drogo as a kind of isolated depository of the centuries-old hope, which becomes the dominating state of his soul. Meanwhile the activity of the foreigners has become visible to the naked eye, showing that it is in fact the construction of a highway. But the work goes very slowly, the anticipation is always the same, and Drogo feels that now time is corrosive, destroying the Fort, aging the men, pulling everything into a kind of

inexorable flight. Weaving back and forth between a rhythm of progress (the duration of the construction that never ends) and a rhythm of regress (the unceasing destruction of the place and the men), he continues to await the great moment.

Fifteen years, noted in a few lines, pass this way before the construction of the paved road is done. The hills and fields are the same, but the fort is decayed and the men changed. Drogo has been promoted to Captain, and the final phase begins with a replica of the beginning: we see him climbing the hill after a leave, in his forties, definitively estranged from his city, where his mother has died and his brothers no longer live. At the beginning of the book the young Lieutenant Drogo, climbing the mysterious mountain, saw Captain Ortiz on the other side of the precipice and called to him with youthful fear. Now Captain Drogo climbs wearily, and from the other side young Lieutenant Moro calls to him in the same way. The recurrence of time is marked by the similarity of the situations, expressed in the rhyming of their surnames, which seem the same: Drogo-Moro. The generations replace each other, time goes on, the Fort continues to await its destiny.

In the following chapter ten more years have passed, Drogo is Major Subcommander, he is fifty-four years old, sick, worn out, without even the strength to get out of bed. And then there occurs the incredible, which was nevertheless expected: from the steppe come powerful enemy battalions, complete with artillery, in a military advance. Finally, after centuries, the great moment seems to have come. Headquarters sends reinforcements, and an excited, bellicose activity begins on the eve of the combat. Drogo, almost an invalid, becomes agitated at the prospect of the ideal realized, but the Commander, Lieutenant Colonel Simeoni, forces him to leave, because he needs Drogo's spacious old room to put up the officers of the arriving reinforcements. In despair, unsteady, his body spilling out of his uniform, he takes the road back to the valley, descending in a coach while the troops come up for the battle.

On the road, he decides to spend the night in a guest house, troubled by the incredible irony of luck, which made him waste his entire life in the Fort and then be posted away from it when the long-awaited hour arrives. The end of the book is written with an easy strength, full of precision and mystery, expressing the convergence of the great themes of the novel—Waiting, Death, and Time—as they modulate and combine.

It is a late, enchanting spring, with the perfume of flowers, a mild sky, and hills the color of violet losing themselves in the heights. Sitting in a poor room, Drogo is on the point of breaking into tears because of his insignificant life, crowned by this forced desertion, when he realizes that he is going to die. Then, he understands that Death was the great adventure he had waited for, there being no reason to lament that it has come thus, obscure, solitary, seemingly completely insignificant and disappointing. Time seems tied down, as if the flight toward constant disappointment had finally collided with a plenitude—which is the consciousness of confronting with strength and tranquility the supreme moment in the life of every man. This battle then seems harder than the others he had dreamed of, and more noble than that which came to Angustina under the eyes of Captain Monti and the soldiers. He has no witnesses, he is absolutely alone, he cannot show anyone the fiber of his character and the temper in which he dies. And thus this death reveals itself as more noble than a death in battle. And Time, which seemed lost during life, emerges at the end as a total victory. Time is redeemed and Death concludes its long game with Waiting. Here are the final lines:

> The room has filled with darkness; only with difficulty can one see the white of the bed and all the rest is black. Soon the moon should rise.
>
> Will Drogo manage to see it or will he have to go before then? The door of the room shakes and creaks slightly. Perhaps it is a breath of wind, merely the air swirling a little as it does on these restless spring nights. But perhaps it is she who has come in with her silent step and is now standing by Drogo's chair. Giovanni makes an effort and straightens his shoulders a little; he puts right the collar of his uniform with one hand and takes one more look out of the window, the briefest of glances, his last share of the stars. Then in the dark he smiles, although there is no one to see him.

Definitions

The Tartar Steppe belongs to the roster of novels of disenchantment, which describe life as bringing nothing but frustration and showing, in the final balance, great losses. Nevertheless (as opposed to certain terrible endings, like that of Machado de Assis's *Epitaph for a Small Winner*), its outcome is a paradoxical case of triumph in defeat, of fullness extracted from privation. This confirms that it is a book of ambiguities on various planes, beginning with the indefinable character of its place and time.

Where does the action occur? In a nameless country impossible to locate, as in folktales, despite the European cut of the customs and costumes, as well as the Italian substratum—the only precise geographic reference is, occasionally, to Holland (and its tulips), where Drogo's sweetheart announces she is going to travel. Otherwise, in a certain sense there is no place, properly speaking, but only a vague city without form and the fantasmal sight of Fort Bastiani, which is at an elastic distance, in no one knows what direction.

The name of the Fort is Italian and a few of the characters' surnames are usual in that language, like Martini, Pietri, Lazzari, Santi, Moro. But there is a preference for less frequent names, like Lagòrio, Andronico, Consalvi; or rare names, like Batta, Prosdoscimo, Stizione, and for those which seem like inventions based on other names, like Drogo, from Drago; Fonzaso, from Fonso or Fonsato; Angustina, from Agostino; Stazzi, from Stasi. The derivations that begin with a name from other languages are significant, like Morel (French), which could have Morelli as a point of departure; or Espina (Spanish), similar to Spina; or Magnus (a Latin form the German naming system finds pleasing), like Magni or Magno. At the extreme, names that are purely foreign: Fernandez, Ortiz, Zimmerman, Tronk, while that of the Commander, Filimore, seems not to belong to any language at all. This anthroponomic game contributes to dissolving the possible identity of the vague universe the Fort is situated in.

Still more: beyond the Fort is a steppe where nomads wander, which might suggest Africa or Asia. The supposed Tartars, who have perhaps never existed, would be in the north, but the troops that come from there to place the boundary markers seem to be of the same nature and degree of civilization as those of the Fort. In truth, who are these awaited enemies? Tartars? Only Russians had them as neighbors in Europe. Note, by the way, that the army doctor wears a fur cap, in the Russian style, and that the kings of the country are called Peter, such as (excluding the case of one king of Serbia at the beginning of this century) are found only in Russia and Portugal. The name of the heroic prince represented as dead in the picture is Sebastian, the same as that of the Portuguese king who died heroically in Alcacer-Quebir.

And the epoch? People travel on horse and by coach, and toward the end of the book there is a reference to the railroad. Nevertheless, there still exist golden carriages, which suggests the eighteenth century. The telescope has only one eye piece, indicating that they still did not have binoculars. The rifles are not repeating and are loaded in an archaic manner, suggesting at least the middle of the nineteenth century. This means that care has been taken to confuse the chronology as well, including that there is no sign of any change in the weapons, uniforms, or objects throughout an action that lasts more than thirty years. There are other signs of things being deliberately mixed up, such as the fact of the garrison of the Fort being (this is what can be inferred) infantry in which, according to rule, only officers have horses; nevertheless, an important episode is dominated by the fact of Private Lazzari's *recognizing his horse*, as if he belonged to the cavalry. We are in a world without substance or data.

With respect to the composition, we see that the narrative seems to order itself in four segments, which are opposed to each other, being opposed also to themselves internally: incorporation and disincorporation, illusion and disillusion, hope and frustration, life and death, fast-moving and slow-moving time. Throughout the episodes there spring up partial significances, some of which we have already seen, which lead us to general significances. To capture them, it is necessary to compare the first pages with the last.

The beginning says openly that Giovanni Drogo has no self-esteem. But the end consists in the acquisition of that self-esteem he lacked. During his entire life he waited for the moment that would permit him a kind of revelation of his being, in such a way that others might recognize his valor, which would let him recognize it in himself. But here arises the supreme contradiction, since this moment turns out to be the moment of death. For this reason, it is death that defines his being and gives him the opportunity to find a justification for his own life. In a way, an affirmation through supreme negation.

Thus, the novel of disenchantment dissolves itself in death, which emerges as the real feeling of life and an allegory of the possible existence of each person. As in all of us, it was always in the fine grain of the narrative, first in the form of the ideal target, dreamed of on a grandiose scale, and then as banal reality, in the cases of Lazzari and Angustina. When time stopped, Death appeared and redeemed it, justifying Drogo, who acquired then the wisdom that the long years of frustrated waiting had not taught him and that, if we do not fear a sententious tone, could be formulated thus: the significance of each person's life lies in the capacity to resist, to confront destiny without thinking of the witness of others and without a scenario for our actions, but in a mode of being; death reveals the nature of our being and justifies our life.

For this reason, *The Tartar Steppe* is a novel unconnected to history or society, without a defined place or a specific epoch. It is a novel of Being, outside Time and Space, without any realistic intention. From the ethical point of view, it is an aristocratic book, where the measure of things and the criterion of valor is the individual, capable of separating himself as a isolated entity, drawing significance above all from himself alone, and for this reason able to accomplish his greatest feat in solitude. The collective and theatrical death of military dreams, longed for as the crowning event of a life, gives place to the undeferrable glory of solitary death, without witnesses and with no reciprocal action, having meaning only through its own power. And we remember Montaigne, when he says that "Courage in death is without doubt the most notable action of life."

FOURTH: ON THE COAST

A Vague Country

The Opposing Shore, by Julien Gracq,[7] published in 1951, forms a curious pair with *The Tartar Steppe* because of their affinities, but above all because of their differences, which are essential, especially since the keynote of *The Tartar Steppe* is existential, while that of *The Opposing Shore* is clearly political. It tells, in the first person, the story of a young aristocrat of Orsenna, Aldo, appointed Observer, that is, Political Commissar, assigned to the weak and antiquated naval forces theoretically in operation in the Sea of Syrtes, which separates Orsenna from Farghestan, and reminds us of the Mediterranean by its situation. He goes to the headquarters, pompously called the Admiralty, as a vestige of olden times of warlike action, at the side of an old half-ruined fort near the coastal city of Maremma.

Orsenna is a patrician republic (obviously inspired by Venice), governed by an old oligarchy that owes its prosperity to commerce, especially with the East, and sustained by strong naval power. Now it is stagnant and decadent, with the refined tone of very mature civilizations, confronted by a Farghestan that perhaps is invigorated by intercourse with its primitive peoples, and whose name recalls Asiatic countries or regions: Azerbaijan, Afghanistan, Turkistan. In the Russian part of Turkistan there is an area called Fergana, which was so named by Arabs, Persians, and Mongols, as was Rhages, situated in ancient Persia and which, in the novel, is an important city of Farghestan, situated near the volcano Tengri, a name given by the Mongols to the sky conceived of as the One God. Beyond these Eastern features, vague allusions suggest that the Farghestanis (referred to in the offical rhetoric of Orsenna as "the infidels," the traditional designation of Muslims for Christians) are dark skinned, have suffered Mongol invasions, and have in their country Saracen nomads, which introduces a touch of North Africa. This would be geographically compatible with a country situated across the Mediterranean from Syrtes, which in reality is the name of the Gulf of Tunisia. Within Orsenna, there are places with Palestinian names, like Engadi and Gaza, beyond the deserts and nomadic groups, without mentioning that in the south there are messianic trends, and apocalyptic religiousity, oriental rites, visionaries and prophets. And since the two countries can communicate by land in certain regions, the reader feels in all this a meeting place between East and West, through the Venetian mediation of a state that links them by mercantile activity.

And also by armed rivalry, since Orsenna and Farghestan fought a great deal and have a history of warfare. Peace has never been officially declared between them, but for three hundred years a kind of tacit armistice has governed their relations. The rule is not to speak of Farghestan, not to leave the territorial waters, and to leave the status quo untouched. The history of Orsenna seems as stagnant as the lagoons from which its capital and the city of Maremma emerged. This Venetian trait is reinforced by various others, which the reader notes: all the names of the people and places are Italian; the aristocracy occupies all public offices and, if the head of the Executive is called Podestà, there were some in the past who were called Orseolo, the name of an historic Venetian family that furnished more than one Doge. Just as the Venetian aristocracy had its country houses along the Brenta Canal, those of the aristocracy of Orsenna are along the banks of the River Zenta. Similarly in the Venetian manner, the designation of the government is Signory, and there are feared organizations, recalling the Council of Ten (here, "The Eyes"). And further: in Orsenna espionage is normal, accusation is a public service, and everything is known by oblique means. The great national painter is called Longhone, a compound probably made from the famous names of two Venetian painters of different epochs: Longh(i) and Giorgi(one).

These data, which the reader infers and arranges little by little for himself from a narrative marked by the dispersion or imprecision of references, shows that Julian Gracq's intention is different from that of Dino Buzzatti: instead of developing a drama of the individual being, he sketches a society, a State, and a complicated political plot. *The Opposing Shore* is a rare type of narrative, in which the individual and the society reveal themselves reciprocally as two sides of reality, by means of a technique that is apparently the most inadequate possible for suggesting political mechanisms, one in which allusion, ellipses, and metaphor reign, creating a universe of implication and information as fragmentary as it is obscure. It seems that the plan is to make Aldo into something coextensive with the country and to imply the reality from a mystery, as if everything were an allegory or a symbol, as if the people, scenes, and places might be half dissolved in a magnetic halo of the kind surrealism cultivated.

In this respect the observation of Maria Theresa de Freitas is correct.[8] For her, the book oscillates between realism and surrealism, having from the first the deliberation of verisimilitude, and later using a transfiguring vision, organized around situations characterized by "decadence," the "unexpected," the "awaiting," and the "meeting." In any event, this dimly drawn country has no literary analogy to others similarly invented but with a realistic framing, like Costaguana, in Joseph Conrad's *Nostromo*, so palpable and well defined, despite some symbolic touches.

This shows that *The Opposing Shore* is a more difficult book, and the analysis more delicate, than the *The Tartar Steppe*. While the latter is short and dry, allowing the critic to arrange it according to a plausible scheme, *The Opposing Shore* is abundant and juicy, elusive, without obvious clues, requiring attentive rereadings so that we might feel how each line is charged with meaning and forms a link in a chain lost in a narrative fog, misleading and insinuating. In consequence, the rereadings show, underneath the text, a latent concatenation, which is not formed by a necessary connection to the previous moment, but obeys something ominous, governed by a strange causality.

Read thus, the narrative appears as an obsessive, almost fatal, journey, juxtaposing hints that bring Aldo to transform the possible into concrete reality: by crossing the prohibited limit of the territorial waters of Orsenna and reaching the shores of Farghestan, he breaks the ancient virtual armistice and the immobility of three hundred years.

With this as an axis, the book is organized in two parts, the first occupying two-thirds and the second one-third. First, there was the mysterious uncertain preparation; later, there will be the consequences, also vague.

The commander of the Flotilla and of the naval station, Captain Marino, feels a vague uneasiness with Aldo's presence. He is a bovine and loyal man, a perfect servant who embodies the tradition of unmoving prudence adopted by the stagnant Republic. His sailors have been transformed into agricultural laborers for the ranches of the region, by means of contracts whose execution he supervises like a man on horseback, with boots and spurs. In this setting Aldo's presence creates something new, and on a second reading we see that, while he has not received any definite instructions and is not nourishing any troubling intentions, he is being driven blindly to break the routine. This is congruent with certain changes having occurred at the heart of the oligarchy in Orsenna, giving influence to people who are restless and even suspect, like Prince Aldobrandi, a member of a family filled with traitors and rebels, who had been in exile and has returned. Appointed in this new phase, Aldo, though unaware of what he represents, has a disquieting aura that interferes with the stability embodied in Marino.

Preparation

Thus, *The Opposing Shore* is divided into two parts, the first the Preparation of the action and the second its Consequence. Everything is organized as a function of this, and the narrative, throughout the first part, consists in an obscure but decisive progression that drives it, in an undulatory structure in which each event is more charged with destiny than the one before, culminating in the crossing to Farghestan.

The first premonitory sign is Aldo's visit to the Map Room, where he feels himself strangely disoriented, under an influence similiar to that which the Russian steppes exerted on the compass. The maritime maps, with a solid line marking the permitted limits of navigation, fascinate him. A little further, a second signal appears, when, lying one night on the beach, he sees a suspicious boat slipping along the coast, in a violation of routine about which he notifies Marino, greatly embarrassing him, since in the three-century peacefulness any novelty is disturbing. Then, riding on horseback to the ruins of Sagra, Aldo sees the same boat (which is clandestine, since it does not carry the obligatory markings on its stern) anchored near a house in which there are armed men, showing that it is probably a hiding place or rendezvous. There then enters onto the scene Princess Vanessa Aldobrandi, who asks him to be silent about what he has seen. The reader suspects that something is up, involving a member of that dangerous family which has already caused so much evil to befall Orsenna. But Aldo not only does what his friend asks, he begins to frequent her summer palace in Maremma, with the other officers of the admiralty, becoming involved, little by little, in an amorous relationship. Belsenza, the policeman, tells him that Maremma is full of rumors. These, of which we learn nothing, never take shape in any report; but we intuit in some way that they concern Farghestan. Everything in Vanessa's words has a premonitory air, but Aldo continues visiting and loving this child of traitors. That there are problems in the air is suggested by the fact that the two principal employers of official labor do not wish to renew their contracts. To occupy the idle sailors, one of the officers, Fabrizio, proposes employing them to clean and repair things in the abandoned fort, which is done as though it were being prepared to function again. After it is cleaned and white, it stands out from the dark tonalities that predominate in the book, and the officers cannot decide, significantly, whether to compare it to a bridal gown or to a shroud.

Fulfilling his obligations, Aldo has written to the Signory about the rumors in Maremma, indicating that he does not attach much importance to them. The official response is nebulous and ambiguous: the government wants him to give some credit to these rumors and insinuates indirectly that the permitted limit for navigation need not be taken at the letter of the law. But at the same time, contradictorily, it reproves the works of reform. In the face of this slippery, bureaucratic style, Aldo sees that something can happen. It is then that Vanessa invites him for a cruise and takes him to the island of Vezzano, in the Sea of Syrtes, the land nearest to the coast of Farghestan.

At this season, Christmastime, there is a great ferment in Maremma. Among the people, visionaries prophesy; among the aristocracy, there is an obscure sentiment of impending catastrophe; in the church of Saint John Damascene, where the old Eastern rite flourishes, the priest delivers a disquieting apocalyptic sermon. Old Carlo, the most important of the ranchers employing the admiralty's sailors, who had not renewed his contract, expresses the same feeling of inauspicious premonition. Marino, who embodies traditional prudence, is absent, en route to the capital, and the younger officers meet in a "last supper." Aldo and Fabrizio then leave for a cruise required by routine procedure, and Aldo gives the order to go beyond the prohibited line, moving in a rhythm of exalted intoxication of the soul to Rhages, where they are received with some cannon fire. But these manifestly do not go beyond a warning salvo, and, curiously, their ship seems to have been expected, since otherwise it would not have been identifiable in the night's darkness, nor would the batteries be ready after three hundred years of tranquillity. There is, thus, a mysterious meeting of intentions, perhaps a kind of tacit understanding between the two countries, to break the three-hundred-year-old truce. On a second reading, it becomes evident that Aldo's disobedience was in fact obedience to external suggestions wedded to his own impulses; and that that is the axis of the story, organized around his slow-moving motivation. It also becomes evident that Marino is the old Orsenna, at a standstill, and Aldo the agent of new tendencies of an Orsenna disposed to exotic adventures. But one must not conclude from my description that the narrative proceeds with such clarity. On the contrary, nothing is explicit and everything proceeds by feeling one's way in the dark. What rumors are circulating? What are the visionaries proclaiming? What catastrophic warnings do the priests give? To what possible events does old Carlo refer? Does Vannesa have some definite purpose? Does the government want Aldo to cross the line, or not? Does Aldo want to do it, or not? Troubled, the reader has available only vague suggestions that come in successive waves of narrative and finally become meaningful with the explosion of the transgressive act. The rich, insinuating narrative, floating among images charged with implications, flows like a dark, magnetic liquid toward possible catastrophes, in sight of a horizon marked by death.

Consequences

In this book, the dubious characters enter the scene imperceptibly, as does the envoy of Farghestan, a vague image that, when it appears suddenly before Aldo, he recognizes as someone connected to the Aldobrandi Palace, probably a boatman who had taken him there. There was, then, a spy in Maremma, and he comes now, dark in the dark room, to suggest that Aldo apologize for his transgression in order to avoid reprisals. But, at the same time, he impedes this apology, by saying that not everyone, that is, Orsenna, deserves the glorious end of a war. In this way he stirs up Aldo's pride and fixes Aldo in a hardened attitude. For her part, Vanessa, who will disappear from the story, makes him feel that he and she are no more than instruments, and that the important thing is to travel consciously toward death. Aldo will perceive later that Vanessa "had been given to him as a guide," and that once he was "in her sway, the daylight part of my mind had been so worthless: she belonged to the sex which presses so hard at the gates of anguish, to the mysteriously docile sex that already consents to whatever looms beyond catastrophe and darkness." He will perceive even that *everyone is an instrument*, including those capable of betrayal on their own initiative, like Vanessa's father and his companions, and that he is only executing a profound design of Orsenna itself, searching for another course. Following this, we are not surprised by the suicide of Marino; he returns tired, without reproaches, ready for the inevitable death of someone who represents an outdated past. When he jumps from the tower into the lagoon, losing himself symbolically in the mud, it is as if there went with him the old, motionless Orsenna.

In the capital, to which Aldo returns, his friend Orlando tells him that his crossing was unimportant and inconsequential, and that everything will remain as it has always been. But in the final interview with old Danielo, one of the leaders of the country, it is evident that Aldo in fact did what the Signory desired without formulating it explicitly. Orsenna needed to precipitate something new, and (the politician says this expressly) if Aldo had not existed, they would have invented him, as they would also have invented Vanessa's dangerous father. Syrtes, being the locus of everything disturbing, was therefore an eventual source of renewal. His mission sought fundamentally to transform him into the fuse of an eventual catastrophe, longed for as perhaps the way to shake off the torpor of the old Republic. Aldo was, in truth, the instrument of Orsenna's destiny. Then he is sent back to his post, now as commander, to prepare for a probable state of war.

But this is not the real end of the book. Faithful to the general tone of the narrative, the narrator stops in this inconclusive state of suspense, which is more than a little vague; but the attentive reader knows that the outcome was camouflaged in a casual phrase halfway through the narrative, a little before Aldo alludes to his "hateful history": "the nightmare veil which hangs over the embers of my destroyed country." Keep the color of those embers in mind for now and see that, in the latent plot of the book, the crossing to Farghestan provoked, between the two countries, a war hidden by ellipsis, whose result was the destruction of

Orsenna, that is, the catastrophe after three centuries of anticipation, the anticipation that was the law of Fort Bastiani in *The Tartar Steppe* and of China behind Kafka's wall. From the clouded exposition of the narrator there emerged an image of total destruction (only suggested in a crack in the text), as the meaning emerges from allusion and ellipsis.

Metaphors and Meanings

The atmosphere of imprecision is singularly reinforced by the fictional ambiance. The action almost always takes place at night, the horizons are all brown, rooms dark, earth and vegetation gray. The Romantic taste (which the surrealists inherited) is visible through the melancholy darkness, the moon and sombre palaces, tall windows opening on the sea or a starlit night, castles in ruins, glimpsed corridors, adventurous princesses and rebellious aristocrats. The epoch is unclear, but the sound of a motor suggests automobiles, as a modern touch in a timeless and fading place.

In truth, the only note of color is red, already present in the emblem of the Republic ("I persist in the blood of the living and the prudence of the dead"). It erupts in the seal of the State or in the already cited image of the final blaze of its fall, but above all in a system of metaphors that trace the undefinable course of the calamity. The reader discerns that the coherence of the book must be sought in the metaphors more than in fugitive announcements or vague allusions.

The first metaphorized appearance of red is in the vast Map Room, where Aldo liked to consult marine charts spread out on an enormous table. On the wall behind it hangs, like a blood stain, the red banner of the flagship that, three centuries earlier, had bombarded the coast of Farghestan. It is the standard of the patron saint of Orsenna, Saint Jude, ambiguously symbolic, perhaps even an obscure stimulus to eventual transgressions, because it alludes indirectly to the traitorous apostle Judas. It seems to point to the maps, in which Aldo examines, fascinatedly, the line, also red, that marks the uncrossable limits of Orsenna's territorial waters. When we later see that he was sent exactly in order to cross it, we understand that the banner is the imperious finger of the Signory itself, sealing his fate as the embodiment of the fate of the Republic. From the Map Room, everything is traced through two complementary indications given a metaphoric force—the banner that suggests the transgression and the line that raises itself as a barrier. In the detail of the text, there begin to appear the signs of a metaphoric politics, and I recall Maria Teresa de Freitas's concept (on page 39 of the study cited): "The ideal surrealist novel would be a story whose development would be obedient to the power and the direction of the images, grouped in events."

Another mysterious hint occurs later when, during the first visit to the Aldobrandi Palace in Maremma, Aldo, despite being alone with Vanessa, feels an undefinable *presence*, which he immediately identifies as that of the portrait of the traitor Piero Aldobrandi, defender of the fortifications of Rhages against his own country. The description of this picture, masterpiece of the painter Longhone, is one of the most beautiful moments of the book. After describing the background, a Farghian landscape convulsed by combat, but at the same time calmed by the aesthetic serenity of its technique, the narrator settles on the central figure:

> All that mere dissociation can communicate of what is cynically natural to the spectacle of war somehow exalted the unforgettable smile on the face which thrust like a clenched fist from within the canvas and seemed to burst through the painting's foreground. Piero Aldobrandi, unhelmeted, was wearing the black cuirass and the red commander's scarf and carrying the baton which linked him forever to this scene of carnage. But the figure, turning its back to the spectacle, relegated it to the mere status of landscape, and the face, strained by a secret vision, was the emblem of a supernatural *detachment*. The half-closed eyes, with their strange inward gaze, floated in an immeasurable ecstasy; a wind from farther away than the sea stirred those locks and reanimated the entire countenance with a fierce chastity. The arm in its polished steel sheath, bright with reflected luster, raised the hand to the face in a gesture of great concentration. Between the fingertips of his gauntlet with its hard chitinous carapace, its cruel and elegant insectlike articulations, in a gesture of perverse and almost amorous grace, as though his nostrils were breathing in a drop of ultimate attar, ears deaf to the cannons' thunder, Piero Aldobrandi was crushing a blood-red, fleshy flower, the red rose of Orsenna.
>
> The room floated away. My eyes were fixed on that face rising out of the armor's sharp collar with the phosphorence of a hydra's newly severed head, like the blinding ostension of a black sun. Its light ascended above a nameless distance of far-away life, devising in me something like a dark and promised dawn.

Obviously, in the chain of strange hints that begin to envelop him, this is the key moment in which Aldo has a presentiment of some vague role he will play in the misty future, making the reader think of the heraldic motto of the Aldobrandi's coat of arms: *Fines transcendam* (We will go beyond the limits). In the palace of this dangerous family, entangled in Vanessa's seduction, he contemplates the symbolic image of treason that can result in catastrophe for Orsenna, represented in the picture by the red rose ready to be crushed in the tentacles of the arthropod formed by the gauntlet, toward which converge the movement of the scene and the ferocious disposition of the outlaw ancestor, girded by the red scarf.

Red of authority, red of barrier, red of transgression, red of catastrophe organize themselves, beginning with the bloody evocation of the standard of Orsenna and its blood red floral emblem, in a metaphorical system that shows the significances of the book. In this setting, as an instrument of its snares, Aldo represents, in a scenario filled with surrealist touches, the drama of Temptation, to which the old politician Danielo refers at the end of the novel, implicitly justifying his own transgression: "The world blossoms through those of us who surrender to temptation. The world is justified only at the eternal cost of its own security."

In classic cases, like those of Faust and Peter Schlemihl, temptation had a relatively simple allegorical character because, while it could be seen as a projection of the tempted, the tempter assumed a definite identity (Mephistopheles, the Man in the gray cassock) and corresponded to a strictly personal situation. In *The Opposing Shore* temptation manifests itself as a deepening of interior contradictions and takes the external form of multiple agents, who do not have the unique or sole function of tempting, who can be a seductive woman, like Vanessa, a symbolic portrait, the rumors carried by Police Officer Belsenza, the sybilline instructions of the government—all tuned deafly to Aldo's impulses, which come closer and closer, though he does not know it, to acts of transgression. Thus his divided personality is the mainspring, on the one hand, but, on the other, the sounding board of an historical conjuncture. One depends on the other.

It would in fact be impossible to imagine the rupture of the status quo beginning with Marino, with his massive fidelity, for example. Being what he is, Aldo comes to be, at bottom, the permanent accomplice of the forces that seek him, and this confers necessity on his act. That is what Danielo intimates in the final interview, when he says that the transgression pushed into the light a hidden part of his personality (which had to express itself). And this gave it a unity that would not have been attained without the transgression. In a more complex way than in *The Tartar Steppe*, the human being is here linked to others, to the milieu, to history. Aldo becomes part of Orsenna, which exists, the entire time, as the strength and the boundary of his self. Thanks to this, the long wait empties into the risk assumed, which explodes in a supreme negation, the destruction of the state, obscurely desired as a possibility of at least provoking a sign of life in a society at a standstill.

NOTES

First published as "Quatro esperas," in *Novos Estudos* 26 (1990), 49–76, and reprinted in *O discurso e a cidade* (São Paulo: Livraria Duas Cidades, 1993), pp. 153–200.

1. *C. P. Cavafy: Collected Poems*, revised edition, translated by Edmund Keeley and Philip Sherrard, and edited by George Savidis (Princeton: Princeton University Press, 1975 and 1992), pp.18–19.

2. "Lembra, corpo: Uma tentativa de descricão crítica da poesia de Konstantinos Kaváfis," in Konstantinos Kaváfis, *Poemas*, selecão, etudo crítico, notas e traducão direta do grego por José Paulo Paes (Rio de Janeiro: Nova Fronteira, 1982), p. 83.

3. C. M. Bowra, "Constantine Cavafy and the Greek Past," in *The Creative Experiment* (London: Macmillan, 1949), p. 38.

4. Guiseppe Ungaretti, "Difficoltà della poesia," in *Vita d'un uomo, saggi e interventi* (Milan: Mondadori, 1974), p. 810.

5. "At the Building of the Great Wall of China," in *Kafka Today*, edited by Angel Flores and Homer Swander (Madison: University of Wisconsin Press, 1958), pp. 77–81.

6. Dino Buzatti, *The Tartar Steppe*, translated by Stuart C. Hood (New York: Farrar, Straus and Young, 1952).

7. Julien Gracq, *The Opposing Shore*, translated by Richard Howard (New York: Columbia University Press, 1986).

8. Maria Teresa de Freitas, "Fiction et surréalisme dans *Le rivage des syrtes* de Julien Gracq," Master's Thesis: University of São Paulo, 1974.

Chapter 4

REPRESSION'S TRUTH

BALZAC, who saw so many things, also saw the role the police were beginning to play in the contemporary world. Fouché had transformed the police apparatus into a precise and omnipotent instrument, necessary to maintain Napoleon's dictatorship, but one that created within it a parallel world, an element that was determining as much as it was determined.

The novelist was about sixteen when Napoleon fell and thus had been able to see how the police force Fouché organized had acquired (in a kind of natural development of functions) its important role in the bourgeois and constitutional world then opening up: to disguise the arbitrariness of the will of the authorities through a simulation of legality.

The police force of an absolute sovereign is open and brutal, because an absolute sovereign does not much concern himself with justifying his actions. But the police of a constitutional State must be more hermetic and refined. For this reason, it becomes organically mixed with the rest of society, putting into practice what we might call a "Venetian" model: one that establishes a subtle network of espionage and irresponsible accusations (made under the cover of anonymity) as the foundation of the State.

To this end, the police make intimate and profound links to every part of society. They disguise themselves and assume a double organization, splitting into a visible part (with its symbols and badges) and a secret part, with its unsuspected army of spies and informers, who seem on the surface to be pursuing some other activity. This double functioning also allows the organization to satisfy an intransigent requirement of the bourgeoisie, dominant since Balzac's time and dispensed with only when their class position is threatened: the police must pursue their work implacably, but without overly offending the sensibilities of those well placed in life. Thus, they must hide as much as possible the most disagreeable aspects of investigation and repression.

To obtain this result, the society needs thousands of individuals with appropriately deformed souls. Like the "comprachicos" in Victor Hugo's *The Man Who Laughs*, who mutilated children to provide dwarfs and cripples to entertain others, society draws from these people the brutality, the need, the frustration, the depravity, the defect—and gives them the repressive function.

This is the source of literature's interest in the police, ever since Balzac saw the organic solidarity between them and society, the power of their hidden sectors, and the way they took advantage of the marginal and the degenerate in order to strengthen order. In his books there is always a point where the transgressor cannot be distinguished from the oppressor, who may even have been a transgressor himself, as in the case of Vautrin, at the same time Balzac's greatest criminal and his greatest policeman.

Dostoyevsky saw something more subtle: the symbolic function of the police as a possible substitute for the conscience—society entering into each person through the pressure it exerts or the secrets it uncovers. In *Crime and Punishment*, the Judge of Instruction Porphyry Petrovitch becomes, through his cross-examination, a kind of double of Raskolnikov.

But it was Kafka, in *The Trial*, who saw that aspect of the police which was, so to speak, essential and at the same time profoundly social. He saw them as inseparable from justice, which itself increasingly came to look like the police. He saw how the repressive function (which Balzac had shown to be a normal function of society) acquired a transcendent sense, until it finally became its own end. When this occurs, it reveals basic aspects of man, repressor and repressed.

To begin functioning, Kafka's police/justice needs no motives, only stimuli. And once in operation it can no longer stop, because its purpose is itself. For this reason, it does not hesitate to push a man off his accustomed track, even to the point of liquidating him completely, physically or morally. It does not hesitate to make him (by whatever means) part of an action or put him under suspicion of an action, or even of the vague possibility of an action, which the State wants to repress, whether or not the person who is the target was involved in it. Because of the importance of the punitive process (whose illegitimate object is simply to function, without any purpose), the materiality of guilt loses its meaning.

The police thus appear as an agency that violates the personality, robbing men of the precarious sources of equilibrium they usually have available: shame, emotional control, loyalty, discretion—all dissolved with skill or with professional brutality. Operating as a powerful reductive force, the police bring to the surface everything we have succeeded in repressing, transforming modesty into impudence, control into disorder, loyalty into denunciation, discretion into tragic meddlesomeness.

By means of these transformations, the police bring into being a kind of monstrous truth, the hidden truth of someone who has painfully presented himself as *other*, who in fact was *other*, in the sense that he was not obliged to descend into his most profound depths. Perhaps it would be more accurate to say that what the police have brought into being is the *other* himself, his truth imposed on him or drawn out by the repressive process, extracted against his will from the depths where it had been more or less imprisoned.

In fact, the police must construct the truth of the *other* in order to manipulate the *self* of their victim. Their strength consists in opposing the *self* to the *other*, so that it may be absorbed by it and, in this way, made ready for what awaits it: collaboration, submission, omission, silence. The police mold the *other* through interrogation, ransacking the past, exposing weakness, and by means of physical and moral violence. In the end, if necessary, they can even employ, for their own ends, this *other*, which is a new *self*, manipulated by a dose of an ingredient of the highest efficacy: fear, in all its degrees and modalities.

An example of this degrading reduction is the behavior of the police officer with the plumber, in Elio Petri's film *Investigation of a Citizen above Suspicion*. The officer, who is also the criminal, resolves to play with destiny and to test the self-determining mechanism of the police as an end in itself. To do this, he addresses himself to a passerby, chosen by chance, and confesses that he is the murderer who is wanted, giving as proof the sky blue tie he is wearing, which had been seen on the criminal. He convinces the poor passerby to go to the police and tell them about the confession, giving him as evidence (and evidently intending to confuse the evidence) a number of similar ties, which would show what the one worn by the killer looked like.

Arriving at the police station, the passerby, who is a plumber, comes face to face with the murderer who confessed to him in the street, who he has come to denounce, but who is now in his role as police officer. The officer interrogates him brutally and pressures him physically and morally to identify the murderer who disclosed himself to him in the street. But the poor devil, completely disorganized by this inexplicable contradiction, does not have that much courage. He thus becomes a suspect himself, being characterized legally as a possible criminal, until he disappears, faltering and exhausted, down dirty corridors that lead to what we suspect only too well.

The force that paralyzes him, and that would eventually paralyze us, stems from an ambiguity, mysterious in appearance, but efficacious, whose nature was suggested above: the repressor and the transgressor are the same, not only physically and from the point of view of social roles, but ontologically (the *other* is the *self*).

Everything in this episode is exemplary: the gratuitous selection of the guilty person; the imposition of an unintended behavior (to go to the police with blue ties in hand, to denounce a nameless criminal, in whom he has no interest); the mixing up of the truth, when he sees that the man he is to denounce as a criminal is also the officer; the transformation of the innocent into a suspect and the suspect into a criminal, accepted by the innocent person himself, in the depths of the mental disorganization the inquiry has forged in him.

The fulcrum of this process is, perhaps, the moment of the interrogation in which the officer asks the poor devil, already stunned, what his profession is.

"I'm a hydraulic engineer," he replies.

The officer mocks him: "Hydraulic engineer, my ass! Today everyone wants to be something prettier. What you are is a plumber, right? Plumber! Why hy-draul-ic en-gin-eer?"

And the unfortunate one, already without courage or backbone: "Yes, I'm a plumber."

(Not having the script, I cite this from memory.)

We see that the poor man, like everyone in his trade, has adopted a technical designation (*idraulico*, in Italian), which separates him from the craft designation of "plumber" (*stagnaro*, in Italian), thus giving the illusion of a level that is apparently more elevated, or at least more scientific and up-to-date. But the policeman *reduces* him to his previous level, *unmasks* his self-promotion, extracts from him the undesirable *truth*. And, in the end, it is as if he were to say:

"Yes, I confess, I'm not a technician with a sonorous name, which innocently evokes something of engineering; I'm only a poor devil, a plumber. I am reduced to my true *self*, liberated from the *other*."

But, in fact, it was the police who imposed the *other* on him as his *self*. The police effectuated the dismantling of his personality, so arduously constructed, and brought back what the man had overcome. Sinister reductive mentality, which obliges us to be, or return to being, what we don't wish to be; and which shows that Alfred de Vigny was right, when he wrote in his diary:

"I'm not afraid of poverty, nor of exile, nor of prison, nor of death. But I'm afraid of fear."

NOTE

First published as "A verdade da repressão," *Opinão* 11 (1972), 15–22, and reprinted in *Teresina etc.* (São Paulo: Paz e Terra, 1992), pp. 103–8.

Chapter 5

DIALECTIC OF MALANDROISM

IN 1894 José Veríssimo defined *Memórias de um sargento de milícias* (The memoirs of a sergeant of the militia), by Manuel Antônio de Almeida, as a novel of manners that, because it describes places and scenes in Rio de Janeiro at the time of Dom João VI [king of Portugal, who lived in Brazil from 1807 until 1822], is characterized by a kind of premature realism; in consequence, he praises it, like a man of an era dominated by the aesthetic of naturalism.

Almost nothing further was said of it until 1941, when Mário de Andrade reoriented criticism, denying that it was a precursor. It was, rather, a late continuation, a novel of a marginal type, a deviation from the mainstream of a literary tradition, like that of Apuleius or Petronius, in antiquity, or of *Lazarillo de Tormes*, in the Renaissance—all with antiheroic characters who are differing types of picaro.

A third step was taken in 1956 by Darcy Damasceno, who approached it from the perspective of a stylistic analysis, beginning with an excellent rejection of these prior positions:

> It is not necessary to consider a book picaresque because there is in it a picaro more apparent than essential, especially if the book lacks the peculiar marks of the picaresque genre; nor would it be historical, even though a certain dose of veracity has served in the creation of types or the evocation of an epoch; still less could we consider it realistic, when the most attentive reading shows us a predominance of the imaginative and the improvised over portraiture or historic reconstitution.

And, after showing how few documentary indications there are, he suggests the designation of novel of manners.[1]

I agree with these appropriate and penetrating opinions (unhappily very brief), which can serve as a point of departure for the present essay. My only doubt is in reference to realism, and perhaps not even that, if Darcy Damasceno was referring to the usual concept in literary classifications, which so designates what occurred in the last half of the nineteenth century, while my purpose is to characterize a somewhat peculiar literary type, which is manifested in Manuel Antônio de Almeida's book.

A Picaresque Novel?

The point of view according to which Almeida's book is a picaresque novel, widely diffused beginning with Mário de Andrade (who, however, did not say exactly that), was stamped as definitive by Josué Montello, who thought he had found its roots in such works as *Lazarillo de Tormes* (1554) and *Vida e hechos de Estabanillo González* (1645).[2]

Had this been so, it would have resolved the problem of the line of descent and, with that, a large part of the critical characterization. But, in truth, Josué Montello based his argument on a petitio principii, taking as proved what was to *be* proved, that is, that the *Memórias* is a picaresque novel. Beginning with that, he overvalued some fugitive analogies and thought what he wanted to, but not what an objective comparison would have shown. In fact, the analysis of Spanish picaresque literature shows that these two books motivated nothing of importance in Almeida's book, although he might possibly have gotten some marginal suggestions from some other novel, Spanish or written in the Spanish style, which was common all over Europe in the seventeenth and part of the eighteenth centuries. What can give us the best assurance is to compare the characteristics of "our hero" (as the novelist says of his character) with the typical picaresque hero or antihero, minutely described by Chandler in his book on the topic.[3]

In general, the picaro himself narrates his adventures, which limits the vision of reality to his restricted viewpoint; and this first person voice is one of the enchantments for the reader, communicating a false candor that the author creates skillfully and uses as a psychological resource in characterization. Manuel Antônio's novel, however, is told in the third person by a narrator (first viewpoint) who is not identified, and he varies the secondary viewpoints uninhibitedly—from Leonardo the father to Leonardo the Son, from there to the Godfather and Godmother, then the Gypsy, and so on, in such a way as to establish a dynamic view of the narrated material. From this perspective, the hero is one character among others, though he has a preferential position; he does not establish and is not the *occasion* for the establishment of the fictional world, as are Lazarillo, Estebanillo, Guzman de Alfarache, the Pícara Justina, or Gil Blas de Santillana.

On the other hand, Leonardo the Son has some affinities with the picaresque narrators: like them, he is of humble origin and, like some of them, is illegitimate. Like them, too, he is set loose in the world, but he is not abandoned, as were Lazarillo or Quevedo's Buscón; on the contrary, his parents have hardly left him to his destiny when he is given a much better father in the person of the Godfather, the good barber who watches over him for the rest of his life and shelters him from material adversity, so much so that he lacks a basic trait of the picaro: the harsh conflict with reality, which leads him to lying, dissimulation, and robbery, and which is the major excuse for the picaro's "tricks." At the beginning, the picaro is ingenuous; it is the brutality of life that slowly turns him clever and unscrupulous, almost as a defense; but Leonardo, well protected by his Godfather, is born a full-blown *malandro*,[4] as if this were an essential quality, not an attribute acquired by force of circumstance.

Further: humble origins and being abandoned by destiny lead necessarily, for the protagonist of the Spanish novels and those that resemble them closely, to a servile status. At some point in his career he is a servant, in such a way that it has been mistakenly supposed that the word "picaro" comes from that fact, and would signify an inferior sort of serf, most often a kitchen helper, dirty and ragged. And it is from the fact of being a servant that an important principle of the novel's organization flows, since, passing from master to master, the picaro is always moving, changing his surroundings, varying his experience, and seeing society as a whole. But our Leonardo is so far from a servile condition that the Godfather is offended when the Godmother suggests that he send him to learn a manual trade; the good man wants to see him a priest or trained in the law, and in this sense tries to get him off to a good start, freeing him of any necessity to earn a living. So subsistence never appears as a serious problem, even when Leonardo gets into a scrape and, almost as a game, goes into service in the royal kitchens, which approximates vaguely the condition of the picaro in the sense referred to above.

Like many picaros, he is amiable and cheerful, spontaneous in his actions, and devoted to reality, as it moves him through life. This submits him, like them, to a kind of external causality, to a motivation that comes from circumstances and makes the character into a puppet, empty of psychological ballast and characterized only by the turns of the plot. The sense of a destiny that motivates conduct is lively in the *Memórias*, when the Godfather refers to the *fate* that follows his godson, heaping misfortunes on him and undoing at every step the favorable situations that come his way.

Like the picaros, he lives by the dictates of chance, without plan or reflection; unlike them he learns nothing from the experience. In fact, an important element of the picaresque is this apprenticeship, which matures the protagonist and makes him review his life in the light of a disenchanted philosophy. But, consistent with the vocation of puppet, Leonardo concludes nothing and learns nothing; the book's being narrated in the third person facilitates this lack of awareness, since it falls to the narrator to make little moral reflections, in general a little cynical and always optimistic, in contrast to the acid sarcasm and relative pessi-

mism of the picaresque novels. The Spanish malandro always ends either
in a resigned mediocrity, accepting it as a shelter after so much agitation,
or more miserable than ever, in a universe without deceptions or illusions, a characteristic feature of Spanish literature of the Golden Age.

Hardened by life, cornered and beaten, the picaro has no feelings,
only reflexes of attack and defense. Betraying his friends, deceiving his
patrons, he has no standard of conduct, does not love and, if he marries,
will marry for profit, ready, like poor Lazarillo, for even the dullest arrangement. Leonardo, while destitute of passion, has more sincere feelings in this area, and the book is in part the story of his obstacle-filled
love for the cunning Luisinha, whom he finally marries, after being promoted, retiring, and receiving five legacies, which fall into his hands
without his having to lift a finger. No model of virtue, he is nevertheless
loyal and commits himself seriously in order not to harm the malandro
Teotônio. An antipicaro, therefore, in these and other circumstances,
who does not seek out or make himself agreeable to "superiors," which
constitutes the supreme aim of the Spanish malandro.

With such a protagonist, we might expect that the book, taken as a
whole, will present the same oscillation between analogies to and differences from the picaresque novel.

Picaresque novels are dominated by a sense of physical and social
space, since the picaro goes to diverse places and comes into contact
with a variety of social groups and strata, both nationally and interna-
tionally, like that of the "Galician Roman" Estabanillo. The fact of being
a classless adventurer is expressed in a change of circumstances, whose
primary type, established in the first novel of its type, *Lazarillo de
Tormes*, is the change of patrons. Servant to a beggar, servant to a poor
squire, servant to a priest, the little vagabond moves through society,
whose social types the book reviews, in such a way as to make it an exploration of social groups and their customs—something that became
common in the picaresque novel, making it one of the models of modern realistic fiction. Though deformed by its satiric angle, its viewpoint
exhibits society in its variation of places, groups, and classes—typically
seen from the position of the inferiors looking up at the superiors, as is
apppropriate to the picaro's eventual social ascent. In this panoramic
view, a vulgar moralism appears at the end, but there is little or no real
moral purpose, despite the constant protests with which the narrator
tries to give an exemplary stamp to the picaro's tricks. And, in relation
to women, he displays an accentuated misogyny. While they are neither
licentious nor sentimental, the picaresque novels are frequently obscene
and use dirty words freely, appropriately for the milieus described.

Manuel Antônio's book, on the contrary, has a *clean* vocabulary. It
uses no vulgar expressions and, when it does enter the zone of licen-

tiousness, is discreet, or does it in such a caricatured way that the irregular element dissolves in good humor—as is notably the case in the sequence of the misfortune of the priest surprised in the Gypsy's room in his underwear. But we see that the book has a certain touch of amorous feeling, despite being described with suitable irony; and the satire, visible throughout, never touches the whole of society since, unlike the picaresque book, its field is restricted.

THE NOVEL OF THE MALANDRO

Let us say, then, that Leonardo is not a picaro, coming out of the Spanish tradition; but, rather, the first great malandro to enter the world of the Brazilian novel, coming from an almost folkloric tradition and corresponding, more than it is customary to say, to a certain comic and folkloresque atmosphere of its time in Brazil. He is the malandro who would be elevated to the category of a symbol by Mário de Andrade in *Macunaima*[5] and who Manuel Antônio probably shaped spontaneously to share, with intelligence and feeling, in the popular tone of the stories that, according to tradition, he heard from a newspaper colleague, a former sergeant commanded by the real Major Vidigal.

The malandro, like the picaro, is one specimen of the larger genre of the clever adventurer, common to all folklores. We have already noted, in fact, that Leonardo engages in cleverness for its own sake (even when he is trying to get himself out of a tight spot), displaying a love for the game itself, which differentiates him from the pragmatism of the picaros, whose rascality almost always looks toward some gain or some concrete problem, frequently injuring third parties in its solution. This being clever for its own sake approximates "our hero" to the classic trickster, even in his zoomorphic incarnations—monkey, fox, turtle—making him less an "antihero" than a creation that may take some features from such popular heroes as Pedro Malasarte. More erudite models, too, may have influenced its elaboration; but what appears to predominate in the book is the dynamism of the clever characters of folklore. For this reason, Mário de Andrade is right to say that in the *Memórias* there is no realism in the modern sense; what is found is something vaster and more timeless, characteristic of this vein of popular humor.

This originally folkloric element perhaps explains certain manifestations of an archetypal stamp—including beginning with the stock phrase of the fairy tale: "It was in the time of the King." To the same universe belongs the constellation of good fairies (the Godfather and Godmother) and the typical bad fairy (who here is the Neighbor), all encircling the child's crib and serving the purposes of destiny, the "fate" invoked more than once in the course of the narrative. To this could also be related the anonymity of various characters, important and second-ary, designated only by profession or their position in a group that, on the one hand, dissolves them into typical social categories, but on the other approximates them to legendary paradigms and the indeterminacy of the fable, where there is always "the king," "a man," "a woodcutter," "the soldier's wife," etc. Similarly, Major Vidigal, beneath the histori-cally documented uniform, is a kind of ogre, a devourer of happy people. And to all this, finally, could be related the curious duplication that es-tablishes two protagonists, Leonardo the Father and Leonardo the Son, not only contrasting with the strong structural unity of picaresque an-tiheroes (at the same time the source of the narrative and its destina-tion), but also revealing one more tie with folk models.

Indeed, father and son embody the two faces of the trickster: foolish-ness, eventually leading to a desired result, and cleverness, often leading, at least temporarily, to disaster. From this point of view, the half-silly bailiff who ends with his life in order, and his clever son who almost brings disaster on himself, would be a kind of inverted projection, on the level of adventure, of the didactic family of Bertoldo, which Giulio Cesare Della Croce and his followers popularized in Italy beginning in the sixteenth century, inspired by ancient oriental sources. It is hardly worth saying that in the bookstore catalogs of Manuel Antônio's time there appeared various editions and collections of the stories of this fa-mous bunch, such as: *Astúcias de Bertoldo*; *Simplicidades de Bertoldinho, filho do sublime e astuto Bertoldo, e agudas respostas de Marcolfa, sua mãe*; *Vida de Cacasseno, filho do simples Bertoldinho e neto de astuto Bertoldo*. In the *Memórias de um sargento de milícias*, a cultivated book linked only remotely to the archetypes of folklore, the father is a simpleton and the son is clever, having beyond this no vestige of any gnomic prophe-cies, characteristic of the series of Bertoldos and of the *Donzela Teodora*, another know-it-all very much alive in Brazilian folklore.

Since we have no reason to mistrust the story that the material of the novel came, at least in part, from the reports of an old police sergeant,[6] we can acknowledge that the first level of the novelist's stylistic work consisted of extracting from the facts and the people a certain element of generality, thus bringing them closer to the underlying paradigms of folk narratives. Thus, for example, a certain judicial official, perhaps called Leonardo Pataca, was trimmed, simplified, reordered, and ficti-tiously reminted, getting rid of his flesh and blood, in order to transform him into a specific instance of a type, the unlucky lover, and, beyond that, of the butt of everyone's joke. In other words, the fiction writer would first have had to reduce the facts and situations to general types, probably because their popular character allowed him to build an easy bridge to the universe of folklore, giving these oral transmissions the solidity of folk tradition.

We could, then, say that the integrity of the *Memórias* arises from the intimate association between the plane of what was created consciously (the representation of customs and scenes of Rio) and a plane that is perhaps in greater part involuntary (semifolkloric features, manifested above all in the tenor of acts and incidents). An ingredient in this integrity is a spontaneous and commonplace realism, based in the feeling of the social dynamic of Brazil in the first half of the nineteenth century. And in this probably resides the secret of the book's strength and of its durability.

There are also, clearly, some learned influences and features related to the literary currents that, at that time, joined with the tendencies peculiar to Romanticism to create a more complicated picture than the one suggested by schematic classifications. In this way, it intersects with the forces at work in Brazilian literature of the time, whose consideration clarifies it as much or more than the invocation of foreign models, and even of a folk substratum.

In fact, to understand a book like the *Memórias* it is worth remembering its affinity with the comic and satiric production of the Regency and the first years of the reign of Emperor Dom Pedro II—in journalism, in poetry, in visual art, and in theater. Written in 1852 and 1853, the book followed a trend that began in the thirties, when small comic and satirical papers began to flourish, such as *O Carupuceiro*, of Father Lopes Gama (1832–34; 1837–43; 1847) and *O Novo Carapuceiro*, of Gama e Castro (1841–42). Both were occupied with political and moral analysis through the satire of customs and portraits of characteristic types, dissolving the individual in the category, as Manuel Antônio tended to do. This line, which comes from La Bruyère, but also from the old Portuguese and Brazilian comic poem, above all the example of Nicolau Tolentino, still shows itself in the veritable mania for the satirical portrait, drawing typical portraits from everyday life that, under the name of "physiology" (for which read "psychology"), increased rapidly in the French press between 1830 and 1850 and from there passed to Brazil. Balzac had cultivated this form with great talent, but it is not necessary to go back to his influence, as a recent study has done,[7] to find the ultimate source of a fashion that was the daily fare of the newspapers.

At the same time, the political caricature appeared in the first drawings of Araujo Porto-Alegre (1837)[8] and then, from 1838 to 1849, in the theatrical activity of Martins Pena, whose conception of life and of literary composition resembled that of Manuel Antônio—the same light touch, the same penetrating sense of typical traits, the same suspension of moral judgment. A lover of the theater like our author could not have been at the margin of a tendency so well represented, one that would still appear, modestly, in the novels and theatrical work of Joaquim Manuel Macedo, full of infrarealism and caricature.

The poets themselves, whom we think of today as a tearful collection of professional mourners, wrote comic poetry, obscene and crazy, at times with great grace, like Laurindo Rabelo and Bernardo Guimarães, whose work has lasted until today. Álvares de Azevedo was an amusing poet, and some latecomers maintained the tradition of good-humored social satire, as is the case of *A festa de Baldo* (1847), by Álvaro Teixeira de Macedo, whose old-fashioned language does not entirely hide a choice perception of provincial customs.

Documentary Novel?

To say that Manuel Antônio de Almeida's book is eminently documentary, a faithful reproduction of the society in which the action develops, would perhaps be to commit again the fallacy of petitio principii—it would then still have to be shown, first, that it reflects the Rio de Janeiro of the era of King Dom João VI and, second, that the book owes its character and its value to this reflection.

The novel of the realistic type, archaic or modern, always communicates a certain vision of society, whose aspect and significance it seeks to translate in terms of art. It is more doubtful that it gives an informative vision, since generally we can only evaluate the faithfulness of the representation through comparisons with the data we take from documents of some other kind. Having said this, there remains the fact that Manuel Antônio's book suggests the lively presence of a society that seems to us quite coherent and existent, and which connects us to the Rio de Janeiro of the beginning of the nineteenth century, so that Astrojildo Pereira has come to compare it to the engravings of Debret, as a representational effort.[9]

Nevertheless, the panorama it traces is narrow. Restricted spatially, its action occurs in Rio, above all in what are today the central areas and at that time comprised most of the city. No character leaves this ambit, and only once or twice does the author take us to a suburb, as in the episode of the Caboclo [a person of mixed Indian and European descent] of Mangue and in Vidinha's family party in the country.

The action is also circumscribed socially to the kind of free people of modest position who we would today call petit bourgeois. Beyond this, there are a rich woman, two priests, a chief of police, and, in a brief glance, a superior officer of the army and a nobleman, through whom we glimpse the world of the Royal Palace. This new world, recently superimposed on the peaceful capital of the Viceregalty,[10] was then a great novelty, with the presence of the King and his ministers, the installation (filled with episodes, half picturesque, half loathsome) of a nobility and a bureaucracy ferried over in refugee ships, surrounded by machinery and crates of books. But of this lively and relevant world, not a word; it is as though Rio had continued to be the city of the Viceroy Luis de Vasconcelos Sousa.

There was, also, an older and more important element affecting daily life, which formed a major part of the population, which no one lived without: the slaves. Now, as Mário de Andrade notes, there are no "people of color" in the book—except for the Bahians in the procession of the Goldsmiths, a mere decorative element, and the servants in the house of Dona Maria, mentioned in passing in order to frame the Master of Prayer. Only the free mulatto Chico-Juca is treated as a character, as a representative of that fringe of disorderly and marginal people which formed a sizable part of the Brazilian society of the time.

The book is a restricted documentary, then, which ignores the ruling classes, on the one hand, and the labor force, on the other. But perhaps the problem should be put in other terms, without trying to see the fiction as a duplication, a frequent attitude in the naturalist criticism that has inspired most of the commentaries on the *Memórias* and that had a conception of realism we could call mechanical.

In truth, what interests the literary analyst is to know, in this case, what role was played by historically localized social reality in constituting the structure of the book, that is, a phenomenon that could be called the formalization or structural reduction of external data.

For this, we must begin by verifying that Manuel Antônio de Almeida's novel is made up of several discontinuous, but discernible, threads, arranged in a manner whose effectiveness varies: (1) the facts narrated, including the characters; (2) the social practices and customs described; and (3) the judgments made by the narrator and some of the characters. When the author organizes them in an integrated way, the result is satisfactory and we sense the reality. When the integration is less happy, we seem to see a more or less precarious juxtaposition of elements that, though interesting and sometimes enchanting as isolated pictures, are insufficiently blended. It is in this last case that the customs and usages appear as *documents*, ready for the files of the folklorists, the curious, and the practitioners of *petite histoire*.

This is what happens, for example, in chapter 17 of part 1, "Dona Maria," where the constitutive elements are not integrated. We have in this chapter a description of customs (the procession of the Goldsmiths); the physical and moral portrait of a new character, who gives the chapter its name; and the current action, which is the debate about the young Leonardo, in which Dona Maria, the Godfather, and the Neighbor participate. Though interesting, everything in the chapter is disconnected. The procession earlier described as an autonomous focus of interest is not the procession-in-fact, that is, a specific procession, concrete, localized, detailed, and made part of the narrative. Though it is linked to the current action, it only functions this way for an instant, at the end, and what dominates the chapter is the procession-as-custom, a nonspecific procession, having the character of picturesque information, of the kind generally considered as constituting Manuel Antônio's strength, when in truth it is the weak point of his composition.

But if we move back to chapter 15 of the same part, we will see something else. It deals with the "Estralada," the Gypsy's amusing party birthday, which Leonardo upsets, paying the *capoeira* Chico-Juca to create disorder and denouncing everything beforehand to Vigidal, who intervenes and makes public the sin of the Master of Ceremonies.

In this chapter, there appear again some *documentary* elements, including the *capoeira* fight, associated with the physical and moral portrait of the *caporeira* and a sequence of facts. But here the *document* does not exist in itself, as in the previous case: it is a constitutive part of the action, in such a way that it never seems that the author has been informing us or diverting our attention to a feature of society. Within the traditional norms of composition, which Manuel Antônio follows, the second of these is the right thing; the first, if not a mistake, is imperfect in a structural sense.

The book's ability to convince us essentially depends, then, on certain devices of its construction, which organize the *data* on the surface of the narrative. These data must be seen as elements of composition, not as information arranged by the author, for to do that would be to reduce the novel to a series of descriptive pictures of customs of the time.

Manuel Antônio's book ran this risk of such a reduction. The criteria suggested above permit it to be read in a more illuminating mode, perhaps because one can see that it succeeds as a novel to the degree that it gives up being a collection of curious types and picturesque customs, which predominate in the first half. It is possible, and even probable, that the composition of the book took place a little at a time, in accordance with its serial publication;[11] and that the sense of unity grew progressively, to the degree that the master line of the hero's destiny was consolidated, emerging from the host of anecdotes. For this reason, the first half is more of a chronicle, while the second is more a novel, strengthening what came before, preserving what was colorful and picturesque in everyday life, without putting it excessively in the foreground.

This duality of stages (which are like two coexisting narrative orders) becomes clear if we note that in the first half Leonardo the Son is still not distinguished from the other characters and that the novel can be thought of as having both him and his father as its principal figures. The facts related to one and the other, and also to the characters associated directly with them, run like alternate lines, while beginning with chapter 28 the line of the son absolutely dominates and the narrative, going beyond static description, diminishes the effect of the frequent inclusion of usage and custom, dissolving them in the dynamic of events.

This being so, it is probable that the impression of reality the book communicates does not come essentially from the relatively limited amount of information it contains on the society of Rio in the time of Dom João VI. It derives from a more profound, though instinctive, vision of people's function or "destiny" in that society; so much so that the real acquires its full force when it becomes an integral part of the act and a constituent part of situations. Manuel Antônio, despite his simplicity, has one thing in common with the great realists: the capacity to see, beyond the fragments described, certain constitutive principles of the society, a hidden element that acts as totalizer of partial aspects.

A Representative Novel

The popular nature of the *Memórias de um sargento de milícias* is one of the sources of its widespread appeal and, therefore, of the effectiveness and durability with which it acts on the imagination of readers. Imagination almost always reacts to the stimulus caused by archetypal situations and characters, endowed with the ability to evoke resonances. But beyond this kind of generality lies another, which reinforces and, at the same time, determines it, restricting its meaning and making it more fitting for the specific ambit of Brazil. In other words: there is in the book a primary universalizing stratum, where there exist archetypes valid for the imagination of a wide circle of culture, such types as the trickster or such situations as those born of the caprice of "fate"; and there is a second universalizing stratum of a more restricted stamp, where one encounters representations of life capable of stimulating the imagination of a smaller universe within the cycle: the Brazilian.

In the *Memórias*, the second stratum is constituted by a dialectic between order and disorder, which express human relations concretely at the level of the book, for which they form the system of reference. This dialectic's character as a structural principle, which generates the supporting skeleton, is due to the aesthetic formalization of social circumstances that are profoundly significant as modes of existence; and for this reason they contribute to the book's reaching readers deeply.

This conclusion can only be clarified by the description of the system of relations between the characters, which shows (1) the construction, in the society described by the book, of an order connected to the disorder that surrounds it on every side; (2) the book's profound correspondence, much more than documentary, to certain aspects of the relationship between order and disorder in Brazilian society in the first half of the nineteenth century.

We will thus see that, elementary as its conception of life and characterization of characters may be, the *Memórias* is a book acute with perception of human relations taken as a whole. If he was not fully conscious of it, there is no doubt that the author had sufficient mastery to organize a number of characters according to intuitions sufficient to the social reality.

We take, to begin with, the central character of the book, Leonardo the Son, imagining that he also occupies a central position in its social space; on the right is his mother, on the left his father, all three on the same plane. With a minimum of arbitrariness we can place the other characters, even some vague figures, above and below the equatorial line they form. Above them are those who live according to established norms, with their great representative, Major Vidigal, standing at the apex ; below the line are those who live in opposition to, or at least dubiously integrated with, those norms. We might say that there is, in this way, a positive hemisphere of order and a negative hemisphere of disorder, functioning as two magnets that attract Leonardo, having already attracted his parents. The dynamic of the book presupposes a seesaw of the two poles, with Leonardo growing and participating now in the one, now in the other, until he is finally absorbed by the conventionally positive pole.

From this point of view, father, mother, and son are three nodes of relations, *positive* (the pole of order) and *negative* (the pole of disorder), the first two constituting a kind of prefiguring of the destiny of the third. Leonardo Pataca, the father, is, as an official of justice, on the side of order; and, despite its illegitimacy, his relation with Maria da Hortaliça is common and almost normal according to the customs of his time and class. But, after he is abandoned by her, he enters a more suspect world, because of his love for the Gypsy, who takes him to the forbidden witchcraft meetings of the Caboclo do Mangue, where Major Vidigal surprises him and puts him in jail. For the sake of the Gypsy, too, he creates a scene at her party, hiring the ruffian Chico-Juca, which causes Vidigal to intervene again and expose the picturesque shame of a priest, the Master of Ceremonies. The Gypsy later comes to live with Leonardo Pataca, until finally, now mature, he established a stable relationship with the Godmother's daughter, though one equally deprived of religious blessing, as (we repeat) would have been almost normal at that time among people of modest means. Thus Leonardo the Father, representing order, descends through successive circles of disorder and eventually returns to a relatively sanctioned position, plagued by the patient and brutal interventions of Major Vidigal—a character who actually existed and must have been of great importance in a city where, according to an observer of the time, "one had to avoid going out alone at night and had to be more attentive to one's security than anywhere else, because robberies and crimes were frequent, even though it was as easy to find police there as to find sand at the beach."[12]

The life of Leonardo the Son is, similarly, an oscillation between the two hemispheres, with a greater variety of situations.

If we analyze the system of relations in which he is involved, we see first the actions of those who try to set him on the road to order: his protectors, the Godfather and the Godmother. Through them, he comes into contact with Dona Maria, a woman well placed in life, who is linked in turn to a rich intriguer, José Manuel, served by a blind man, the Master of Prayer, who teaches religious doctrine to children; Dona Maria, who is linked above all to her niece Luisinha, a well-provided-for heiress and Leonardo's future wife, after first marrying the already mentioned José Manuel. We are in a world of alliances, of careers, of inheritances, of people of settled position: at a modest level, the Godfather, a barber, and the Neighbor; at a more elevated level, Dona Maria. They are all on the *positive* side that the police respect and whose parties Major Vidigal does not keep an eye on.

Seen from this angle, the story of Leonardo the Son is the old story of a hero who passes through many dangers to reach happiness, but expressed through a peculiar social constellation, which transforms it into the story of a youth who vacillates between the established order and transgressive conduct, in order finally to be integrated into the first, after having had plenty of experience of the other. The special stamp of the book consists in a certain absence of moral judgment and in the cheerful acceptance of "man as he is," a mixture of cynicism and good nature that demonstrates to the reader a relative equivalence between the universe of order and that of disorder, between what would conventionally be called good and evil.

In the construction of the plot this equivalence is represented objectively by the state of mind in which the narrator displays the moments of order and disorder, presented as being on the same level to a reader incapable of judging, because the author has removed the scale necessary for that. But there is something more profound, which supports the more superficial levels of interpretation: the equivalence of order and disorder in the very economy of the book, as can be verified in the descriptions of situations and relations. We will take only two examples.

Leonardo has liked Luisinha since he was a boy, since the beautiful episode of "Fire in the Field," when he sees her shy little peasant face

transfigured by the emotion of the colored rockets. But since circumstances (or, in the terms of the book, "destiny") have separated him
from her through her conventional marriage to José Manuel, Leonardo,
who has no capacity for suffering (since, despite what the narrator says,
he does not have his father's amorous character), moves easily to other
loves and to the enchanting Vidinha. She evokes, by the spontaneity of
her behavior, the little brunette who was "friendly" with the cattle
driver, who eased the stay of the German mercenary Schlichthorst in Rio
at that time by singing popular songs, sitting on a mat together with her
complacent mother.[13]

Luisinha and Vidinha constitute an admirably symmetric pair. The
first, on the plane of order, is the bourgeois young girl with whom there
can be no viable relationship outside of marriage, since she brings with
her an inheritance, family, position, and obligations. Vidinha, on the
plane of disorder, is the woman whom one can only love, but with
whom neither marriage nor obligations are possible, since she brings
with her nothing beyond her charm and her curious family, which recognizes neither obligation nor sanction, and in which everyone behaves
more or less according to the promptings of instinct or pleasure. It is
during the phase of his affair with Vidinha, or soon after, that Leonardo
gets himself into more serious and more picturesque fixes, now that he
is freed of the respectable projects his godfather and godmother have
planned for his life.

But, when "destiny" once more brings him near Luisinha, now prov-
identially a widow, and he begins again the courtship that will lead directly to marriage, we note that the tone of the account is not more ap-
proving and, on the contrary, that the sequences with Vidinha are
warmer and more charming. Like Leonardo, the narrator seems to be approaching marriage with due circumspection, but without enthusiasm.

At this point, we compare the situation to everything we know of the
beings in the universe of the book and cannot help making an extrapola-
tion. Given the structure of that society, if Luisinha could become a
faithful, home-loving wife, what is most probable is that Leonardo
would follow the norm for husbands and, descending happily from the
hemisphere of order, again make the descent through the circles of
disorder, where Vidinha or her equivalent waits for him, so that they
could together form a supplementary household, which he will unmake
in favor of newer arrangments, according to the customs of the traditional Brazilian family. Order and disorder are, therefore, extremely
relative, and connected in innumerable ways, which make the official
of justice a fomenter of riots, the professor of religion an agent of in-
trigue, the Cadet's sin the source of the Lieutenant colonel's goodness,

illegitimate unions honorable situations, and proper marriages excused irregularities.

"Tutto nel mondo è burla" [Everything in the world is a joke] sing Falstaff and the chorus, to summarize the confusions and unforeseen events of Verdi's opera. "Tutto nel mondo è burla," the narrator of the *Memórias de um sargento de milícias,* a novel that has traces of opera buffa, seems to say. So much so that (and here we come to the second example) the happy ending is prepared for by a surprising opinion of Major Vidigal, who in the book is the incarnation of order, being a manifestation of an exterior conscience, the only kind imaginable in his universe. In fact, the conventional order to which people's behavior is obedient, but to which, finally, consciences remain indifferent is here more than in any other place like the policeman on the corner, that is, Vidigal, with his prudence, his vigilance, his whip, and his relative fair play.

He is the representative of a world only glimpsed during the narrative, when the Godmother starts a campaign to obtain Leonardo's freedom. As everyone knows, she goes to ask for the protection of the Lieutenant Colonel, a member of the grotesque guard of old officers, who doze in a room in the Royal Palace. The Lieutenant Colonel, for his part, seeks the interest of the Fidalgo (who lives with his cape and his clogs in a cold and ill-furnished house), so that he will speak to the King. The King, who does not appear but hovers overhead as the source of everything, will speak to Vidigal, the instrument of his will. More than a picturesque character, Vidigal embodies order; for this reason, in the structure of the book, he is the keystone of the vault and, from the dynamic aspect, the only regulatory force of a disorganized world, pressuring it from above and reaching, one by one, the agents of disorder. He catches Leonardo the Father in the house of the Caboclo, and the Master of Ceremonies in that of the Gypsy. He patrols the party for the baptism of Leonardo the Son and intervenes many years later in his brother's birthday party, a consequence of the father's new love affairs. He persecutes Teotônio, breaks up Vidinha's picnic, tramples Toma-Largura, and pursues and then catches Leonardo the Son, forcing him to join the army. People fear him and flee at his name.

This being the case, when the Godmother resolves to obtain a pardon for her godson it is to Vidigal that she turns, by means of a new series of mediations which are very significant in the dialectic of order and disorder suggested here. Of modest social position, troublemaking and complacent, she strengthens herself by association with the prosperous Dona Maria, who would be a strong recommendation for the representatives of the law, always accessible to well-placed property owners. But Dona

Maria easily changes her course and goes to a woman whose ways had
been easy, as was said when such things were still difficult. And it is with
pure order, embodied in Dona Maria, on one side and, on the other,
disorder made into apparent order, embodied in her picturesque name-
sake Maria Regalada, that the Godmother sets out to assail the intracta-
ble citadel, the hobgoblin, the killjoy Major.

The scene is worthy of an age that produced the comedies of Martins
Pena. Everyone remembers how, to the surprise of the reader, Vidigal is
declared "an idiot" and melts with pleasure among the skirts of the three
old ladies. Lest he resist, encased in the intransigence of the conscien-
tious policeman, Maria Regalada calls him to the side and whispers
something to him, alluding to some pleasing relation in the past, with,
who knows, possibilities for the future. The fortress of order collapses
and not only frees Leonardo, but gives him the post of sergeant, which
will appear in the title of the novel and with which he, retired from the
service, will marry Luisinha triumphally, bringing together five estates in
order to give greater solidity to his position in the positive hemisphere.

His position in this hemisphere is now so firm that, as we have suggested, he will fall eventually into the agreeable world of disorder, now
that he has the supreme example of Major Vidigal, who yielded to the
petition of an "easy" lady supported by a capitalist lady, in a smooth
collusion of the two hemispheres, on the initiative of a third lady, who
circulates freely between the two and could be called, like Belladonna in
Eliot's poem, "the lady of situations." Order and disorder are therefore
articulated solidly; the world, hierarchized in appearance, is revealed as
essentially subverted, when the extremes meet and the general lability of
characters is justified by the great slipperiness that brings the Major from
the sanctioned heights of the law to a dubious complaisance with the
strata he had so endlessly repressed.

A delicious feature blends, symbolically, these confusions of hemispheres and this final subversion of values. When the women arrive at his
house (Dona Maria in a sedan chair, the others panting at her side), the
Major appears in a cotton print dressing gown and wooden clogs, in a
slovenliness that contradicts the uprightness he has displayed throughout the narrative. Perplexed by the visit, dissolving in the smiles and
chills of senile eroticism, he runs inside and returns arrayed in his uniform dress coat, properly buttoned up and shining in his gold braid, but
with his everyday trousers and the same clogs pounding on the floor.
And thus we have our severe dragon of order, the ethical conscience of
the world, reduced to a lively image of the two hemispheres, because in
that moment when he transgresses his own norms in the face of the seduction of his old and, perhaps, new lovers, he has really become the
equal of any of the malandros he has persecuted: of the two Leonardos,

Teotônio, Toma-Largura, or the Master of Ceremonies. Just as the Master of Ceremonies, who, appearing contradictorily in priestly skullcap and underpants in the Gypsy's room, mixed the majesty of the Church and the delights of sin in comic symbols, the Major is now in uniform from the belt up, in informal clothing from the belt down—armoring reason in the standards of the law and easing the solar plexus in amiable disorder.

This stroke gives the deep meaning of the book and of its capricious balancing of order and disorder. Everything has been arranged on a plane more meaningful than that of the conventional norms; and we remind ourselves that the good, the excellent, Godfather, "took care of himself" in life by perjuring, betraying his word given to a dying man, robbing the heirs of the gold the man had entrusted to him. But didn't this gold serve to turn him into an honest citizen and, above all, to care for Leonardo? "Tutto nel mondo è burla."

It is a joke and it is serious, because the society that swarms through the *Memórias* is suggestive, not so much because of the descriptions of festivities or indications of behavior and places; but because it manifests on a deeper and more effective plane the dialectic game of order and disorder, functioning as a correlative of what existed in Brazilian society at that time. Order imposed and maintained with difficulty, surrounded on every side by a lively disorder, which opposed twenty situations of concubinage to every marriage and a thousand chance unions to every situation of concubinage. A society in which only a few free people worked and the others abandoned themselves to idleness, reaping the surplus of parasitism, of contrivance, of munificence, of fortune, or of petty theft. Eliminating the slave, Manuel Antônio eliminated labor almost totally; elminating the ruling classes, he eliminated the controls of power. What remained was the gamelike air of this feeble organization fissured by anomie, translated into the dance of the characters between licit and illicit, in such a way that we cannot say which was the one and which the other, because they all, finally, circulate from one to the other with a naturalness that recalls the mode of formation of families, prestige, fortunes, and reputations in urban Brazil in the first half of the nineteenth century. A novel profoundly social, then, not by being documentary, but by being constructed according to the general rhythm of the society, seen through one of its sectors. And above all because it dissolves what is sociologically essential in the twists and turns of literary construction.

In fact, it is not the representation of particular concrete data that produces the feeling of reality in fiction, but rather the suggestion of a certain generality, which sees the two sides and gives consistency as much to the specific data of the real as to the specific data of the fictional world. In the diagram, let OD be the general phenomenon of order and disorder, as indicated; AB the particular facts, whatever they might be, of the society of Rio in the time of Dom João VI; A′B′ the particular facts, whatever they might be, of the society described in the *Memórias*.

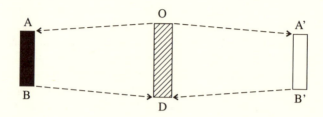

OD, the dialectic of order and disorder, is a valid principal of generalization, which organizes in depth AB as much as A′B′, making them intelligible, being at the same time real and fictitious—a common dimension in which the two meet, and which explains one as much as the other. AB does not directly give rise to A′B′, since the sense of reality in a fiction presupposes the data of reality but does not depend on them. It depends on the mediating principles, generally hidden, which structure the work and thanks to which the two series, the real and the fictitious, become coherent.

At this point, we realize that the structure of the book expresses the tension of the two lines that constitute the author's vision and translates them in two narrative directions, dynamically interrelated. On the one hand, the stamp of the popular introduces archetypal elements, which bring with them the presence of what is most universal in cultures, pulling it toward the legendary and the unreal, without recognizing the particular historical situation. On the other hand, the perception of the social rhythm pulls it toward the representation of a concrete, historically delimited society, which anchors the book and intensifies the realism infused in it. To the uncharacteristic and conformist realism of common sense and popular irreverence is joined the realism of the social observation of the universe described. Perhaps we could say that the peculiar characteristics of the *Memórias* are due to the reciprocal contamination of the archetypal and the social: the almost folkloric universality evaporates much of the realism; but, in compensation, the realism gives concreteness and effectiveness to the uncharacteristic patterns. There derives, from the tension between the two, a curious alternation of eruptions of the picturesque and reductions to socially penetrating models—avoiding the accessory character of anecdote, the banal excesses of fantasy, and the pretentious affectation that compromised the greater part of Brazilian fiction of that period.

THE WORLD WITHOUT GUILT

Unlike almost all Brazilian novels of the nineteenth century, even those making up the small minority of comic novels, the *Memórias de um sargento de milícias* creates a world that seems free of the weight of error and of sin. A universe without guilt and even without repression, except for the external repression that weighs on everyone all the time through Vidigal and the results of which we have already seen. The perception of the human appears in the book as a kind of superficial curiosity, setting in motion the interest of the characters in one another and of the author in his characters, creating a web of relations lived and described. To this curiosity corresponds a very tolerant, almost charming, vision. People do things that could be described as reproachable but do other things worthy of praise, which compensate for them. And, since everyone has defects, no one merits censure.

The Godmother makes a false accusation against José Manuel but does so in order to help the good cause of the lovers; and, in any event, José Manuel is a scoundrel. The compensation comes with his reaction through the intercession of the Master of Prayer, a petty intriguer who succeeds in putting an end to the calumny. Things get straightened out, but we ask ourselves if it would not have been better to leave the calumny alive . . .

As we saw, the Godfather has "taken care of himself" through perjury. But the narrator only tells us this after our sympathy for him is already assured by the dedication he displays to his godchild. For us, he is so good that this bad trait cannot compromise him. This is so much so that the evilly acquired gold is in no way cursed and becomes part of the inheritance that will guarantee Leonardo's prosperity.

One of the greatest efforts of societies, through their organization and the ideologies that justify them, is to establish the objective existence and real value of antithetical pairs, between which it is necessary to choose, expressed as licit or illicit, true or false, moral or immoral, just or unjust, the political left or right, and so on. The more rigid the society, the more strictly defined the terms and the more constrained the choice. For this reason, accommodations of a casuistic type are developed in parallel, which make hypocrisy a pillar of civilization. And one of the great functions of satirical literature, of demystifying realism, and of psychological analysis is to show, each in its own way, that these pairs are reversible, not watertight, and that, beyond ideological rationalizations, the antinomies coexist in a curious twilight zone.

From what we have seen, the moral principle of the *Memórias* seems to be, exactly like the facts narrated, a kind of balancing between good and bad, balanced at every instant by each other but never appearing as a whole. From this derives the idea of symmetry or equivalence that, in a half-chaotic society, continuously reestablishes the normal, so to speak, position of each character. The extremes negate each other, and the morality of events is as balanced as the relations of men.

Everything gives off an air of freedom, a relaxed view of customs, which may or may not coincide with what occurred "in the time of the king," but which lies at the base of the society established in the *Memórias*, as the product of a coherent perception of the mode of life of men. Remorse does not exist, since actions are evaluated according to their effectiveness. Only a secondary character, the old Lieutenant Colonel, has a heavy conscience because of bad behavior of his son, the Cadet, in relation to the mother of "our hero"; and this heavy conscience is amusing in contrast.

If that is so, it is clear that moral repression can only exist, as was said, outside of conscience. It is a "police question" and is concentrated entirely in Major Vidigal, whose comic slide into the sphere of transgression ends, at the conclusion of the novel, by confusing definitively the relation of the planes.

In this, and in all of this, the *Memórias de um sargento de milícias* contrasts with Brazilian fiction of the times. A young society, which seeks to discipline the irregularity of its vigor in order to make itself the equal of the old societies that serve it as models, normally develops certain ideal mechanisms of containment, which appear in every sector: in the juridical field, as rigid and impeccably formulated norms, creating the appearance and illusion of a perfect organization that does not exist and for that very reason constitutes the idealized target; in literature, as an accentuated taste for repressive symbols, which seem to control the expression of impulses. It is what we see, for example, in the perception of the corruption of love, so frequent among the ultra-Romantics. It is what we see in Peri, the heroic Indian, who suppresses in himself, to the point of negating, the aspirations that could realize him as an autonomous being, in a renunciation that permits him to construct in compensation an alienated, automatic self, identified with the ideal patterns of colonization. In *O Guarani*, the strength of the vital impulse, the naturalness of feelings, only occurs as a characteristic of villains or, sublimated, in the exuberant picture of nature—that is, the forces that must be controlled by civilization and the morality of the conqueror, of whom D. Antônio de Mariz is a paradigm and the Romantic Indian a homologue or an ally. (Remember the "torchholding Indian. The Indian son of Maria, godchild of Catherine de Medici and son-in-law of D. Antônio de Mariz," of the *Manifesto antropófago* of Oswald de Andrade.) A mutilating repression of personality is still what we find in other novels of Alencar, those called urban, like *Lucíola* and *Senhora*, where the woman oppressed by patriarchal society confers on the plot a penumbra of suppressed energies. In the midst of all this, the almost magical liberty of the fictional space of Manuel Antônio, free of guilt and remorse, of repression and interior sanctions, colors and mobilizes the firmament of Romanticism, like the rockets in "Fire in the Field," or the Bahians dancing in the processions.

Thanks to this, it differentiates itself from the habitual superego of Brazilian fiction, effecting a kind of demystification that approximates the spontaneous forms of social life, connecting to them in a more profound way. Let us make a parallel that may help.

In the historical development of the United States there was, from very early on, a constricting presence of law, civil and religious, that shaped groups and individuals, limiting their behavior through the punitive force of exterior penalties and the internalized feeling of sin. From this arose a *moral* society, which finds expression in such novels as Hawthorne's *Scarlet Letter*, and which created the setting for such dramas as the witchcraft trials of Salem.

This hardening of the group and individual confers a great strength of identity and resistance on both; but it dehumanizes relations with others, above all with individuals of other groups, who do not belong to the same *law* and therefore can be manipulated at will. Alienation becomes at the same time a mark of rejection and a punishment for the rejected; the stern biblical model of an elect people, justifying its brutality toward the nonelect, the *others*, reappears in these communities of daily readers of the Bible. Order and liberty—that is, internal and external policing, arbitrary rights, and violent action against the stranger—are formulations of this state of affairs.

In Brazil, neither groups nor individuals ever effectively encountered such forms; they never had an obsession with order, except as an abstract principle, nor with liberty except as caprice. The spontaneous forms of sociability operated with great ease and thus mitigated the collisions between norm and conduct, making conflicts of conscience less dramatic.

The two diverse situations are linked to the mechanisms of the respective societies; one that, under the assertion of a deceptive fraternity, sought to create and maintain a group that would be, ideally, monoracial and monoreligious; the other that in fact incorporated racial and, later, religious pluralism into its most intimate nature, despite certain ideological fictions that might have been postulated to the contrary. With no desire to constitute a homogenous group and, in consequence, no need to defend it strongly, Brazilian society opened itself broadly to the penetration of dominated and foreign groups. And gained in flexibility what it lost in integrity and coherence.

The deep meaning of the *Memórias* is linked to its not being related to any of the ideological rationalizations then reigning in Brazilian literature: Indianism, nationalism, the grandeur of suffering, redemption through pain, pompous style, etc. In its more intimate structure and its latent vision of things, this book expresses the vast general accommodation that dissolves the extremes, confuses the meaning of law and order, manifests the reciprocal penetration of groups, of ideas, of the most disparate attitudes, creating a kind of moral no-man's-land, where transgression is only a nuance in the spectrum that runs from norm to crime. All this because, not manifesting these ideological attitudes, Manuel Antônio's book is perhaps the only one in Brazilian literature of the nineteenth century that does not express the vision of the dominant class.

This fact is evidenced in its style, which distinguishes itself from the preferred language of the novel of the times, searching for a tonality that can be called colloquial. Because he was a novice, with no commitments to established literature, and protected by anonymity as well, Manuel Antônio was free, and open to the influence of popular rhythms. This brought with it a kind of irreverent common sense, which is precritical, but which, reducing everything to the comprehensive scale of "human nature," becomes in the end more demystifying than the almost militant intent of an Alencar, marred by the style of his class. Being neutral, Manuel Antônio's charming style is translucent and shows the other side of each thing, exactly like the balancing of certain sentences. "The Godmother was a woman of the lower class, excessively fat, goodnatured, simple or stupid up to a certain point, and sly up to another." "The old Lieutenant Colonel, despite being virtuous and good, had on his conscience a few regular sins." From this flows the equivalence of opposites and the nullification of good and evil, in a discourse deprived of mannerism. Even in a book so willingly critical and *social* as *Senhora*, Alencar's style in the end closes the door on reality, because it inclines to the conventional language of a restricted group, committed to a certain vision of the world; and, in so doing, carries the weight of its times, remains too much imprisoned in the contingencies of the moment and of its social class, preventing the facts described from acquiring sufficient generality to become convincing. Now the language of Manuel Antônio, detached from what is fashionable, makes the details of reality seem comprehensive, significant, and exemplary, because they are immersed in the flow of the popular culture—which tends to kill place and time, putting the objects it touches beyond the frontiers of social groups. It is thus on the level of style that we can best understand the detachment of the *Memórias* from the ideology of the dominant classes of its time—so present in the liberal rhetoric and florid style of the "bellelettrists." This is a liberation, which functions as if the moral neutrality corresponds to a social neutrality, stirring the pretensions of class ideology indiscriminately in the pot of popular irreverence.

This is connected to a broader, and very Brazilian, attitude of corrosive tolerance, presupposing a reality not regulated by norm or law, and at times manifesting itself in literature in the form of devastating jokes, which betray paradoxically a vague nostalgia for more legitimate values, while attacking those traits that, stiff and crystallized, threaten that flexibility which is one of the fruitful dimensions of our cultural universe.

This sense of humor, avoiding the sanctioned spheres of bourgeois norms, moves instead toward the irreverence and amorality of certain popular expressions. It manifests itself in Pedro Malasarte at the level of folklore and finds in Gregório de Matos glittering expressions, which reappear periodically—reaching their maximum in Modernism, with *Macunaíma* and *Serafim Ponte Grande*. It smooths the edges and makes room for every manner of accommodation (or negation), which at times make us seem inferior in the face of a vision stupidly nourished by puritan values, like those of capitalist societies; but which will facilitate our entrance into an eventually open world.

With much less virulence and stylization than the two books cited, Manuel António's belongs to a branch of this line, which takes various forms. It is not surprising that only after Modernism did his book finally find the glory and the favor of readers, with a rhythm of publication that in the last twenty-five years has gone beyond one printing a year, in contrast to an earlier time, when it had one every eight years.

In the limpid transparency of its universe without guilt, we see dimly the outlines of a world without definitive or irremediable evils, ruled by a charming moral neutrality. There one does not work, one leaves necessity behind, every trouble is taken care of. The parasitic and indolent society, which was then that of the free men of Brazil, was very much like that, thanks to the brutality of slave labor, which the author elides along with other forms of violence. But since he aims at the type and the paradigm, we glimpse beyond the concrete social situations a kind of archetypal world of legend, where realism is counterbalanced by elements that are unobtrusively fabulous: an adventurous birth, tutelary spirits, dragons, pilfering of the economic order, the failure of chronology, the absurdity of relations. For this reason, we must take with a grain of salt the idea that the *Memórias* is a documentary panorama of Brazil in the time of Dom João VI; and after having suggested that it is rather its ghostly anatomy, much more totalizing, better to think nothing at all and let ourselves be lulled by this realist fable composed in tempo allegro vivace.

NOTES

First published as "Dialética da malandragem," in *Revista do Instituto de Estudos Brasileiros* 8 (1970) and republished in *O discurso e a cidade* (São Paulo: Livraria Duas Cidades, 1993), pp. 19–53.

1. José Verissimo, "Um velho romance brasileiro," *Estudos brasileiros*, 2nd series (Rio de Janeiro: Laemmert, 1895), pp, 107–24; Mário de Andrade, Introduction to Manuel Antônio de Almeida, *Memórias de um sargento de milícias*, Biblioteca de literatura brasileira, I, (São Paulo: Martins, 1941), pp. 5–19; Darcy Damasceno, "A afetividade lingüística nas *Memórias de um sargento de milícias*," *Revista Brasileira de Filologia* 2 (December, 1956), 155–77, especially 156–58 (the citation is from p. 156).

2. Josué Montello, "Um precursor: Manuel Antônio de Almeida," *A literatura do Brasil*, Direção de Afrânio Coutinho, II (Rio de Janeiro: Editorial Sul Americana S.A., 1955), pp. 37–45.

3. *The Literature of Roguery*, 3 vols. (New York: Houghton Mifflin, 1907). See also Ángel Valbuena Prat, "Estudio preliminar," *La novela picaresca española*, 4th ed. (Madrid: Aguilar, 1942), pp. 11–79, the edition of the principal Spanish picaresque novels used in this essay.

4. ["Malandro" (pronounced "mahl-AHN-droo") is a classically untranslatable word, referring to a cultural conception common in Brazil, but nonexistent in North America. It is often translated as "rogue" or "scamp" or "rascal" or "trickster." If I had to choose, I would, using contemporary idiom, say "hustler." But each of these leaves something to be desired, and I have chosen to leave the word in Portuguese and the let the reader fill in its meaning contextually, since the essay is in some ways devoted to explaining what it means. HSB]

5. "It is in this mode that Manuel Antônio de Almeida described the character Leonardo, which results in a *hero without any character*, or better, one who represents the fundamental traits of the stereotype of the Brazilian. Manuel Antônio de Almeida is the first to fix in literature the national character of the Brazilian, which then will have a long life in our literature. . . . I believe that we meet in Leonardo the ancestor of *Macunaíma*." Walnice Nogueira Galvão, "No tempo do rei," in *Saco de gatos: Ensaios críticos* (São Paulo: Duas Cidades, 1976), p. 32. This beautiful essay, one of the most penetrating on our author, first appeared, under the title "Manuel Antônio de Almeida," in the "Suplemento Literário" of the *Estado de São Paulo*, March 17, 1962.

6. Marques Rebelo, *Vida e obra de Manuel Antônio de Almeida*, 2nd ed. (São Paulo: Martins, 1963), pp. 38–39 and 42.

7. Alan Carey Taylor, "Balzac, Manoel Antonio de Almeida et les débuts du réalisme au Brésil," summary of a paper, *Le réel dans la littérature et le langage*, Actes du Xe. Congrès de la Fédération des Langues et Littératures Modernes, published by Paul Vernois (Paris: Klincksieck, 1967), pp. 202–3.

8. Herman Lima, *História da caricatura no Brasil*, 4 vols. (Rio de Janeiro: José Oympio, 1963), vol. 1, pp. 70–85.

9. Astrojildo Pereira, "Romancistas da cidade: Macedo, Manuel Antônio and Lima Barreto," *O romance brasileiro (de 1752 a 1930)*, Coordenação etc., de

Aurélio Buarque de Holanda, (Rio de Janeiro: O Cruzeiro, 1952), pp. 36–73. See p. 40.

10. [This refers to the move of the court of the Portuguese king from Lisbon to Rio de Janeiro, the royal court thus taking over from the previous colonial administration. HSB]

11. Marques Rebelo, *op. cit.*, pp. 40–41.

12. T. von Leithold e L. von Rango, *O Rio de Janeiro visto por dois prussianos em 1819*, translated and annotated by Joaquim de Sousa Leão Filho (São Paulo: Editora Nacional, 1966), p. 166.

13. C. Schlichthorst, *O Rio de Janeiro como é, 1824–1826 (Huma vez e nunca mais) etc.*, translated by Emy Dodt and Gustavo Barroso (Rio de Janeiro: Getúlio Costa, n.d.), pp. 78–80.

Chapter 6

AN OUTLINE OF MACHADO DE ASSIS

AS OUR SENSIBILITY is still Romantic, we have an almost invincible tendency to attribute to great writers a heavy and conspicuous quota of suffering and of drama, since normal life seems incompatible with genius. Dickens disordered by a passion of maturity, after having suffered, as a child, the humiliation of seeing his father imprisoned; Dostoyevsky nearly executed, thrown into the squalor of the Siberian prison, shaken by neurological disease, staking the money for household expenses at roulette; Proust jailed in his bedroom and his remorse, suffocated with asthma, sunk in forbidden passions—images like these seize our imagination.

For this reason, critics who have studied Machado de Assis never fail to inventory and emphasize the potential causes of torment, social and individual: dark color, humble origin, difficult career, humiliations, nervous ailments.

But in truth his sufferings do not seem to have been greater than those of others, nor was his life particularly arduous. Racially mixed people of humble origin were among the representative men of our liberal Empire, men who, though being of his color and having begun poor, ended by receiving titles of nobility and carrying ministerial portfolios. Let us not exaggerate, therefore, the theme of genius versus fate. On the contrary, it would, rather, be fitting to note the exterior normality and relative ease of his public life. Typographer, reporter, minor government official, finally an official of higher rank, his career was placid. Color seems not to have been the cause of any loss of prestige, and perhaps caused trouble, quickly overcome, only when he married a Portuguese lady. And his social condition never impeded his being intimate from youth with Counselor Nabuco's children, Sizenando and Joaquim, upper-class young men full of talent.

If we analyze his intellectual career, we see that he was admired and supported early, and that for fifty years he was considered the major writer of the country, the object of a general reverence and admiration, such as no other Brazilian novelist or poet, before or after, knew. Only Silvio Romero sounded a dissonant note, neither understanding nor wishing to understand Machado's work, which escaped the schematic and massively naturalistic orientation of his mind. When the founding of a Brazilian Academy of Letters was considered, Machado de Assis was chosen as its adviser and president, a post he occupied until he died. He was by then, before he entered his sixties, a kind of patriarch of letters.

Patriarchal (to be frank) in both the good and bad sense. Very conventional, much taken with formalisms, he was capable, in this respect, of being as ridiculous, and even as mean, as any president of the Academy. Perhaps owing to a certain timidity, he was from childhood gregarious and, without neglecting his good relations with a large number of people, seemed to feel more at home in the closed circle of the *happy few* [English in the original]. The Academy emerged, in the last part of his life, as one of those closed groups in which his personality found support; and, as the approval of new members depended in large part on him, he acted with a singular mixture of social conformism and the feeling of a clique, admitting among the founders a beginner like Carlos Magalhães de Azeredo, simply because he held Azeredo, who was dedicated to him, in high estimation—motives that led him to let in, a few years later, Mário de Alencar, still more mediocre. Nevertheless, he barred others of an equal or superior level, like Emílio de Meneses, not for intellectual reasons, but because they did not behave according to the conventional norms he respected in social life.

So there seems to be no doubt that his life was not only without adventures, but relatively placid, though marked by the rare privilege of recognition and glorification as a writer, the love and homage growing until he became a symbol of what is considered highest in creative intelligence.

On the other hand, if we look at his work, not in the narrow panorama of the Brazilian literature of the times, but in the broader current of Western literature, we see the ironic, at times melancholy, counterpart of his unfailing success. Though a writer of international stature, he remained almost totally unknown outside Brazil; and, since literary glory depends so much on the political radiance of the country, only now has he begun to have a *succès d'estime* in the United States, England, and some Latin American countries. His almost hypertrophic national glory was the counterpart of a discouraging international obscurity.

This circumstance seems shocking because, in his stories and novels, especially between 1880 and 1900, we find, concealed by curious archaizing features, some of the themes that would be characteristic of the fiction of the twentieth century. The fact that his work now meets with a certain success abroad shows that it has the capacity to survive, that is, to adapt itself to the spirit of the times, having meaning for the generations that read Proust and Kafka, Faulkner and Camus, Joyce and Borges. Moving into the realm of conjecture, we can imagine what could have happened had he been known outside Brazil at a time when the most famous practitioners of the novel, in the world of the Romance languages, were men like Anatole France and Paul Bourget, or Antonio Fogazzaro and Emile Zola, who, save the last, are irremediably dated and no longer have any meaning for our time.

Of the Western languages, ours [Portuguese] is the least known, and if the countries where it is spoken matter little today, in 1900 they mattered even less in the political game. For this reason, two novelists who wrote in our language and who are the equals of the best then writing remain marginal: Eça de Queirós, well suited to the spirit of naturalism; and Machado de Assis, enigmatic and Janus-headed, looking to the past and to the future, hiding a strange and original world under the apparent neutrality of stories "everyone could read."

Clearly, then, the man is of little interest and the work of great interest. Beneath the cheerful youth and the temperate bourgeois who tried to adapt himself to outward appearances, who passed through life conventionally, respecting that he might be respected, functioned a powerful and tormented writer, who covered his books with a cuticle of human respect and good manners in order to be able, beneath it, to unmask, investigate, experiment, discover the world of the soul, laugh at society, and expose some of the strangest components of the personality. In inverse ratio to the elegance and discretion of his prose, to his humorous yet academic tone, the attentive reader will find the most disconcerting surprises. Its contemporary quality comes from the almost timeless enchantment of his style and of that hidden universe which suggests the abysses prized by twentieth-century literature. And for this reason it is interesting to reexamine the different stages of his fame in Brazil, in order to evaluate his many faces and the rhythm of their discovery.

II

The polyvalence of literary expression is most visible in the works of great writers. They are great because they are extremely rich in meaning, permitting each group and each epoch to find in them their own obsessions and their own necessities of expression. For this reason, successive generations of Brazilian readers and critics have found different levels in Machado de Assis, esteeming him for diverse reasons, and seeing him as a great writer by virtue of qualities that are at times contradictory. The most curious thing is that all these interpretations are probably right, since to pick out one angle does not mean that the others could not have been chosen.

As soon as he reached maturity, around the age of forty, what perhaps first attracted attention were his irony and his style, conceived of as "good language." One depends on the other, it is clear, and the word that best united them for the criticism of the time was perhaps *finesse*. *Fine* irony, *refined* style, evoking the idea of a sharp and penetrating point, of delicacy and power joined. To this was added a general notion of a suave urbanity, of discretion and reserve. At a time when naturalists flung detailed descriptions of physiological life at a frightened public, he took pride in implications, in allusions, in euphemisms, writing stories and novels that did not collide with the requirements of conventional morality. To explain him, it was usual to evoke Almeida Garrett, who was in effect one of the models for his prose—whose slightly archaic touch paid the tribute of colonial peoples to grammatical correctness. Toward the end of Machado's life readers also emphasized his pessimism, the disenchantment that emanated from his stories. What cannot be doubted is that these first generations found in him a "philosophy" sufficiently acid to give the impression of audacity, but expressed in an elegant and restrained way that reassured them and made reading him an experience that was agreeable and without major consequence. It could be said that he courted the average public, including the critics, giving them the feeling of being intelligent at a moderate price. His taste for moral maxims, inherited from the French of the classic centuries and from reading the Bible, led him to compose lapidary formulas, which escaped their context and pursued their own destiny, spreading a facile idea of *wisdom*. For cultivated, or semicultivated, opinion at the beginning of the century, he appeared as a kind of local Anatole France, with the same feline elegance but with less licentiousness of the spirit. The anthologies did not fail to choose from his work things like the ingenious and at bottom banal "Apologue" on the needle and the thread, or the episode of the muledriver in *Epitaph for a Small Winner* [*Memórias póstumas de Brás Cubas*], which, extracted from the whole, shows (in a manner which is only apparently profound) the force of greed.

This first Machado de Assis, "philosophizing" and classic, appears in two good studies published soon after his death: Oliveira Lima's talk at the Sorbonne, and the small book by Alcides Maya, which pointed out, beyond the Voltairean irony, the more complicated components of *humor*, of the English type. Alfredo Pujol's book, published at the end of the First World War, crystallized the conventional vision of his life and the "philosophizing" vision of his work, establishing and accentuating the mythological features, the unusual story of a poor boy who attained, in compensation, the pinnacle of literary expression. A little later, Graça Aranha proposed an ingenious theory of the crisscrossing movements of Nabuco, descending from the aristocracy to the people, and Machado de Assis, rising from the people to aristocratic ways.

A new kind of interpretation had to wait until the 1930s, with the biography by Lúcia Miguel-Pereira, the analyses of Augusto Meyer, and the subtle biographical interpretations of Mário Matos. That was the stage we could properly call psychological, when critics tried to establish a reciprocal flow of understanding between the life and the work, focusing on them in accord with the disciplines then in style, above all psychoanalysis, somatology, and neurology. Parenthetically, I will not take into account the extreme versions of this tendency, represented by physicians who took hold of Machado de Assis as though he were a defenseless posthumous patient, multiplying diagnoses and wishing to extract from his work and the few known elements of his life interpretations whose scientific value must be small. Before and after, but especially in the 1930s, the obsolete shadows of Lombroso and Max Nordau hovered, in new clothing, over the great writer.

From all this there resulted something positive for criticism: the notion that it was necessary to read Machado, not with conventional eyes, nor with academic subtleties, but with a sense of the disproportionate and even of the abnormal; of that which seems rare in us in the light of a psychology of the surface, and nevertheless comprises the deepest layers in which everyone's behavior germinates. In this new style of reading, Augusto Meyer, without doubt, loomed large. Inspired by the work of Dostoyevsky and of Pirandello, he went beyond the humorous and "philosophizing" view, showing that in Machado's work there is much of the "underground man" of the first, and of the multiple, impalpable being of the second. He and Lúcia Miguel-Pereira called attention to the phenomena of ambiguity that appear in abundance in Machado's fiction, requiring a more exacting reading, thanks to which the normality and the sense of decorum only disguise a more complicated, at times troubled, universe. What can be criticized, in them and in Mário Matos, is the excessive preoccupation with finding in the author's life a basis for what appears in his work or, vice versa, using the work to clarify his life and personality. But there is no doubt that it was these studies and some others, generally preceding or following shortly after the commemorations of the centenary of his birth in 1939, that began to make a place for him in our modern vision. He was already no longer the "gentle ironist," the elegant engraver of sentences, of academic convention; he was the creator of a paradoxical world, the experimenter, the lonely chronicler of the absurd.

In the 1940s we note a turn to philosophy (above all Christian) and to sociology. The first wished to emphasize, in Machado de Assis, without introducing biographical contaminants, chiefly what could be called existential anguish. This is true of one of his best critics, Barreto Filho, whose book is one of the most mature interpretations of his work we possess. These critics resisted psychologism and biographism, while trying to clarify matters metaphysically. In this position, neither psychological nor biographical, we might also situate Astrojildo Pereira, who was preoccupied with the social aspects of Machado's work, but who erred to the degree that he did in this direction what the biographers had done in the other, that is, considered the work insofar as it described the society, thereby dissolving it into a document of events. But by then there had already begun to appear freer and less ambitious essays, such as the one by Roger Bastide, which, contradicting the old assertion that Machado did not sense the nature of his country, showed that, on the contrary, he saw it with penetration and steadfastness but incorporated it into the fine grain of the narrative, as a functional component of literary composition, instead of representing it by the methods of Romantic descriptivism. It was in the same spirit that Bastide was accustomed to tell his students at the University of São Paulo that the "most Brazilian" writer was not Euclides da Cunha, ornamental and almost exotic, but Machado de Assis, who gave universality to his country through the exploration, in our context, of fundamental themes.

III

What first claims the attention of the critic in the fiction of Machado de Assis is his heedlessness of the dominant styles and the apparent archaicism of his technique. At a time when Flaubert had systematized the theory of the "novel that narrated itself," hiding the narrator behind the objectivity of the narrative, at a time when Zola praised the massive inventory of reality, observed in its least details, Machado cultivated freely the elliptical, the incomplete, and the fragmentary, intervening in the narrative with tasty gossip, reminding the reader that behind the story was this conventional voice. It was a way of maintaining, in the second half of the nineteenth century, the capricious tone of Sterne, whom he esteemed, to effect Sterne's temporal jumps, and to toy with the reader. There was also an echo of the "conte philosophique," in the manner of Voltaire, and there was above all his own way of leaving things half in the air, creating unresolved perplexities.

Curiously, the archaicism seemed brusquely modern, in the style of the vanguard in our century, which also tried to suggest the whole by the fragment, the structure by the ellipsis, emotion by irony, and grandeur by banality. Many of his tales and some of his novels seem open, with no necessary conclusion, or permitting a double reading, as occurs with our contemporaries. And the most piquant thing is the heightened and somewhat precious style he worked in, which, if it seemed on the one hand academicism, on the other appeared without doubt as a subtle form of provocation, as if the narrator were laughing a little at the reader. The style maintained a kind of impartiality, which is the personal mark of Machado, making the strange cases he presents with thoughtless moderation seem doubly intense. It is not in the passionate naturalists of his time, theoreticians of objectivity, that we find the aesthetic distancing that reinforces the vibration of reality, but rather in his technique of the spectator.

It is from this formal origin, what could be called the "Machadian tone," that we can comprehend the profundity and complexity of a lucid and disenchanted work, which hides its riches deeply. Like Kafka and like Gide, the contrary of Dostoyevsky, Proust, or Faulkner, the torments of man and the iniquities of the world appear in Machado's work bare and without rhetoric, intensified by the stylistic impartiality referred to above.

His technique consists essentially in suggesting the most tremendous things in the simplest way (like the ironists of the eighteenth century); or in establishing a contrast between the social normality of events and their essential abnormality; or in suggesting, under the appearance of doing the contrary, that the exceptional act is normal, and the commonplace act is what is abnormal. Here is the cause of his modernity, despite his superficial archaicism.

It is not possible to pack into one paper the analysis adequate to deal with his diverse manifestations. But I can try to present a few cases, to give an idea of the originality that today seems to exist in the work of Machado de Assis, which was uncovered slowly by the generations of critics referred to earlier.

1. Perhaps we can say that one of the fundamental problems of his work is identity. Who am I? What am I? To what degree do I exist only through others? Am I more authentic when I think or when I exist? Is there more than one person in me? These are some questions that seem to form the substratum of many of his stories and novels. In a mild form, it is the problem of the division of the self or of the unfolding of the personality, studied by Augusto Meyer. In an extreme form, it is the problem of the border between reason and madness, which early on drew the attention of critics, as one of the principal themes of Machado's work.

The first of these is the object, for example, of the story "The Mirror," in which there emerges the old allegory of the lost shadow, present in demonology and made famous in Romanticism by Adalbert von Chamisso's *Peter Schlemihl*. A young man, named to the position of *Alferes* (ensign) in the National Guard (the militia, which in imperial Brazil soon became a simple pretext for giving posts and showy uniforms to people of a certain social position), comes to spend a few days at his aunt's estate. She, proud of his appointment, creates an atmosphere in which his position is extremely highly valued, calling him, and requiring the slaves to call him, at all times, "Senhor Alferes," in such a way that this social feature ends up being a "second soul," indispensable to the character's psychological integrity.

Some days later the aunt has to make an urgent trip and leaves the estate in his charge. The slaves take advantage of her departure to run away, and he is left completely alone, coming to the edge of spiritual dissolution, since he no longer has the laudatory chorus that evoked his position at every instant. The dissolution goes so far that, looking in the mirror one day, he sees that his image seems almost dissolved, blurred and unrecognizable. Then the idea occurs to him to dress in his uniform and spend some time every day in front of the mirror, which tranquilizes him and reestablishes his equilibrium, since his figure is again normally projected, owing to his dressing up in the social symbol of the uniform. This means that his personal integrity lay above all in the opinions and actions of others, in the society the uniform represents, and in that part of the being which is a projection in and of society. The Ensign's uniform is also the Ensign's soul, one of the two that every man possesses, according to the narrator, because he manifests his "being through others," without whom we are nothing. It is clear that the strength of the story does not come from this banal conclusion, enunciated explicitly by the author, as is his custom in such cases. It comes from the admirable utilization of the symbolic uniform and the monumental mirror in the desert of the abandoned estate, constructing a kind of modern allegory of the division of the personality and the relativity of the self.

With respect to the problem of madness, we can cite the tale "The Psychiatrist," elaborated according to a structure Forster would call "hourglass." A doctor opens an asylum for the insane of the city and begins diagnosing all the manifestations of mental abnormality he observes. In a short time, the asylum is full; in time it holds half the population; then almost all of it, until the psychiatrist feels that the truth, as a consequence, is in contradiction with his theory. He then orders that those who have been hospitalized should be freed and that the small minority of well-balanced people should be picked up because, being the exception, it is they who are really abnormal. The minority is given the "second soul" treatment, to use the terms of the preceding story. Each is tempted by a weakness. Finally giving in, and thus becoming the same as the majority, each is then liberated, until the asylum is again empty. The psychiatrist sees then that the germs of disequilibrium prospered so easily because they were already latent in everyone; therefore, the cure is not due to his therapy. Is there not one normal man, immune to the enticements of manias, to vanities, to lack of balance? Analyzing himself, he sees that this is his case exactly and resolves to intern himself, alone in the vast empty asylum, where he dies some months later. And we ask ourselves: who was mad? Or was everyone mad, in which case no one was? We note that this tale and the earlier one displayed, at the end of the nineteenth century, what would be the style of Pirandello in the 1920s.

2. Another problem that comes up frequently in the work of Machado de Assis is that of the relation between the real event and the imagined one, which will be one of the axes of Marcel Proust's great novel, and which both analyzed principally in relation to jealousy. The same reversibility of reason and madness, whose frontiers it becomes impossible to delineate and, therefore, to define satisfactorily, exists between what has happened and what we think has happened. One of his novels, *Dom Casmurro*, tells the story of Bento Santiago, who, after the death of his greatest and most faithful friend, Escobar, is convinced that Escobar was the lover of Bento's own wife, Capitu, the novelist's most famous female character. The wife denies it, but, in order to elaborate his conviction, Bento combines many clues, the most important of which is the similarity of his son's appearance to that of his dead friend. A North American scholar, Helen Caldwell, in her book *The Brazilian Othello of Machado de Assis*, puts forth the hypothesis, viable just because it is so Machadian, that in fact Capitu did not betray her husband. Since the book is narrated by him, in the first person, it is necessary to agree that we only know *his* view of things, and that, by the furious negative "crystallization" of a jealousy, it is even possible to find nonexistent similarities, or those that are the results of chance (like that of Capitu to the mother of Sancha, Escobar's wife, a circumstance to which my American colleague, Alfred Hower, has called my attention). But the fact is that, within the Machadian universe, it doesn't matter much whether Bento's conviction is false or true, because the consequence is exactly the same in both cases: imaginary or real, it destroys his home and his life. And we conclude that in this novel, as in other situations in Machado's work, what is real can be what appears to be real. And since the friendship and the love seem, but cannot really be, friendship or love, a psychological ambiguity is joined to the philosophical ambiguity, in order to dissolve moral concepts and evoke a slippery world, where contraries meet and dissolve into one another.

3. What meaning does the act then have? Here is another fundamental problem in Machado de Assis, which brings him near to the preoccupations of writers like the Conrad of *Lord Jim* or *The Secret Sharer*, and which was one of the central themes of contemporary literary existentialism, as in Sartre and Camus. Could I be something more than the act

which expresses me? Will life be more than a succession of choices? In one of his best novels, *Esau and Jacob*, he takes up again, now at the end of his career, this problem that is scattered through the entire body of his work. He takes it up again in a symbolic form, in the permanent rivalry of two twin brothers, Pedro and Paulo, who invariably represent the alternatives of any act. One always does the contrary of the other, and it is clear that the two possibilities are both legitimate. The great problem this raises is that of the validity of the act and of its relation to the intention that sustains it. At every moment in the apparently trivial story of a bourgeois family from Rio at the end of the Empire and the beginning of the Republic, this argument arises, which is completed by the third key character, the girl Flora, whom both brothers love, it is clear, but who, placed between them, does not know how to choose. It falls to her, as to other women in the work of Machado de Assis, to embody the ethical decision, the commitment, of self and act, which does not turn back, because once done it defines and obligates the self of whoever has done it. The brothers act and choose without pausing, because they are the opposed alternatives; but she, who must identify herself with one or the other, would feel reduced by half were she to do that, and only the possession of the two halves can realize her; this is impossible, because it would suppress the very law of the act, which is choice. Symbolically, Flora dies without choosing. And we feel in her the same breath of moral paralysis that was Heyst's illusion in Joseph Conrad's *Victory*.

4. It seems clear that the theme of choice is the complement of one of the fundamental obsessions of Machado de Assis, well analyzed by Lúcia Miguel-Pereira—the theme of perfection, the aspiration to the complete act, the total work, which we find in a variety of stories and, above all, in one of the most beautiful and poignant he ever wrote: "A Famous Man."

It deals with a composer of polkas, Pestana, the most famous composer of the time, recognized and lauded wherever he goes, sought after by publishers, financially secure. Nevertheless, Pestana hates his polkas, which everyone sings and plays, because his wish is to compose a classical piece of the highest quality—a sonata, a mass—like those of Beethoven or Mozart that he admires. At night, seated at the piano, he spends hours seeking the inspiration that eludes him. After many days, he begins to feel something that presages the visit of the goddess, and his emotion grows, he can almost feel the longed-for notes budding at his fingertips, he hurls himself at the keyboard and . . . composes yet another polka! Polkas and always polkas, ever more brilliant and popular, is what he does until he dies. The alternative is also denied him; it only remains to him to do what is possible, not what would please him. In this terrible story, under the apparent levity of humor, the spiritual impotence of man cries out from the depths of a dungeon.

5. Then the question arises: if the fantasy functions as reality; if we do not succeed in acting without mutilating the self; if what is most profound in us is in the end the opinion of others; if we are condemned not to attain what seems to us really precious—what is the difference between good and evil, just and unjust, right and wrong? Machado de Assis spent his life illustrating this question, which is expressed in an examplary manner in the first and most well-known of the great novels of his maturity: *Epitaph for a Small Winner.* In it, even life is judged relatively, since it is a dead man who tells his own story.

This profound feeling of the total relativity of acts, of the impossibility of judging them adequately, gives way to a feeling of the absurd, of the act with no origin and the judgment with no basis, which is the fountainhead of Kafka's work and, before him, of the gratuitous act of Gide. It was already present in the work of Dostoyevsky and runs, discreetly, through the work of Machado de Assis, as in the story "Singular Occurrence," where we can furthermore find a good example of Machado's Victorianism. Not daring to put a married woman in the scene, he describes the quasi-conjugal situation of a former "girl of easy ways," who lives with a lawyer and comports herself as a respectable and faithful wife. Nevertheless, one day she gives herself, for no apparent reason, to a vagabond of the streets, after having aroused him. The act is discovered accidentally by the lawyer, and there follows a violent rupture that excites in the girl a desperation so sincere and profound that their relations are renewed, with the same dignity of feeling and attitude as before. The lawyer dies and she remains faithful to his memory, as the yearning widow of a great and unique love.

Why, then, this inexplicable act? Impossible to know. And which behavior expresses her better: the fidelity or the transgression? Impossible to determine. These acts and these feelings are surrounded by a halo of absurdity, of gratuitousness, which makes it difficult to make not only moral evaluations, but also psychological interpretations. Some decades later, Freud would demonstrate the fundamental importance of the lapse and of behaviors considered irrelevant. They occur frequently in the work of Machado de Assis, revealing to the attentive reader a profound sense of the contradictions of the soul.

6. What attracted me most in his books, personally, is another theme, different from these: the transformation of man into the object of man, which is one of the curses linked to the lack of true economic and spiritual liberty. This theme is one of the familiar devils in Machado's work, from the attenuated forms of simple egoism to the extremes of sadism

and monetary plunder. To it is linked the famous theory of Humanitism, elaborated by one of his characters, the philosopher Joaquim Borba dos Santos, crazy and just for this reason Machadianly lucid, figuring secondarily in two novels, one of which carries his name: *Epitaph for a Small Winner* and *Quincas Borba [Philosopher or Dog?]*.

The critics (above all Barreto Filho, who has studied the case best) interpreted Humanitism as a satire on positivism and, in general, on the philosophical naturalism of the nineteenth century, principally in the form of the Darwinian theory of the struggle for life as the survival of the fittest. But beyond this is, notably, a wider connotation, which transcends satire and sees man as a devouring being in whose dynamic the survival of the strongest is only an episode and a specific case. This general and silent devouring tends to transform man into the instrument of man, and in this aspect the work of Machado is linked, much more than might be seen at first glance, to the concepts of alienation and its related reification of personality, dominant in contemporary Marxist thought and criticism, and illustrated in the work of the great realists, men as different from him as Balzac and Zola.

In the novel *Philosopher or Dog?* a modest primary-school teacher, Rubião, inherits a fortune from the philosopher Quincas Borba, with the condition that he take care of his dog, to whom Borba gave his own name. But with the money, which is a kind of cursed gold, as in the legend of the Nibelungen, Rubião also inherits his friend's madness. His fortune is squandered in ostentation and in the support of parasites; but it serves above all as capital for the commercial speculations of a scheming arriviste, Cristiano Palha, with whose wife, "the beautiful Sophia," Rubião has fallen in love. Love and madness emerge here, Romantically, hand in hand; but the *tertius gaudens* is the economic ambition, the basso continuo of the novel, of which Rubião becomes an instrument. In the end, poor and crazy, he dies abandoned; but in compensation, as the philosophy of Humanitism required, Palha and Sophia are rich and well regarded, socially perfectly normal. The weak and the pure were subtly manipulated as things and afterward put aside by the mechanism of the narrative itself, which, in a way, spits them out and concentrates itself in the winners, finally leaving in the reader a doubt that is sarcastic and filled with overtones: does the name of the book refer to the philosopher or the dog, the man or the animal, both of whom influence Rubião's fate? He begins as a simple man, comes in his madness to think himself emperor, and ends as a poor beast, battered by hunger and rain, at the same level as his dog.

There is a story, "The Secret Cause," where the devouring relation of man to man assumes the character of a paradigm. Fortunato, a cold and rich man, demonstrates an interest in suffering, helping the wounded, looking after the sick with an exceptional dedication. Married in middle age, he is good to his wife, but she displays a constraint toward him, which seems to be fear.

The couple are friends with a young doctor, whom Fortunato convinces to found, in partnership with him, a nursing home, for which he furnishes the capital. In it, he gives steadfast assistance to the sick, with an absorbing interest that leads him to study anatomy through the vivisection of cats and dogs. The painful noises they make upset his wife's delicate nerves, who asks the doctor to get her husband to stop these experiments. Already the familiarity has awakened in the youth a quiet, pure passion, clearly reciprocated by his friend's wife. The mortifying moment of the story is the scene in which the doctor encounters the wife panic stricken and, in the other room, sees Fortunato torturing a rat in a dreadful and loathsome way. With one hand, he holds a strap tied to the animal's tail, lowering him into a plate full of alcohol in flames, raising him repeatedly in order not to kill him too quickly; with the other, he is cutting his paws with a scissors. The description is long and terrible, going beyond the discrete summary descriptions Machado de Assis usually gives of what is crude or disagreeable. The doctor sees then what kind of man he has for a friend: someone who finds his greatest pleasure in the pain of others.

Shortly afterward, the wife worsens and finally dies. The husband shows an extreme dedication, as always, but in the final phase of the agony what predominates is his pleasure in the spectacle. In the funeral vigil, he surprises the doctor kissing the forehead of the cadaver and grasps everything in a flash of anger; but the friend bursts into desperate tears and Fortunato, observing without being seen, "savored tranquilly this explosion of moral pain which was long, very long, deliciously long."

It is not difficult to see that, beyond everything that is seen on the manifest plane, this sadist virtually transformed his wife and his friend into an amorous pair, inhibited by scruple and as a result suffering constantly; and that both became the supreme instruments of his monstrous pleasure, of his manipulative habit, of which the rat is the symbol. "Of mice and men," we could say with a little black humor, in order to indicate that man, transformed into an instrument of man, falls practically to the level of the violated animal.

It is at this level that we meet the most terrible and the most lucid Machado de Assis, extending his demystifying gaze to the organization of relationships. If it had stayed on the plane of disenchanted aphorisms that fascinated the first generation of critics, or even on that of ambiguous pyschological situations, which later became his principal attraction, perhaps he would have been no more than one of those "heroes of decadence" of whom Viana Moog speaks. But beyond this there is in his work a broader interest, proceeding from the fact of having included, discreetly, a strange social thread in the canvas of his relativism. Throughout his entire body of work there is a profound sense, nothing documentary, of *status*, of the duel of salons, of the movement of social strata, of the power of money. Gain, profit, prestige, the sovereignty of interest—these are the springs of action of his characters, appearing in *Epitaph for a Small Winner*, enlarged in *Esau and Jacob*, predominating in *Philosopher or Dog?*, always transformed into *modes* of being and doing. And the most disagreeable, the most terrible, of his characters are men of an impeccable bourgeois cut, perfectly geared into the *mores* of their class. From this point of view, it is interesting to compare the essential abnormality of Fortunato in "The Secret Cause," with his perfect social normality as a wealthy and sober proprietor, who lives on rents and collective respect. The Machadian sense of secrets of the soul is often connected to an equally profound comprehension of social structures, which function in his work with same powerful immanence Roger Bastide demonstrated to be the case with the landscape. And to his alienations in the psychiatric sense correspond certain alienations in the social and moral sense.

.   .   .

This essay should be called "An Outline of *one particular* Machado de Assis," because it describes above all the underground writer (whom Augusto Meyer situated better than anyone else), seen in various planes and referred to later tendencies in literature. There are others, including a Machado de Assis quite anecdotal and even trivial, author of numerous circumstantial tales that do not go beyond the level of a newspaper column or a pastime. It is he who sometimes comes quite close to a certain snobbish air and a certain constraining affectation. But this one, thank God, is less frequent than another, related to him, pleasant and witty, moved by a kind of narrative pleasure that brings him to create incidents and weave easily solved complications. This unpretentious and good-humored Machado de Assis perhaps constitutes a point of reference for the others, because from him comes the *tone*, casual and reticent, digressive and colloquial, of the majority of his stories and novels. In him is manifested the love of fiction as fiction and of the art of weaving stories that, seeming to be only a game, in truth pursues a clear project. From this clever and diverting author branches off the Machado de Assis focused on here—in an imperceptible passage that goes from the quasi melancholy of "The Admiral's Night" to the dubiousness of "Dona Paula," from there to the perturbing indecision of "Dona Benedita," that reaches the blunt surprise of "The Senhora of Galvão," already at the doorway of a strange world—showing the almost imperceptible transitions that unify the writer's diversity.

This is said in order to justify a final piece of advice: let us look in his work neither for a collection of allegorical fables nor for a gallery of eccentric types. Let us look above all for the *fictional situations* he invented, as much those where the fates and the events are organized according to a kind of gratuitous enchantment as the others, rich with significance in their apparent simplicity, manifesting, with a deceptive neutrality of tone, the human being's essential conflicts with himself, with other men, with classes, and with groups. The resulting vision has a power this essay would not even be capable of suggesting. The best I can do is to advise each of you to forget what I have said, summarizing the critics, and immediately open the books of Machado de Assis.

NOTE

First published as "Esquema de Machado de Assis," in *Varios escritos* (São Paulo: Livraria Duas Cidades, 1970), pp. 15–32.

Chapter 7

LITERATURE AND UNDERDEVELOPMENT

MÁRIO VIEIRA DE MELLO, one of the few writers to approach the problem of the relations between underdevelopment and culture, makes a distinction for the Brazilian case that is also valid for all of Latin America. He says that there has been a marked alteration of perspectives; until the 1930s the idea of "the new country," still unable to realize itself, but attributing to itself great possibilities of future progress, predominated among us. With no essential modification in the distance that separates us from the rich countries, what predominates now is the notion of an "underdeveloped country." The first perspective accentuated potential strength and, therefore, a still unrealized greatness. The second pointed out the present poverty, the atrophy; what was lacking, not what was abundant.[1]

The consequences Mário Vieira de Mello drew from this distinction do not seem valid to me, but taken by itself it is correct and helps us to understand certain fundamental aspects of literary creation in Latin America. In fact, the idea of a new country produces in literature some fundamental attitudes, derived from surprise, from the interest in the exotic, from a certain respect for the grandiose, and from a hopeful sense of possibilities. The idea that America constituted a privileged place was expressed in utopian projections that functioned in the physiognomy of conquest and colonization; and Pedro Henríquez Ureña reminds us that the first document about our continent, Columbus's letter, inaugurated the tone of seduction and exaltation that would be communicated to posterity. In the seventeenth century, mixing pragmatism and prophesy, Antônio Vieira recommended the transfer of the Portuguese monarchy, fated to realize the highest ends of History as the seat of the Fifth Empire, to Brazil. Later, when the contradictions of colonial status led the dominant strata to a political separation from the mother countries, there emerged the complementary idea that America had been predestined to be the country of liberty, and thus to consummate the destiny of Western man.

This state of euphoria was inherited by Latin American intellectuals, who transformed it into both instruments of national affirmation and an ideological justification. Literature became the language of celebration and tender affection, favored by Romanticism, with support from hyperbole and the transformation of exoticism into a state of the soul. Our sky was bluer, our flowers more luxuriant, our countryside more inspiring than that of other places, as in a Brazilian poem that, from this point of view, is valuable as a paradigm: the "Song of Exile," by Gonçalves Dias, who could stand for any of his Latin American contemporaries from Mexico to Tierra del Fuego.

The idea of *country* was closely linked to that of *nature* and in part drew its justification from it. Both were conducive to a literature that compensated for material backwardness and the weakness of institutions by an overvaluation of regional features, making exoticism a reason for social optimism. In the *Santos Vega*, of the Argentine Rafael Obligado, on the verge of the twentieth century, the nativist exaltation is projected onto a patriotism properly speaking, and the poet implicitly distinguishes *country* (institutional) and *land* (natural), nevertheless linking them in the same gesture of identification:

> La convicción de que es mía
> La patria de Echeverría,
> La tierra de Santos Vega.

> [The conviction of what is mine
> The country of Echeverría
> The land of Santos Vega.]

Country for the thinker, *land* for the singer. One of the assumptions, explicit or latent, of Latin American literature was this mutual contamination, generally euphoric, of land and country, the grandeur of the second being considered as a kind of unfolding of the strength of the first. Our literatures are nourished in the "divine promises of hope," to cite a famous verse by the Brazilian Romantic poet Castro Alves.

But, the other side of the coin, the discouraged visions shared the same order of associations, as if the weakness or the disorganization of institutions constituted an inconceivable paradox in the face of the grandiose natural conditions. ("In America everything is great, only man is small.")

Now, given this causal link of "beautiful land—great country," it is not difficult to see the repercussions a consciousness of underdevelopment could produce in a change of perspective that made evident the reality of the poor lands, the archaic technologies, the astonishing misery of the people, the paralyzing lack of culture. The resulting vision is pessimistic with respect to the present and problematic with respect to the future, and the only remnant of the previous phase's millenarianism, perhaps, might be the confidence with which it is acknowledged that the removal of imperialism could bring, in itself, an explosion of progress. But, in general, it is no longer a matter of a passive point of view. Deprived of euphoria, the point of view is combative, and this leads to a decision to struggle, since the trauma of consciousness caused by the confirmation of how great the backwardness is is catastrophic, and invites political reformulations. The preceding gigantism, based on a hyperbolic view of nature, then appears in its true essence—as an ideological construction transformed into a compensatory illusion. From this comes the disposition to combat that is diffused through the continent, the idea of underdevelopment becoming a propulsive force, which gives a new stamp to the political obligation of our intellectuals.

The consciousness of underdevelopment followed the Second World War and was manifested clearly from the fifties on. But there had been, since the thirties, a change in orientation, which could be taken as a thermometer, given its generality and persistence, above all in regionalist fiction. It then abandoned pleasantness and *curiosity*, anticipating or perceiving what had been disguised in the picturesque enchantment or ornamental chivalry with which rustic man had previously been approached. It is not false to say that, from this point of view, the novel acquired a demystifying force that preceded the coming-to-awareness of economists and politicians.

In this essay, I will speak, alternatively or comparatively, of the literary characteristics of the mild phase of backwardness, corresponding to the ideology of the "new country"; and of the phase of catastrophic consciousness of backwardness, corresponding to the notion of "underdeveloped country." The two are intimately meshed with one another, and we see the lines of the present in both the immediate and remote past. With respect to method, it would be possible to study the conditions of the diffusion of, or of the production of, literary works. Without forgetting the first focus, I prefer to emphasize the second by means of which, though we leave aside statistical rigor, we come close, in compensation, to the specific interests of literary criticism.

II

If we think of the material conditions of literature's existence, the basic fact, perhaps, is illiteracy, which in the countries of advanced pre-Columbian culture is aggravated by the still present linguistic plurality, with diverse languages seeking their place in the sun. In fact, illiteracy is linked to the manifestations of cultural weakness: lack of the means of communication and diffusion (publishers, libraries, magazines, newspapers); the nonexistence, dispersion, and weakness of publics disposed to literature, due to the small number of real readers (many fewer than the already small number of literates); the impossibility, for writers, of specializing in their literary jobs, generally therefore realized as marginal, or even amateur, tasks; the lack of resistance or discrimination in the face of external influences and pressures. The picture of this weakness is completed by such economic and political factors as insufficient levels of remuneration and the financial anarchy of governments, coupled with inept or criminally disinterested educational policies. Except in the contiguous meridional countries that form "white America" (in the European phrase), there would have to be a revolution to alter the predominant condition of illiteracy, as occurred slowly and incompletely in Mexico and rapidly in Cuba.

These features are not combined mechanically, nor always in the same way, there being diverse possibilities of dissociation and grouping among them. Illiteracy is not always a sufficient explanation of the weakness in other sectors, although it is the basic feature of underdevelopment in the cultural area. Peru, to cite an example, is less badly situated than various other countries with respect to the index of schooling, but it presents the same backwardness with respect to the diffusion of culture. In another sector, the publishing boom of the 1940s in Mexico and Argentina showed that the lack of books was not uniquely a consequence of the reduced number of readers and of lower buying power, since all of Latin America, including the Portuguese-speaking part, absorbed significant numbers of its publications. Perhaps we can conclude that the bad publishing habits and the lack of communication further accentuated the inertia of the public; and that there was an unsatisfied capacity for absorption.

This last example reminds us that the problem of publics presents distinctive features in Latin America, since it is the only group of underdeveloped countries whose people speak European languages (with the exception, already noted, of the indigenous groups) and have their origins in countries that today still have underdeveloped areas themselves (Spain and Portugal). In these ancient mother countries literature was, and continues to be, a good of restricted consumption, in comparison with the fully developed countries, where publics can be classified according to the kind of reading they do, such a classification permitting comparisons with the stratification of the entire society. But, as much in Spain and Portugal as in our own countries of Latin America, there is a basic negative condition, the number of literates, that is, those who could eventually constitute the readers of works. This circumstance brings the Latin American countries nearer to the actual conditions of their mother countries than are, in relation to theirs, the underdeveloped countries of Africa and Asia, which speak different languages than those of the colonizers and confront the grave problem of choosing the language in which to display literary creation. African writers in European languages (French, like Léopold Sendar Senghor, or English, like Chinua Achebe) are doubly separated from their potential publics; and are tied either to metropolitan publics, distant in every sense, or to an incredibly reduced local public.

This is said to show that the possibilities of communication for the Latin American writer are greater, compared to the rest of the Third World, despite the present situation, which reduces greatly his eventual public. Nevertheless, we can imagine that the Latin American writer is condemned always to be what he has been: a producer of cultural goods for minorities, though in this case that does not signify groups of high aesthetic quality, but simply the few groups disposed to read. But let us not forget that modern audio-visual resources might change our processes of creation and our means of communication, so that when the great masses finally acquire education, who knows but what they will look outside the book to satisfy their needs for fiction and poetry.

Put another way: in the majority of our countries large masses, immersed in a folkloric stage of oral communication, are still beyond the reach of erudite literature. Once literate and absorbed by the process of urbanization, they come under the dominion of radio, television, and comic strips, constituting the foundation of a mass culture. Literacy would then not increase the number of readers of literature, as conceived here, proportionally; but would fling the literate, together with the illiterate, directly from the phase of folklore into this kind of urban folklore that is massified culture. During the Christianization of the continent the colonial missionaries wrote documents and poetry in the indigenous language or the vernacular in order to make the principles of religion and of the metropolitan civilization accessible to those being indoctrinated by means of consecrated literary forms, equivalent to those destined for the cultivated man of the times. In our time, a contrary process rapidly converts rural man to urban society, by means of communicative resources that even include subliminal inculcation, imposing on him dubious values quite different from those the cultivated man seeks in art and in literature.

This problem is one of the gravest in the underdeveloped countries, by virtue of the massive pressure of what could be called the cultural know-how and the very materials already elaborated for massified culture coming from the developed countries. By such means, these countries can not only diffuse their values in the normal fashion, but also act abnormally through them to orient, according to their political interests, the opinions and the sensibility—the political interests—of underdeveloped populations. It is *normal*, for example, that the image of the cowboy hero of the Western is diffused because, independent of judgments of value, it is one of the features of North American culture incorporated into the average sensibility of the contemporary world. In countries with a large Japanese immigration, such as Peru and above all Brazil, there is diffused in a similarly *normal* manner the image of the samurai, especially by means of the cinema. But it is *abnormal* that such images serve as the vehicle for inculcating in the publics of the underdeveloped countries attitudes and ideas that identify them with the political and economic interests of the countries in which those images were made. When we realize that the majority of the animated cartoons and comic strips have a North American copyright, and that a large proportion of detective and adventure fiction comes from the same source, or is copied from it, it is easy to evaluate the negative effect it could eventually have, as an *abnormal* diffusion among a defenseless public.

In this respect it is convenient to point out that in erudite literature the problem of influences (as we will see later) can have either a good aesthetic effect or a deplorable one; but only in exceptional cases does it have any influence on the ethical or political behavior of the masses, since it reaches a restricted number of restricted publics. Even so, in a massified civilization, where nonliterary, preliterary, or subliterary media, such as those cited, predominate, such restricted and differentiated publics tend to unify themselves to the point of being confounded with the mass, which receives the influence on an immense scale. And, what is more, by means of vehicles whose aesthetic element is reduced to a minimum, thus rendering them capable of being confounded with ethical or political designs that, in the limiting case, penetrate the entire population.

Seeing that we are a "continent under intervention," an extreme vigilance is proper for Latin American literature, in order not to be taken in by the instruments and values of mass culture, which seduce so many contemporary artists and theorists. It is not a case of joining the "apocalyptics," but rather of alerting the "integrated"—to use Umberto Eco's expressive distinction. Certain modern experiences are fruitful from the point of view of the spirit of the vanguard and the connection of art and literature to the rhythm of the time, as in Concretism and other currents. But it costs nothing to remember what can occur when they are manipulated politically by the wrong side in a mass society. In fact, even though they present at the time an hermetic and restrictive aspect, the principles in which they are based, having as resources an expressive sonority, graphical elements, and syntagmatic combinations of great suggestive power, can eventually become much more penetrating than traditional literary forms, functioning as nonliterary instruments, but more penetrating for just this reason, reaching massified publics. And there is no point, for the literary expression of Latin America, in moving from the aristocratic segregation of the era of oligarchies to the directed manipulation of the masses in an era of propaganda and total imperialism.

III

Illiteracy and cultural debility influence more than the exterior aspects just mentioned. For the critic, their action in the consciousness of the writer and in the very nature of his work is more interesting.

In the time of what I called the mild consciousness of backwardness, the writer shared the *enlightened* ideology, according to which schooling automatically brought all the benefits that permitted the humanization of man and the progress of society. At first, schooling was recommended only for the *citizens*, the minority from which were recruited those who shared economic and political advantages; later, for all the people, seen dimly, vaguely, and from afar, less as a reality than as a liberal conception. Emperor Dom Pedro II said that he would have preferred to be a teacher, which denoted an attitude equivalent to the famous point of view of Sarmiento, according to which the predominance of civilization over barbarism had as a presupposition a latent urbanization, based in schooling. In the continental vocation of Andrés Bello it is impossible to distinguish the political vision from the pedagogic project; and in the more recent group, Ateneo, of Caracas, the resistance to tyranny of Juan Vicente Gómez was inseparable from the desire to diffuse enlightened ideas and to create a literature full of myths of redemptive education—all projected in the figure of Rómulo Gallegos, who ended up as the first President of a renascent Republic.

A curious case is that of a thinker like Manuel Bonfim, who published in 1905 a book of great interest, *A América Latina*. Unjustly forgotten (perhaps because it based itself on outmoded biological analogies, perhaps because of the troublesome radicalism of its positions), it analyzes our backwardness as a function of the prolongation of colonial status, embodied in the persistence of oligarchies and in foreign imperialism. In the end, when everything leads to a theory of the transformation of social structures as a necessary condition, a disappointing weakening of the argument occurs, and he ends by preaching schooling as a panacea. In such cases, we touch the core of the illusion of the *enlightened*, an ideology of the phase of hopeful consciousness of backwardness that, significantly, does little to bring what is hoped for to realization.

It is not surprising, then, that the idea already referred to, according to which the New Continent was destined to be the country of liberty, has undergone a curious adaptation: it would be destined, equally, to be the country of the book. This is what we read in a rhetorical poem in which Castro Alves says that, while Gutenberg invented the printing press, Columbus found the ideal place for that revolutionary technique (the italics are the poet's):

> Quando no tosco estaleiro
> Da Alemanha o velho obreiro
> A ave da imprensa gerou,
> O Genovês salta os mares,
> Busca um ninho entre os palmares
> E *a pátria da imprensa* achou.

> [While in the rough workshop
> Of Germany the old worker
> Begot the bird of printing,
> The Genoese leaped over the seas,
> Seeking a home among the palms
> and discovered the *country of printing.*]

This poem, written in the 1860s by a young man burning with liberalism, is called, expressively, "O livro e a América" (The book and America), displaying the ideological position I refer to.

Thanks to this ideology, these intellectuals constructed an equally deformed vision of their own position, confronted by a dominant lack of culture. Lamenting the ignorance of the people and wishing it would disappear so that the country might automatically rise to its destined heights, they excluded themselves from the context and thought of themselves as a group apart, really "floating," in a more complete sense than that of Alfred Weber. They floated, with or without consciousness of guilt, above the lack of culture and the backwardness, certain that it could not contaminate them, or affect the quality of what they did. Since the environment could only give them limited shelter, and since their values were rooted in Europe, it was to Europe that they projected themselves, taking it unconsciously as a point of reference and a scale of values; and considering themselves the equals of the best there.

But in truth the general lack of culture produced, and produces, a much more penetrating debility, which interferes with all culture and with the quality of the works themselves. Seen from today, the situation of yesterday seems different from the illusion that reigned then, since today we can analyze it more objectively, due to the action of time and to our own efforts at unmasking.

The question will become clearer as we take up foreign influences. In order to understand them best, it is convenient to focus, in the light of these reflections on backwardness and underdevelopment, on the problem of cultural dependency. This is, so to speak, a natural fact, given our situation as peoples who are colonized, or descendants of colonizers, or who have suffered the imposition of their civilization, but a complicated fact, with positive and negative aspects.

This cultural penury caused writers to turn, necessarily, toward the patterns of the mother countries and of Europe in general, creating a group that was, in a way, aristocratic in relation to the uneducated man. In fact, to the degree that a sufficient local public did not exist, people wrote as if their ideal public was in Europe and thus often dissociated themselves from their own land. This gave birth to works that authors and readers considered highly refined, because they assimilated the forms and values of European fashion. Except that, for lack of local points of reference, they often could go no farther than exercises of mere cultural alienation, which were not justified by the excellence of their realization—and that is what occurred in what there is of the bazaar and of affectation in the so-called "Modernism" of the Spanish language, and its Brazilian equivalents, Parnassianism and Symbolism. Clearly, there is much that is sound in Rubén Darío, as in Herrera y Reissig, Bilac, and Cruz e Sousa. But there are also many false jewels unmasked by time, much contraband that gave them an air of competitors for some international prize for beautiful writing. The refinement of the *decadents* was provincial, showing the mistaken perspective that predominates when the elite, with no base in an uncultivated people, has no way of confronting itself critically and supposes that the relative distance that separates them translates of itself into a position of absolute height. "I am the last Greek!"—so shouted theatrically in 1924 in the Brazilian Academy the enormously affected Coelho Neto, a kind of laborious local D'Annunzio, protesting against the vanguardism of the modernists, who eventually broke the artistocratic pose in art and literature.

Let us recall another aspect of alienated aristocratism, which at the time seemed an appreciable refinement: the use of foreign languages in the production of works.

Certain extreme examples were involuntarily saturated with the most paradoxical humorousness, as in the case of a belated Romantic of the lowest rank, Pires de Almeida, who published, as late as the beginning of this century, in French, a nativist play, probably composed some decades earlier: *La fête des crânes, drame do moeurs indiennes en trois actes et douze tableaux* (The festival of the skulls: A drama of Indian customs in three acts and twelve tableaux).[2] But this practice is really significant when it is linked to authors and works of real quality, such as those of Cláudio Manuel da Costa, who left a large and excellent body of work in Italian. Or Joaquim Nabuco, a typical example of the cosmopolitan oligarchy of liberal sentiment in the second half of the nineteenth century, who wrote autobiographical passages and a book of reflections in French—but above all a play whose conventional alexandrines debated the problems of conscience of an Alsatian after the Franco-Prussian War of 1870! A variety of minor symbolists (and also one of the most important, Alphonsus de Guimaraens) wrote all of their work, or at least a part thereof, in the same language. The Peruvian Francisco García Calderón wrote, in French, a book that had value as an attempt at an integrated vision of the Latin American countries. The Chilean Vicente Huidobro wrote part of his work and of his theory in French. The Brazilian Sérgio Milliet published his first poetic work in French. And I am certain that we could find innumerable examples of the same thing in every country of Latin America, from the vulgar official and academic work of pedants to productions of quality.

All this did not happen without some ambivalence, since the elites, on the one hand, imitated the good and bad of European models; but, on the other hand and sometimes simultaneously, they displayed the most intransigent spiritual independence, in an oscillating movement between reality and a utopia of an ideological stamp. And thus we see that illiteracy and refinement, cosmopolitanism and regionalism, could all have roots that mingled in the soil of the lack of culture and the effort to overcome it.

More serious influences of cultural weakness on literary production are the facts of backwardness, anachronism, degradation, and the confusion of values.

All literature presents aspects of backwardness that are *normal* in their way, it being possible to say that the media of production of a given moment are already tributary to the past, while the vanguard prepares the future. Beyond this there is an official subliterature, marginal and provincial, generally expressed through the Academies. But what demands attention in Latin America is the way aesthetically anachronistic works were considered valid; or the way secondary works were welcomed by the best critical opinion and lasted for more than a generation—while either should soon have been put in its proper place, as something valueless or the evidence of a harmless survival. We cite only the strange case of the poem *Tabaré*, by Juan Zorrilla de San Martín, an attempt at a national Uruguayan epic at the end of the nineteenth century, taken seriously by critical opinion despite having been conceived and executed according to the most obsolete patterns.

At other times the backwardness is not shocking, simply signifying a cultural tardiness. This is what occurred with naturalism in the novel, which arrived a little late and has prolonged itself until now with no essential break in continuity, though modifying its modalities. The fact of our being countries that in the greater part still have problems of adjustment and struggle with the environment, as well as problems linked to racial diversity, prolonged the naturalist preoccupation with physical and biological factors. In such cases the weight of the local reality produces a kind of legitimation of this delayed influence, which acquires a creative meaning. So, when naturalism was already only a survival of an outdated genre in Europe, among us it could still be an ingredient of legitimate literary formulas, such as the social novel of the 1930s and 1940s.

Other cases are frankly disastrous: those of cultural provincialism, which leads to a loss of a sense of measure, the result of which is to evaluate works of no value at all by the standards applied in Europe to works of quality. This leads, further, to phenomena of true cultural degradation, causing spurious work to *pass*, in the sense in which a counterfeit banknote *passes*, due to the weakness of publics and the absence of a sense of values in both publics and writers. We see here the routinization of influences already dubious in themselves, such as Oscar Wilde, D'Annunzio, and even Anatole France, in the books of our own Elísio de Carvalho and Afrânio Peixoto in the first quarter of this century. Or, bordering on the grotesque, the veritable profanation of Nietzsche by Vargas Villa, whose vogue in all of Latin America reached milieus that in principle should have been immune, on a scale that astonishes us and makes us smile. The *profundity* of the semicultured created these and other mistakes.

IV

A problem that touches on the topics of this essay and is worth being discussed in light of the dependence caused by cultural backwardness is that of influences of various types, good and bad, inevitable and unnecessary.

Our Latin American literatures, like those of North America, are basically branches of the literature of a mother country. And if we give up the sensitivities of national pride, we see that, despite the autonomy gained from those mother countries, these literatures are still partly reflections. In the case of the Spanish- and Portuguese-speaking countries, the process of autonomy consisted, in good part, of transferring the dependency, in such a way that, beginning in the nineteenth century, other European literatures, not those of the metropole, and above all French, became the model; this had also occurred in the intensely Frenchified mother countries. These days it is necessary to take into account North American literature, which became a new focus of attraction.

This is what could be called the inevitable influence, sociologically linked to our dependency, since the colonization itself and the at times brutally forced transfer of cultures. As the respected Juan Valera said at the end of the last century:

> From both sides of the Atlantic, I see and admit it, in the people of the Spanish language, our dependence on the French, and, to a certain point, I believe it ineluctable; but I neither diminish the merit of the science and poetry of France so that we can shake off its yoke, nor want us, that we may become independent, to isolate ourselves and not accept the proper influence that civilized peoples must exert on one another.
>
> What I maintain is that our admiration must not be blind, nor our imitation uncritical, and that it is fitting that we take what we take with discernment and prudence.[3]

We must therefore confront our placental link to European literatures calmly, since it is not an option, but a quasi-natural fact. We never created original frameworks of expression, nor basic expressive techniques; we never created such things as Romanticism, on the level of tendencies, or the psychological novel, on the level of genres, or indirect free style, on that of writing. And while we have achieved original results on the level of expressive realization, we implicitly recognize the dependency, so much so that we never see the diverse nativisms disputing the use of imported *forms*, since that would be like opposing the use of the European languages we speak. What these nativisms required was the choice of new *themes*, of different *sentiments*. Carried to an extreme, nativism (which at this level is always ridiculous, though sociologically understandable) would have implied rejecting the sonnet, the realistic story, and free associative verse.

The simple fact of the question never having been raised reveals that, at the deepest levels of creative elaboration (those that involve the choice of expressive instruments), we always recognize our inevitable dependence as natural. Besides, seen thus, it is no longer dependency, but a way of participating in a cultural universe to which we belong, which crosses the boundaries of nations and continents, allowing the exchange of experiences and the circulation of values. And when we in turn influence the Europeans through the works we do (not through the thematic suggestions our continent presents to them to elaborate in their own forms of exoticism), at such moments what we give back are not inventions but a refining of received instruments. This occurred with Rubén Darío in relation to "Modernism" (in the Spanish sense);[4] with Jorge Amado, José Lins do Rego, Graciliano Ramos in relation to Portuguese neorealism.

Spanish-American "Modernism" is considered by many as a kind of rite of passage, marking a literary coming of age through the capacity for original contribution. But, if we correct our perspectives and define the fields, we see that this is more true as a psychosocial fact than as an aesthetic reality. It is evident that Darío, and eventually the entire movement, for the first time reversing the current and carrying the influence of America to Spain, represented a rupture in the literary soverignty Spain had exercised. But the fact is that such a thing is not accomplished with original expressive resources, but rather by adapting French processes and attitudes. What the Spaniards received was the influence of France, already filtered and translated by the Latin Americans, who in this way substituted themselves as cultural mediators.

This in no way diminishes the value of the "modernists" nor the meaning of their accomplishment, based on a deep awareness of literature as art, not document, and an at times exceptional capacity for poetic realization. But it permits the interpretation of Spanish "Modernism" according to the line developed here, that is, as an historically important episode in the process of creative fertilization of dependency—which is a peculiar way in which our countries are original. The corresponding Brazilian movement was not innovative at the level of general aesthetic forms either, but it was less deceptive because, by calling its two large branches "Parnassianism" and "Symbolism," it made clear the French fountain from which they all drank.

A fundamental stage in overcoming dependency is the capacity to produce works of the first order, influenced by previous national examples, not by immediate foreign models. This signifies the establishment of what could be called, a little mechanically, an internal causality, which makes borrowings from other cultures more fruitful. Brazilian Modernism derived in large part from European vanguard movements. But the poets of the succeeding generation, in the 1930s and 1940s, derived immediately from the Modernists—as is the case with what is the fruit of these influences in Carlos Drummond de Andrade or Murilo Mendes. These, in turn, were the inspiration of João Cabral de Melo Neto, even though he also owes much to Paul Valéry, and then to the Spaniards who were his contemporaries. Nevertheless, these high-flying poets were not influential outside their own countries, and much less in the countries from which the original suggestions came.

This being the case, it is possible to say that Jorge Luis Borges represents the first case of incontestable original influence, exercised fully and recognized in the source countries, through a new mode of conceiving of writing. Machado de Assis, whose originality was no less from this point of view, and much greater as a vision of man, could have opened new directions at the end of the nineteenth century for the source countries. But he was lost in the sands of an unknown language, in a country then completely unimportant.

It is for this reason that our own affirmations of nationalism and of cultural independence are inspired by European formulations, an example being the case of Brazilian Romanticism, defined in Paris by a group of youths, who were there and who founded in 1836 the magazine *Niterói*, symbolic landmark of the movement. And we know that today contact between Latin American writers is made above all in Europe and in the United States, which, in addition, encourage, more than we do, the consciousness of our intellectual affinity.[5]

The case of the vanguards of the 1920s is interesting, because it marked an extraordinary liberation of expressive means and prepared us to alter sensitively the treatment of themes proposed to the writer's consciousness. As a matter of fact, these vanguards have been, throughout Latin America, elements of autonomy and self-affirmation; but what did they consist of, examined in the light of our theme? Huidobro established "Creationism" in Paris, inspired by the French and the Italians; he wrote his poems in French and made his position public in French, in magazines like *L'Esprit Nouveau*. Argentine ultraism and Brazilian Modernismo are directly descended from these same sources. And none of this prevented such currents from being innovative, nor those who propelled it from being, par excellence, the founders of the new literature: Huidobro, Borges, Mário de Andrade, Oswald de Andrade, and others.

We know, then, that we are part of a broader culture, in which we participate as a cultural variant. And that, contrary to what our grandparents sometimes ingenuously supposed, it is an illusion to speak of the suppression of contacts and influences, simply because, the law of the world now being interrelation and interaction, the utopias of isolationist originality no longer survive as a patriotic attitude that was understandable when the young nations were being born, a time that called for a provincial and umbilical position.

In the present phase, that of the consciousness of underdevelopment, the question presents itself, therefore, in a more nuanced way. Could there be a paradox here? Indeed, the more the free man who thinks is imbued with the tragic reality of underdevelopment, the more he is imbued with revolutionary aspirations—that is, with the desire to reject the political and economic yoke of imperialism and to promote in every country the modification of the internal structures that nourish the situation of underdevelopment. Nevertheless, he confronts the problem of influences more objectively, considering them as normal linkages on the level of culture.

The paradox is only apparent, since in fact it is a symptom of a maturity that was impossible in the closed and oligarchic world of jingoistic nationalisms. So much so that the recognition of linkage is associated with the beginning of the capacity to innovate at the level of expression, and to fight at the level of economic and political development. Conversely, the traditional affirmation of originality, with a sense of elementary particularism, led and leads, first, to the picturesque and, second, to cultural servility, two diseases of growth, perhaps inevitable, but nevertheless alienating.

Beginning with the aesthetic movements of the 1920s; the intense aesthetic-social consciousness of the 1930s and 1940s; the crisis of economic development and of technical experimentalism of recent years— we began to see that dependency was a step on the road to a cultural interdependency (if it is possible to use this expression, which has recently acquired such disagreeable meanings in the political and diplomatic vocabulary, without misunderstanding). This not only will give writers in Latin America an awareness of their unity in diversity, but will favor works of a mature and original tone, which will slowly be assimilated by other peoples, including those of the metropolitan and imperialist countries. The road of reflection on underdevelopment leads, in the field of culture, to transnational integration, since what was imitation increasingly turns into reciprocal assimilation.

One example among many: in the work of Vargas Llosa there appears, extraordinarily refined, the tradition of the interior monologue, which, Proust's and Joyce's, is also that of Dorothy Richardson and Virginia Woolf, of Döblin and of Faulkner. Perhaps certain modalities preferred by Vargas Llosa are due to Faulkner, but in every case he has deepened them and made them more fruitful, to the point of making them into something of his own. An admirable example maybe found in *The City and the Dogs*: the monologue of the nonidentified character leaves the reader perplexed, since it intersects with the voice of the third person narrator and with the monologue of other named characters, thus being capable of being confused with them; and, in the end, when this character reveals himself as Jaguar, it illuminates the structure of the book retrospectively, like a fuse, requiring us to rethink everything we had established about the characters. This seems like a concretization of an image Proust uses to suggest his own technique (the Japanese figure revealing itself in the water of the bowl): but it signifies something very different, on a different plane of reality. Here, the novelist of the underdeveloped country received ingredients that came to him as a cultural loan from the countries from which we are accustomed to receive literary formulas. But he adapted them profoundly to his intention, compounding from them a peculiar formula, in order to represent problems of his own country. This is neither imitation nor mechanical reproduction. It is participation in resources that have become common through the state of dependency, contributing to turn it into an interdependency.

Awareness of these facts seems integrated into the way of seeing of Latin American writers; and one of the most original, Julio Cortázar, writes interesting things on the new appearance local fidelity and world mobility present, in an interview in *Life* (vol. 33, no. 7). And, with respect to foreign influences on recent writers, Rodríguez Monegal assumes, in an article in *Tri-Quarterly* (nos. 13–14), an attitude that could with justification be called a critical justification of assimilation. Nevertheless, opposing points of view, linked to a certain localism appropriate to the "gentle phase of backwardness," still survive. For those who defend them, such facts as we have mentioned here are manifestations of a lack of individuality or of cultural alienation, as can be seen in an article in the Venezuelan magazine *Zona Franca* (no. 51), where Manuel Pedro González makes clear that, in his view, the true Latin American writer would be one who not only lives in his land, but who also uses its characteristic themes and expresses, without any exterior aesthetic dependency, its peculiar features.

It seems, nevertheless, that one of the positive features of the era of the consciousness of underdevelopment is the overcoming of the attitude of apprehension, which leads to indiscriminate acceptance or the illusion of the originality of work and the charm of local themes. Whoever fights against real obstacles is more balanced and recognizes the fallacy of fictitious obstacles. In Cuba, that admirable vanguard of the Americas in the fight against underdevelopment and its causes, is there artificiality or flight in the surrealist suffusion of Alejo Carpentier, or in his complex transnational vision, including the thematic point of view, as it appears in *Siglo de las luces*? Is there alienation in the bold experiments of Cabrera Infante or Lezama Lima? In Brazil, the recent concrete poetry movement adopts inspirations of Ezra Pound and aesthetic principles of Max Bense and other Europeans; but it produces a redefinition of the national past, reading ignored poets, such as Joaquim de Sousa Andrade, a precursor lost among the Romantics of the nineteenth century, in a new way; or illuminating the stylistic revolution of the great modernists, Mário de Andrade and Oswald de Andrade.

V

Taken as a derivation of backwardness and the lack of economic development, dependency has other aspects that have their repercussions in literature. Recall again the phenomenon of ambivalence, translated into impulses of copying and rejection, apparently contradictory when viewed alone, but which can be seen as complementary when confronted from this angle.

Backwardness stimulates the servile copying of everything the fashion of the advanced countries sometimes offers, as well as seducing writers with migration, an interior migration, which corrals the individual in silence and in isolation. Backwardness, nevertheless, the other side of the coin, suggests what is most specific in the local reality, insinuating a regionalism that, appearing to be an affirmation of the national identity, can in truth be an unsuspected way of offering the European sensibility the exoticism it desires, as an amusement. In this way, it becomes an acute form of dependency within independence. In the present perspective, it seems that the two tendencies are mutual, born of the same situation of retardation or underdevelopment.

In its crudest aspect, the servile imitation of styles, themes, attitudes, and literary usages, it has a comical or embarrassing air of provincialism, having been the compensatory aristocratism of a colonial country. In Brazil this reaches an extreme, with the Academia de Letras, copied from the French, installed in a building that is a reproduction of the Petit Trianon in Versailles (and the Petit Trianon is, in all seriousness, what the institution is called), with forty members who call themselves *Immortals* and, further like their French models, wear embroidered uniforms, cocked hats, and swords . . . But the functional equivalent of that Academy for all of Latin America might often be, in the guise of an innovative rebellion, the imitated Bohemias of Greenwich Village or Saint-Germain-des-Prés.

Perhaps no less crude, on the other hand, are certain forms of nativism and literary regionalism, which reduce human problems to their picturesque element, making the passion and suffering of rural people, or of the populations *of color*, the equivalent of papayas or pineapples. This attitude may not only be the same as the first, but combine with it to *furnish* the urban European (or artificially Europeanized) reader the quasi-touristic reality it would please him to see in America. Without recognizing it, the most sincere nativism risks becoming an ideological manifestation of the same cultural colonialism that its practitioners would reject on the plane of clear reason, and that displays a situation of underdevelopment and consequent dependency.

Nevertheless, in light of the focus of this essay, it would be a mistake to utter, as is fashionable, an indiscriminate anathema against regionalist fiction, at least before making some distinctions that allow us to see it, on the level of judgments of reality, as a consequence of the effect of economic and social conditions on the choice of themes.[6] The areas of underdevelopment and the problems of underdevelopment (or backwardness) invade the field of consciousness and the sensibility of the writer, proposing suggestions, setting themselves up as topics impossible to avoid, becoming positive or negative stimuli to creation.

In French or English literature there have occasionally been great novels whose subject is rural, such as those of Thomas Hardy; but it is clear that this is a matter of an external framework, in which the problems are the same as those of urban novels. In the main, the different modalities of regionalism are in themselves a secondary and generally provincial form, among much richer forms that occupy a higher level. Nevertheless, in such underdeveloped countries as Greece, or those that still have major underdeveloped areas, like Italy or Spain, regionalism can be a valid manifestation, capable of producing works of quality, such as those of Giovanni Verga at the end of the last century, or of Federico García Lorca, Elio Vittorini, or Nikos Kazantzakis in our time.

For this reason, in Latin America regionalism was and still is a stimulating force in literature. In the phase of "new country" consciousness, corresponding to the situation of backwardness, it gives a place, above all, to the decoratively picturesque and functions as a discovery, a recognition of the reality of the country and its incorporation into the themes of literature. In the phase of the consciousness of underdevelopment, it functions as a premonition and then as a consciousness of crisis, motivating the documentary and, with a feeling of urgency, political engagement.

In both stages, there occurs a kind of selection of thematic areas, an attraction for certain remote regions, in which the groups marked by underdevelopment are localized. They can, without doubt, constitute a negative seduction for the urban writer, through a picturesqueness with dubious consequences; but, beyond this, they generally coincide with areas of social problems, which is significant and important in literatures as engaged as those of Latin America.

An example is the Amazonian region, which attracted such Brazilian novelists and storytellers as José Veríssimo and Inglês de Sousa, from the beginnings of naturalism, in the 1870s and 1880s, in a fully picturesque phase; it furnished the material for *La vorágine*, by José Eustasio Rivera, a half century later, situated between the picturesque and the denunciation (more patriotic than social); and it became an important element in *La casa verde* of Vargas Llosa, in the modern phase of high technical consciousness, in which exoticism and denunciation are latent in relation to the human impact that is displayed, in the construction of style, with the immanence of universal works.

It is not necessary to enumerate all the other literary areas that correspond to the panorama of backwardness and underdevelopment—such as the Andean *altiplano* or the Brazilian *sertão*. Or, also, the situations and places of the Cuban, Venezuelan, or the Brazilian Negro, in the poems of Nicolás Guillén and Jorge de Lima, in *Ecué Yamba-Ó* of Alejo Carpentier, *Pobre negro* of Romulo Gallegos, or the *Jubiabá* of Jorge Amado. Or, still further, the man of the plains—*llano, pampa, caatinga*—the object of a tenacious compensatory idealization that comes from such Romantics as José de Alencar in the 1870s; which occurred largely among the peoples of the Rio de la Plata, Uruguayans like Eduardo Acevedo Díaz, Carlos Reyles, or Javier de Viana, and Argentines, from the telluric José Hernández to the stylized Ricardo Güiraldes; which tends to the allegorical in Gallegos, in Venezuela, and reaches, in Brazil, in the full phase of preconsciousness of underdevelopment, an elevated expression in *Vidas Secas* of Graciliano Ramos, without the vertigo of distance, without tournaments or duels, without rodeos or cattle roundups, without the centaurism that marks the others.

Regionalism was a necessary step, which made literature, above all the novel and the story, focus on local reality. At times it was an opportunity for fine literary expression, although the majority of its products have dated. But from a certain angle, perhaps, it can't be said that it is finished; many of those who today attack it, at bottom practice it. The economic reality of underdevelopment maintains the regional dimension as a living object, despite the urban dimension's ever-increasing importance. It is enough to remember that some of the best writers find substance for books that are universally significant in it: José María Arguedas, Gabriel García Marquez, Augusto Roa Bastos, João Guimarães Rosa. Only in countries where the culture of big cities has absolute dominion, such as Argentina and Uruguay, has regional literature become a total anachronism.

For this reason, it is necessary to redefine the problem critically, seeing that it is not exhausted by the fact that, today, no one any longer considers regionalism a privileged form of national literary expression; among other reasons because, as was said, it can be especially alienating. But it is appropriate to think about its transformations, keeping in mind that the same basic reality has been prolonged under diverse names and concepts. In fact, in the euphoric phase of consciousness of the new country, characterized by the idea of backwardness, we had picturesque regionalism, which in various countries was inculcated as *the* literary truth. This modality was long ago left behind, or survives, if at all, at a subliterary level. Its fullest and most tenacious manifestation in the golden phase was perhaps the gauchoism of the countries of the Río de la Plata, while the most spurious form was certainly the sentimental Brazilian "sertanejismo" [from *sertão* = backlands] of the beginning of the twentieth century. And it is what has irremediably compromised certain more recent works, such as those of Rivera and Gallegos.

In the phase of preconsciousness of underdevelopment, through the 1930s and 1940s, we had problematic regionalism, which called itself the "social novel," "indigenism," "novel of the northeast [of Brazil]," depending on the countries and, though not exclusively regional, in good part it was. It interests us more for having been a precursor of the consciousness of underdevelopment—it being fair to record that, much earlier, writers like Alcides Arguedas and Mariano Azuela were already guided by a more realistic sense of the conditions of life, as well as of the problems of unprotected groups.

Among those who then proposed, with analytic vigor and at times in artistic forms of good quality, the demystification of American reality are Miguel Ángel Asturias, Jorge Icaza, Ciro Alegría, José Lins Rego, and others. All of them, in at least some part of their work, created a kind of social novel that was still related to the universe of regionalism, including what was negative in it, such as a sentimental picturesqueness, or kitsch; these remnants of regionalism amounted at times to a schematic and banal humanitarianism, which could compromise what they wrote.

What characterizes them, still, is the overcoming of patriotic optimism and the adoption of a kind of pessimism different from what was present in naturalist fiction. While that fiction focused on the poor man as a refractory element in the march of progress, these uncovered the situation in its complexity, turning against the dominant classes and seeing in the degradation of man a consequence of economic plunder, not of his individual *fate*. The paternalism of *Doña Bárbara* (which is a kind of apotheosis of the good master) suddenly seems archaic, in the face of the traces of George Grosz we observe in Icaza or the early Jorge Amado, in whose books what remains of the picturesque and exotic is dissolved by social unmasking—making it a presentiment of the passage from the "consciousness of the new country" to the "consciousness of the underdeveloped country," with the political consequences that introduces.

Even though many of these writers are characterized by spontaneous and irregular language, the weight of social consciousness acts in their styles as a positive factor, making room for the search for interesting solutions to problems of the representation of inequality and injustice. Without speaking of the consummate master Asturias is in some of his books, even a facile writer like Icaza owes his durability less to his indignant denunciations or to the exaggeration with which he characterizes the exploiters than to some stylistic resources he found to express misery. In *Huasipungo* it is a certain diminutive use of words, of the rhythm of weeping in speech, of the reduction to the level of the animal that, taken together, embody a kind of diminution of man, his reduction to elementary functions, which is associated with the linguistic stuttering to symbolize privation. In *Vidas secas*, Graciliano Ramos carries his customary verbal self-restraint to the maximum, elaborating an expression reduced to the ellipsis, to the monosyllable, to the minimum syntagmas, to express the human suffocation of the cowhand confined to minimum levels of survival.

The Brazilian case is perhaps peculiar, since here the initial regionalism, which began with Romanticism, earlier than in the other countries, never produced works considered first class, even by contemporaries, having been a secondary, when not frankly subliterary, tendency in prose and in verse. The best products of Brazilian fiction were always *urban*, most often stripped of any element of the picturesque; its major representative, Machado de Assis, showed since the 1880s the fragility of descriptivism and of local color, which he banished from his extraordinarily refined books. It was only beginning more or less around 1930, in a second phase that we are trying to characterize, that regionalist tendencies, already sublimated and transfigured by social realism, attained the level of significant works, while in other countries, above all Argentina, Uruguay, Chile, it was already being put to one side.

Overcoming these modalities, as well as the attacks they suffer from critics, is a demonstration of maturity. For this reason, many authors would reject as a blemish the name of "regionalist," which in fact no longer has meaning. But this does not prevent the regional dimension from continuing to be present in many works of major importance, though without any feeling of an imperative tendency, or of any requirement of a dubious national consciousness.

What we see now, from this point of view, is a blooming world of the novel marked by technical refinement, thanks to which regions are transfigured and their human contours subverted, causing formerly picturesque features to be shed and to acquire universality.

Discarding sentimentalism and rhetoric; nourished by nonrealist elements, such as the absurd, the magic of situations, or by antinaturalist techniques, such as the interior monologue, the simultaneous vision, the synthesis, the ellipsis—the novel nevertheless explores what used to be the very substance of nativism, of exoticism, and of social documentary. This would lead to proposing the distinguishing of a third phase, which could be (thinking of surrealism, or superrealism) called *superregionalist*. It corresponds to a consciousness distressed by underdevelopment and explodes the type of naturalism based on reference to an empirical vision of the world, a naturalism that was the aesthetic tendency peculiar to an epoch in which the bourgeois mentality triumphed and that was in harmony with the consolidation of our literatures.

To this superregionalism belongs, in Brazil, the revolutionary work of Guimarães Rosa, solidly planted in what could be called the universality of the region. And the fact that we have gone beyond the picturesque and the documentary does not make the presence of the region any less alive in works such as those of Juan Rulfo—whether in the fragmentary and obsessive reality of *Llano en llamas*, or in the fantasmal sobriety of *Pedro Páramo*. For this reason it is necessary to nuance drastic judgments that are basically fair, like those of Alejo Carpentier in the preface to *El reyno de este mundo*, where he writes that our nativist novel is a kind of official high school literature that no longer finds readers in its places of origin. Without doubt—if we think of the first phase of our attempt at classification; to a certain point—if we think of the second; not at all—if we remind ourselves that the third carries an important dose of regional ingredients, due to the very fact of underdevelopment. As was said, such ingredients constitute a stylized realization of dramatic conditions peculiar to it, intervening in the selection of themes and of topics, as well as in the very elaboration of the language.

Criticism will no longer require, as previously it would have, explicitly or implicitly, that Cortázar sing the life of Juan Moreyra, or that Clarice Lispector use the vocabulary of the Brazilian backland. But it will, equally, not fail to recognize that, writing with refinement and going beyond academic naturalism, Guimarães Rosa, Juan Rulfo, Vargas Llosa practice in their works, in the whole and in their parts, as much as Cortázar or Clarice Lispector in the universe of urban values, a new species of literature, which still is connected in a transfiguring way to the very material of what was once nativism.

NOTES

This article first appeared, in French, in *Cahiers d'Histoire Mondiale* (UNESCO), 12, no. 4 (1970), 618–40; and was reprinted in Antonio Candido, *A educação pela noite e outros ensaios* (São Paulo: Editora Ática, 1987), pp. 140–62.

1. Mário Vieira de Mello, *Desenvolvimento e cultura: O problema do estetismo no Brasil* (São Paulo: Nacional, 1963), pp. 3–17.

2. I owe this citation to Decio de Almeida Prado.

3. Juan Valera, "Juício crítico," in Juan Zorrilla de San Martin, *Tabaré*, edición ilustrada (Mexico City: Casas Editoriales, 1905), pp. 9–10.

4. In Latin American literature in Spanish, the reaction against Romanticism at the end of the nineteenth century is called Modernism. In Brazilian literature, the vanguard literary movement of the 1920s is called Modernism. To distinguish the two, I use quotation marks in referring to the Spanish case.

5. The situation today is different and, besides, was already changing when I wrote this essay (1969). In this change the role of Cuba was decisive, promoting intensely in its territory the meeting of Latin-American artists, scientists, writers, and intellectuals, who could thus meet and exchange experiences without the mediation of the imperialist countries.

6. I use the term *regionalism* here in the manner of Brazilian criticism, which extends it to all the fiction linked to the description of regions and of rural customs since Romanticism; and not in the manner of most of modern Spanish-American criticism, which generally restricts it to the era more or less between 1920 and 1950.

Chapter 8

CRITICISM AND SOCIOLOGY
(AN ATTEMPT AT CLARIFICATION)

NOTHING is more important, in calling attention to a truth, than to exaggerate it. But, likewise, nothing is more dangerous, because one day comes the unavoidable reaction and relegates that truth, unjustly, to the category of error, to such a point that it requires a difficult operation to arrive at an objective point of view, without misrepresenting one side or the other. This is what has occurred with the study of the relation between the work of art and its social conditioning, which had at one time in the past century come to be seen as the key for understanding the work, and then was demoted to an error of vision—and perhaps only now can begin to be proposed in the requisite terms. It could perhaps be said, with an air of paradox, that we evaluate the link between the work and the ambiance better after arriving at the conclusion that aesthetic analysis precedes considerations of any other order.

In fact, some had earlier tried to show that the value and significance of a work depend on whether or not it expresses a certain aspect of reality, and that this aspect constituted what was essential in it. Then, the opposite position was arrived at, which tried to show that the content is secondary, and that the importance of a work derives from the formal operations at work in it, which confer on it a peculiarity that is in fact independent of any conditioning whatsoever, especially social, which is considered inoperative as an element of comprehension.

Today we know that the integrity of the work does not permit us to adopt any of these dissociated visions; and that we can only understand the work by mixing text and context in a dialectically integrated interpretation, in which the old point of view that explained it by external factors, as much as the other, guided by a conviction that the structure is practically independent, are combined, when necessary, in the interpretive process. We know, further, that the *external* (in this case, the social) is important, not as a cause, nor as a meaning, but as an element that performs a certain role in the constitution of the structure, becoming, therefore, *internal.*

Here it is necessary to establish a distinction of disciplines, remembering that the *external* treatment of *external* factors can be legitimate when we deal with the sociology of literature, since this does not address the question of the value of the work and can be interested, properly, in everything that conditions it. It is appropriate, for example, to study the vogue for a book, the statistical preferences for a genre, the taste of classes, the social origins of authors, the relations between works and ideas, the influence of social, economic, and political organization, etc. It is a discipline of a scientific stamp, without the aesthetic orientation necessarily assumed by criticism.

The problem has several aspects and can be illustrated by a question formulated by Lukács at the beginning of his intellectual career, before he adopted Marxism, which led him to concentrate, at times excessively, on the political and economic aspects of literature. Discussing modern theater, he set up the following alternative: "Does the historical-social element possess, in itself, significance for the structure of a work, and to what degree?" Or "Is the sociological element in the dramatic form only a possibility of the realization of aesthetic value . . . but not a determinant of it?"[1]

This is, in effect, the nucleus of the problem since, in the field of literary criticism we analyze works in intimate detail, and what interests us is the investigation of how factors work in the internal organization, in such a way as to construct this specific structure. Taking the social factor, we would seek to determine if it furnishes only the matter (ambiance, customs, group features, ideas), which serve as a vehicle to carry the creative current (in Lukács's terms, if it only makes the realization of aesthetic value possible); or if, beyond this, it is an element that acts in the constitution of what is essential in the work as a work of art (in Lukács's terms, if it is a determinant of aesthetic value).

This is what is perceived or intuited by various contemporary students who, interesting themselves in social and psychic factors, try to see them as agents of structure, not as a framework nor as material recorded by the creative work; and this permits aligning them among the aesthetic factors. Critical analysis, in fact, intends to go much deeper, being basically the search for the elements responsible for the form and significance of the work, unified in order to form an indissoluble whole, about which we could say, like Faust of the Macrocosmos, that everything is woven into a whole, each thing nourishing itself from and acting on the others:

> How each the Whole its substance gives,
> Each in the other works and lives!

We take a simple example: the novel *Senhora* of José de Alencar. Like all books of this type, it has certain obvious social dimensions, which to indicate would be part of any study, historical or critical: references to places, fashions, practices; manifestations of group or class attitudes; the expression of a conception of life lying between the bourgeois and the patriarchal. To note these is a routine task and is not enough to define the sociological character of a study.

But it happens that, beyond this, the subject itself rests on social conditions that it is necessary to understand and indicate in order to penetrate the work's meaning. The book deals with the purchase of a husband; and we will have taken a step forward if we reflect that this purchase has a symbolic social significance, since it represents at the same time the unmasking of such customs of the time as marrying for money. By inventing the crude situation of the spouse who sells himself in a contract, by means of a stipulated payment, the novelist lays bare the roots of the relationship, that is, he makes a radical social analysis, reducing the act to its essential aspect of buying and selling. But, seeing this, we are still not at the deepest layers of analysis—which we reach only when this evident social fact is seen functioning to shape the structure of the book.

If, with this in mind, we attend to the composition of *Senhora*, we see that it rests on a long and complicated transaction—with scenes of advance and retreat, dialogues constructed as pressures and concessions, a latent plot of secret maneuvers—in whose development the position of the spouses alternates. We see that the behavior of the protagonist expresses, in each episode, an obsession with the act of buying to which he yielded, and that the human relations have deteriorated because of these economic motives. The heroine, hardened in her desire for the vengeance made possible by the possession of money, stiffens her soul as if she were the agent of an operation of crushing the other by means of capital, which reduces him to something possessed. And the images of the style themselves manifest a mineralization of the personality, affected by capitalist dehumanization, until the romantic dialectic of love recovers its conventional normality. Taken as a whole, as in the details of each part, the same structural principles inform the material.

Referring this examination to earlier ones, made on a simpler level, we see that if the book is ordered around this long duel, it is because the duel represents a transposition, to the plane of the book's structure, of the mechanism of buying and selling. And, in this case of relations that should be guided by a higher moral necessity, the buying and selling function as a true perversion. This is not affirmed abstractly by the novelist, nor only illustrated with examples, but is suggested in the very composition of the whole and its parts, in the way he organizes the material to give it a certain expressivity.

When we make an analysis of this type, we can say that we take the social into account, not externally, as a reference that permits us to identify in the substance of the book the expression of a certain epoch or a specific society, nor as a scaffold that permits us to situate it historically, but as a factor of artistic construction itself, studied at the explicative, and not the illustrative, level.

In this case, we leave the peripheral aspects of sociology, or of a sociologically oriented history, in order to arrive at an aesthetic interpretation that assimilates the social dimension as an element of the artwork. When this is done, there occurs the paradox pointed out initially: the *external* becomes *internal*, and criticism ceases to be sociological and becomes just criticism. The social element becomes one of the many that intervene in the economy of the book, alongside the psychological, religious, linguistic, and others. At this level of analysis, in which the structure constitutes the point of reference, these divisions matter little, since everything is transformed, by the critic, in an organic ferment from which results the cohesive diversity of the whole.

We see that, from this point of view, the sociological angle acquires a greater validity than it had. In compensation, it can no longer be imposed as the only criterion, or even given preference, since the importance of each factor depends on the case being analyzed. A criticism that wants to be integrated will stop being unilaterally sociological, psychological, or linguistic, in order to utilize freely the elements capable of leading to a coherent interpretation. But nothing prevents each critic from emphasizing the element of his preference, if it is used as a component of the structuring of the book. And we discover that what modern criticism overcomes is not the sociological orientation, always possible and legitimate, but critical sociologism, the devouring tendency to explain everything by means of social factors.

Something similar occurred, furthermore, in sociology itself, whose evolution modified its relations with criticism. Scholars are accustomed to think, on this topic, according to positions established in the nineteenth century, when sociology was in the phase of grand systematic generalizations, which led its practitioners to conceive of a global conditioning of the work, of the literary personality, or of the collection of works in a social system, principally from the historical angle. Nevertheless, the progress of research and theory have brought a more acute sense of the relation between feature and context, permitting the turning of attention to the structural and functional aspects of each unit considered. This occurred at the same time that our critical and analytical studies took up the role of stylistic unities, considered as keys for getting to the sense of the whole, in both cases with the absolute predominance of the synchronic over the diachronic.

Therefore, to speak today of the sociological point of view in literary studies would have to signify something quite different from what it meant fifty years ago. The change in the two fields will certainly provoke

a reaction in the sociology of literature, which not only will move toward concrete research (as is suggested, for example, in the book of
Robert Escarpit, *La sociologie de la littérature*), but will leave aside ambitious causal explanations with their nineteenth-century flavor. The danger, for sociology as much as for criticism, is that the tendency to analysis will obliterate the basic truth, that is, that the logical and empirical
priority goes to the whole, though apprehended through a constant reference to the function of the parts. Another danger is that the scholarly
preoccupation with the integrity and autonomy of the work exaggerates,
beyond appropriate limits, the sense of the internal function of the elements, to the detriment of the historical aspects, an essential dimension
for understanding the meaning of the object studied.

In whatever way, it is convenient to avoid new dogmatisms, always
remembering that contemporary criticism, so much more interested in
formal aspects, cannot dispense with or disdain such independent disciplines as the sociology of literature or sociologically oriented literary
history, as well as the entire gamut of disciplines applied to the the investigation of the social aspects of works, frequently for a nonliterary
purpose.

II

In order to settle our ideas and delimit fields, we can attempt an enu-
meration of the most common kinds of sociological studies in literature,
made according to more or less traditional criteria and moving back and
forth between sociology, history, and the criticism of content.

The first type is made up of works that seek to relate the whole of a
literature, a period, or a genre, to social conditions. It is the traditional
method, sketched in the eighteenth century, which found perhaps its
major representative in Taine and was attempted in Brazil by Silvio
Romero. Its major virtue consists in the effort to discern a general order,
an arrangement, that facilitates the understanding of historical sequences and traces the panorama of epochs. Its defect is the difficulty of
showing effectively, at this scale, the linkage between social conditions
and works of literature. From this difficulty there almost always flows, as
a disappointing result, a parallel structure, in which the student enumer-
ates the factors, analyzes the political and economic conditions, and
then, incapable of linking the two orders of reality, talks about the works
according to his intuitions or his inherited preconceptions. This is that
much more serious when, as with the majority of scholars who take this
line, there is a causal nexus of a deterministic type between the two. This
is what can be observed not only in works of lesser intellectual reach, but
also in works of rigorous information and good quality, such as *Drama
and Society in the Age of Johnson*, by L. C. Knights.

Studies of this type are even more disappointing when the student, giving up the job of correlating the society and the whole of a literature or genre, transports the parallelism I referred to to the interpretation of isolated works and writers, who serve as a mere pretext for speaking about social features and problems, whose exposition would not require this kind of dubious mediation, as is the case in Heitor Ferreira Lima's book on Castro Alves.

A second type consists of studies that try to investigate the degree to which works of art mirror or represent the society, describing its various aspects. It is the simplest and most common modality, consisting basically in establishing correlations between actual aspects of society and those that appear in the book. When sociological criticism is spoken of, or the sociology of literature, this modality, which has its illustrious archetype in Taine's *La Fontaine et ses fables*, is what is generally thought of; an example of high quality is W. F. Bruford's study (*Chekhov and His Russia*) of the fidelity with which Chekhov's plays and stories represent the Russian society of his time.

If this second type tends more toward an elementary sociology than toward literary criticism, the third is only sociological, and much more coherent, consisting in the study of the relation between the work and the public, that is, the work's fate, its acceptance, the reciprocal action of the two. A well-known example is the essay by Lewin Schücking, in Vierkandt's *Handwörterbuch der Soziologie*, "The Sociology of Literary Taste," later published as a book and translated into various languages. Despite its renown, it does not go beyond indicating the kind of studies that could be done from this point of view.

Others, less systematic, are in compensation more anchored in the facts; such works include *Le public et le vie littéraire à Rome*, by A. M. Guillemin. *Fiction and the Reading Public*, by Q. D. Leavis, explores the function of literature with respect to readers. When the author approaches the historical problem of public acceptance over time, there arises a variant that is less sociological and more based in the traditional surveys of erudition; this is what is observed, equally, in similar studies in comparative literature, such as *Byron et le Romantisme français* by Edmond Estève.

A fourth type, still situated almost exclusively within sociology, studies the position and social function of the writer, seeking to relate his position to the nature of his production, and both of these to the organization of the society. In the field of genre, we have a series of works outside the literary ambit, such as that of Geiger on the status and work of the intellectual (*Aufgabe und Stellung der Intelligenz in der Gesellschaft*), or the important considerations of the sociology of knowledge, in particular those of Mannheim. The spirit with which, in the historical field, Henri Brunschvicg utilizes this angle to analyze the situation and the role of the intellectuals in the formation of modern German society is exemplary (*Le crise de l'etat prussien à la fin du XVIIIe siècle*). In the literary field, Alexandre Beljame's monograph on the man of letters in seventeenth-century England is well known.

A further development of this last is the fifth type, which investigates the political function of works and authors, generally with a marked ideological intention. In our time, this has been the preference of Marxists, from the primary formulations of party criticism to the more variegated and not uncommonly powerful observations of Lukács, in his work after 1930. In Italy, beyond the fragments of Gramsci, there is a significant flowering of works of this type, with a freedom much less frequent in authors of a Marxist orientation in other countries, as in the case of Galvano della Volpe.

We recall, finally, a sixth type, turned toward the hypothetical investigation of origins, whether of literature in general or of specific genres. There are certain classic works in this key, such as Gunmere's on the roots of poetry, Bucher's on the correlation between work and poetic rhythm, or Christopher Caudwell's Marxist investigation of the nature and origins of poetry. George Thomson's study of the social roots of Greek tragedy, equally guided by the directives of Marxism (*Aeschylus and Athens*), is much more solid.

All these modalities and their numerous variants are legitimate and, when well done, fruitful, to the degree that we take them not as criticism, but as the sociological theory and history of literature, or as the sociology of literature, though some of them also satisfy the requirements of criticism proper. We note in all of them the dislocation of interest from the work to the social elements that form its matter, to the circumstances of the milieu that influence its elaboration, or to its function in the society.

Now such aspects are important for the historian and sociologist, but may be secondary and even useless for the critic interested in interpretation, if they are not considered according to their function in the internal economy of the book, to which they can contribute in a manner so remote as to become, in the clarification of concrete cases, dispensable.

In fact, everyone knows that literature, as a phenomenon of civilization, depends, for its constitution and characterization, on the interweaving of various social factors. But from there to the determination of whether those factors intervene directly in the essential characteristics of a specific work there is an abyss that is not always crossed felicitously. In the same way, we know that our neuroglandular constitution and the first experiences of infancy lay out the course of our mode of being. Will it necessarily follow that the neuroglandular constitution and the first experiences of infancy of a given writer hold the key to the understanding and evaluation of his work, as J. P. Weber recently tried to show in so exclusivist and radical a manner in *La genèse de l'oeuvre poétique?* These questions, easy to approach speculatively, become difficult to answer when we move to the individual author, but help to stabilize the basic notion in this field, which is: it is not a matter of affirming or denying an evident dimension of literary fact; but it is, rather, to investigate, from the specific angle of criticism, if it is decisive or only useful for understanding particular works.

The first step (which, though obvious, must be pointed out) is to be aware of the arbitrary and deforming relation artistic work establishes with reality, even when it intends to observe and convey it rigorously, since mimesis is always a form of poiesis. The physician Fernandes Figueira tells, in his book *Velaturas* (written under the pseudonym of Alcides Flávio), that his friend Aluísio Azevedo consulted him, while he was writing *O homem*, about strychnine poisoning; but he did not use the information he received. Despite naturalism's scrupulous attempt to be informative, he disregarded the data given by science and gave the poison a more rapid and dramatic action, because his design required that it be that way.

This liberty, even within the documentary orientation, belongs to fantasy, which at times needs to modify the world's order exactly to make it more expressive, in such a way that the feeling of truth constitutes itself in the reader thanks to this methodical treachery. Such a paradox is at the core of literary work and guarantees its effectiveness as a representation of the world. To think, then, that it is enough to compare the work to external reality in order to understand it is to run the risk of a dangerous causal simplification.

But if we take care to consider the social factors (as explained here) in their role as shapers of structure, we see that they, as much as the psychic, are decisive for literary analysis, and that to pretend to define the aesthetic integrity of the work without them is to wish to do what only the Baron Munchausen succeeded in doing, to pull yourself out of the swamp by your own hair.

III

We have already seen, in many sociologically oriented critics, the effort to show this interiorization of data of a social nature, made into nuclei of aesthetic elaboration. Lukács himself, when he did not run into certain limitations of political sectarianism, indicated in a convincing manner that, for example, Manzoni's *I promessi sposi* is a superb historical novel because the literary construction expresses a coherent vision of the society it describes (*Der historische Roman*). In a more detailed manner,

Arnold Kettle suggests that the structure of Dickens's *Oliver Twist* is literarily effective and suggestive while its author develops the contrast between the egoism *bien-pensant* and lack of awareness of the bourgeoisie, and the world that revolves around crime, which mutually presuppose one another, and between which the little protagonist is tossed. But, when Oliver is protected in the bosom of his grandfather's conciliating kindness, which attenuates the bitterness of the inequality and of the social contradictions, the composition loses its bite and even its profound coherence, causing a drop in quality that every sensitive reader observes at a certain point (Kettle, *The English Novel*, vol. 1). In the one case as in the other, we have the effect of a specific vision of society acting as an aesthetic factor and permitting us to understand the economy of the book.

This problem occurs, amplified in a different sense, and prejudiced by a certain speculative luxuriance, in the work of Lucien Goldmann, who has tried to show how creation, despite its singularity and autonomy, derives from a certain vision of the world, which is a collective phenomenon to the degree that it has been elaborated by a social class, according to its own ideological angle. Though he does not consider problems of construction (as Kettle does), he tries to show that the peculiar vision transmitted by Racinian tragedy is related to that derived from the thought of Pascal; and that both have their roots, in a special and independent manner, in Jansenist pessimism, by means of which an important sector of the French bourgeoisie, badly adjusted to the then dominant caste structure, expressed this lack of adjustment ideologically (*Le dieu caché*).

In all these cases, the social factor is invoked to explain the structure of the work and the tone of its ideas, furnishing elements that determine its validity and its effect on us. On a less explicit and more subtle plane, we mention the attempt of Erich Auerbach, mixing stylistic processes with historicosociological methods to investigate literature (*Mimesis: Dargestellte Wirklichkeit in der abendländischen Literatur*). It was in relation to similar attempts that Otto Maria Carpeaux alluded to a synthetic method, which he called "stylistic-sociological," in the introduction to his magnificent *História da literatura ocidental*. Such a method, whose perfecting will certainly be one of the jobs of the second half of the century in the field of literary studies, will permit bringing a synthetic point of view to the intimacy of interpretation, undoing the traditional dichotomy between *internal* and *external* factors, which still serves today in place of adequate criteria. We will see then, probably, that social elements will be filtered through an aesthetic conception and brought to the level of literary construction, in order to understand the singularity and autonomy of the work. And this will be the reverse of what we observe in determinist criticism, against which many critics of this century have justly rebelled, since it annuls the individuality of the work, incorporating it in an overly broad and generic vision of the social elements, as is seen in its major example, the brilliant schematism of Taine, in his study of English literature.

In this still unsatisfactory provisional stage in which we find ourselves, the situation has a polemic character, given the insecurity of points of view. This makes comprehensible certain compensatory exaggerations, which go to the other extreme and assert that what is meaningful in the work is a whole that is explicable in itself, like a closed universe. This radically structural point of view, appropriate as one of the moments of analysis, is not viable in the practical work of interpretation, because it undervalues, among other things, the historical dimension, without which contemporary thought does not adequately confront the problems that preoccupy it. But to its diverse modalities we owe fruitful results, such as the concept, already referred to, of the organicity of the work, which, while known to earlier criticism, received from these modern currents what it had lacked: instruments of investigation, including an adequate terminology.

Today we feel that, contrary to how things might seem at first glance, it is exactly this conception of the work as an organism that permits us, in its study, to take into account and diversify the play of factors that condition and motivate it; since, when interpreted as an element of structure, each factor becomes an essential component of the case in focus, whose legitimacy can be neither contested nor glorified a priori.

NOTES

First published as "Crítica e sociologia," in *Literatura e sociedade* (São Paulo: Companhia Editora Nacional, 1965), pp. 3–17.

1. Georg Lukács, "Zur Soziologie des modernen Dramas," in *Schriften zur Literatursoziologie* (Neuwied: Hermann Luchterhand Verlag, 1961), p. 262.

Chapter 9

TERESINA AND HER FRIENDS

INITIAL ACCOUNT

When one thinks of the pious and conformist atmosphere in which Teresina was born and grew up, it is only by remembering her volcanic personality that it is possible to understand how she could change her ideas so fundamentally when she was about thirty.

Teresa Maria Carini was born on August 27, 1863, in the village of Fontanellato, in the new province of Reggio-Emilia in the newly founded Kingdom of Italy, in the shadow of a famous feudal castle, the Rocca of the Sanvitales, a family of the upper nobility (of which her family was a dependent), who in the Middle Ages alternated with others as the governors of Parma. When she was born, the head of the house was Count Luigi Sanvitale, married to Princess Albertina Montenuovo, a daughter, "legitimated by subsequent marriage," of Marie Louise of Austria—the sovereign duchess of Parma until 1847, and former wife of Napoleon I—and Adalbert, count of Neiperg (Neipperg = Neuperg = Neu Berg = Monte Nuovo).[1]

The Sanvitales had an enormous palace of 365 rooms in the city of Parma, which they donated at the end of the nineteenth century for a school for girls.

Teresina's parents were the engineer Anacleto Carini, born in the same village, administrator of the Sanvitale estate, and his wife, Virginia Pasquale. Before Teresina, the couple had two children, who grew up to be Camilo Carini, a general, and Gino Carini, an agronomist.

Teresina was a little girl when her mother died, and her grandmother, a severe woman, came to take charge of the house, in the central square of the village, across from the Rocca. Teresina had grown up in a provincial and aristocratic world, among her own relatives, some of whom were half rustic, and their noble patrons, who no longer believed in their own *status*. "We nobles are no longer of any use and had better disappear," her agemate Giannino Sanvitale said bitterly; moving from the idea to the act, he later married his nephews' governess and was the last male in his line. Giannino had two older sisters: Albertina, married to the Marquess Montecucoli degli Erri, and Guglielmina, who married the Marquess Paveri-Fontana and inherited the Rocca. They were all children of Count Alberto and Contessa Laura Malvezzi dei Medici,

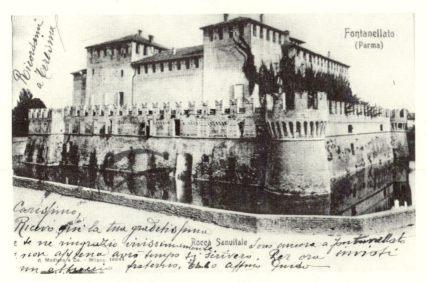

1. Rear facade of the castle (*Rocca*) of the Counts Sanvitale in the town of Fontanellato, near Parma.

thus being grandchildren of the Count Luigi and Princess Albertina already mentioned. Teresina grew up near these people, saying her beads, knitting things for the poor, embroidering coverlets, painting watercolors, retelling family stories—oriented toward the fear of God and King, whose all powerful representatives in the home were first the Father and later the Husband.

She used to say that the Sanvitales were related to many European kings and were descended from Saint Louis; and that in the castle there were many portraits of *antenati* (ancestors) and many coats of arms (including the French fleur-de-lis) emblazoning the coverings of the ceilings and the walls. The public was allowed to visit the castle periodically, an illiterate porter who spoke very badly serving as guide. In the Portrait Gallery he explained the portraits on the walls to them summarily: "They're all Sanvitales." He took them to the Gallery of Arms and then to the small room decorated by Parmigianino, who lived for a time in the castle in the 1530s under the protection of the then count, before retiring with some disciples to the isolation of Casalmaggiore. There were there (and still are) a series of frescos representing the legend of Diana and Acteon, with nude or seminude mythological figures before whom the visitors, in general modest people, stood openmouthed in amazement, asking who they were. The guide described these too as "all Sanvitales." These naked ones too? Yes, sir, all of them. "All Sanvitales." As a child, Teresina and the *contessina* used to eavesdrop on the visitors

2. Teresina's father, the engineer Anacleto Carini.

in order to hear the porter's picturesque generalization; it was one of her most diverting reminiscences. Throughout her life she used to die laughing when she repeated the phrase and used it to describe unusual things.[2]

She was very close to her father, who died relatively young of cancer of the throat on the last day of the year 1889, causing in her a hopeless and irreconcilable suffering throughout her life. She was twenty-six years old, and her brothers, as well as the count and countess, wanting to resolve her situation and, according to her, to get rid of their responsibilities, arranged her wedding to the cellist Guido Rocchi, who had long been in love with her. They married, and the count and countess, whom her father had served with dedication all his life, gave her a wedding present of five hundred lire, a fact Teresina always complained about.[3]

Music and Brazil

Rocchi, born in 1865, was the beloved disciple of an uncle of hers, the well-known maestro Leandro Carini, professor of cello at the Royal Conservatory of Parma and badly thought of then because of his intransigent love of German music, which seemed unpatriotic at that time of the recent unification of Italy against the Austrian occupation. His other beloved disciple was Arturo Toscanini, born near Piacenza in March of 1867. The maestro brought them together semisecretly, in a kind of conspiracy, to play Beethoven, and they were called "i tedeschi" [the Germans].

The newly married couple went to live in Milan, where Rocchi played in the orchestra at La Scala. Teresina used to observe, with curiosity, a handsome young neighbor, with a gold earing, one green sock and the other red, who played some easy pieces, which she eventually learned by heart, on the piano. One day she accompanied her busband to La Scala for the premiere of *Cavalleria Rusticana*, which had just had a spectacular opening in Rome. Then she recognized the music and saw that the fiery neighbor was Mascagni (but she always thought that *Cavalleria* was a bore).

Shortly afterward the couple came to Brazil with the orchestra of an opera company, which arrived in Rio de Janeiro on St. Peter's Day, June 29, 1890. Rockets were going off, there were fireworks and firecrackers everywhere, and she thought it was some feature of the local savagery—a sentiment she kept till her death, complaining loudly about the Portuguese and Brazilian abuse of fireworks.

She was also shocked by the bad behavior of audiences, who did not respect the artists and booed for no reason at all (Brazilians considered this a mark of connoiseurship). Night after night she indignantly observed some young women who, from the front of their box, threw copper coins at the bald head of the drummer. What a country! And still worse was the yellow fever, which decimated the company and the orchestra as well.

When she told of these things, Teresina evoked what had occurred in Rio four years before her arrival, in 1886, when there arose an unexpected opportunity, one full of future consequences, for their friend Toscanini, an obscure nineteen-year-old cellist, who knew many scores by heart. One night, when *Aida* was being done, the conductor quit, and the impresario didn't know what to do. Toscanini, pushed forward by his colleagues, assumed the baton and conducted, perfectly and to great applause, continuing to conduct for the rest of the engagement.

(In 1940 Teresina heard a radio broadcast of a concert by Toscanini, by then quite famous, in the city where he had, by chance, begun his

3. Group photographed in 1922 in front of the Restaurante Trianon, in the Avenida Paulista (where the Museum of Art of São Paulo stands today). The fourth from the left is Maestro Guido Rocchi. (The sixth from the left is the well-known Brazilian writer Mário de Andrade.)

career as a conductor. It was the June 13, three days before Italy entered the war, and she saw in the coincidence a dramatic parallel. From a reflection she wrote in her notebook, I transcribe the following: "I cannot explain the emotion I felt, such pleasure and such pain! . . . Fate had him seize the baton of an eminent conductor while a monster, also Italian, grasped the sword in order to massacre his brothers. . . . Toscanini and Mussolini: life and death."[4]

She never saw her friend Arturo again, but got news and messages about him from her cousin and faithful correspondent Gino Nastrucci, who was his favorite "violino di spala" as long as he lived in Italy.)

Returning to 1890 and the thread of the story: the Rocchis had not caught the disease, despite Teresina having dedicated herself as a nurse of her countrymen to the point of exhaustion; their own country was in an economic crisis; they had local offers and decided to stay in Brazil for a while. But in fact they stayed their entire lives and never saw their country again. They lived in Santos, and later bought an estate in the area of Iguape, in Pariquera-Açu, which occupied them for several years; more her than him, because he frequently left her there alone. After that they moved to São Paulo, sometime before 1895. In 1906, Rocchi participated in the founding of the Conservatório Dramático e Musical, where he was the permanent professor of cello. There is an excellent portrait of the faculty of the Conservatory, taken in 1922, Rocchi standing near Mário de Andrade, short and stocky, with his face flashing like that of a Renaissance tyrant (later, after he let his mustache and goatee grow, he would come to look like Trotsky).

He and his wife shared the cult of Beethoven and in general preferred German music; of the Italian, they preferred the instrumental works of the seventeenth and eighteenth centuries, then little esteemed. (When he founded his own Conservatory, located at the beginning of Liberty Street, Rocchi gave it the name of Benedetto Marcello.) In opera, Teresina liked, in general, the lighter and comic works: Pergolesi, Mozart, Cimarosa, Rossini, Donizetti; she liked Wagner very much and some of Verdi. And she thought operas in the style of *verismo* "vile music."

The Out-of-Tune Couple

Both husband and wife had strong spirits and, despite points of affinity, had many differences that were hard to reconcile. She was always reading and writing, looking for lectures to attend, interesting herself in the movement of ideas; and she finally adopted socialist convictions with a passion that her husband did not understand. He read nothing, nor was he interested in politics, which provoked her to say: "Rocchi is a celebrity; but he has a head full of sawdust with some musical notes in the middle." By "celebrity" she meant great competence; and in fact she had the most profound and justified admiration for her husband as musician.

In São Paulo she joined the radical movements that had developed at the end of the nineteenth century, participating in the formation of alliances, the promotion of lectures, the support of workers' schools and strike movements, interesting herself greatly in the political and intellectual emancipation of her sex, in which respect she liked to mention a phrase of Zola's, translated into Italian: "Dalla donna, e per la donna verrà fatta la Società futura" [The future society will be made for woman and by woman]. She was the friend and comrade-in-arms of socialists, anarchists, and revolutionary syndicalists, Italians and Brazilians, as we will soon see. She was an essential figure at workers' meetings, at working-class cultural events, in movements of protest and of solidarity, but also at the lectures, courses, and concerts of the bourgeoisie. Her house was frequented by coreligionists and people of the musical world, including Maestro Antonio Carlos Ribeiro de Andrada Machado e Silva Júnior, who always excited the same joke from Rocchi whenever he appeared: "Non c'è posto per tanta gente!" [We don't have room for such people!]. Almost like a son to the couple was the cellist Alfredo Gomes,

4. Teresina in 1915.

who later became eminent (a participant in the Week of Modern Art in 1922), nephew of the author of *O Guarani* and son of Maestro Santana Gomes, who composed the opera *Semira* and the prelude to *Pastoral*, the play by Coelho Neto. Alfredo lived with them for many years, from childhood, as a disciple of Rocchi's, from whose severity Teresina defended him.

Around 1910 she decided to separate from her husband, whom she had never really loved, and who had given her cause for this decision; the decision was made easier by the fact that they had no children. She then went to Poços de Caldas, on the advice of a good friend of the couple, Francisco Escobar, a friend of Euclides da Cunha, an amateur musicologist and pianist, and a man of advanced ideas and great culture, who was the mayor of the town and later a state senator.

Rocchi was not happy with the separation and, after a little while, went to Poços de Caldas too. He lived there intermittently, finally dying there around 1940. She no longer wished to see him, despite his attempts to get together again; but from time to time she would communicate with him by means of tempestuous letters.

He constructed an enormous house on Rio de Janeiro Street, beside the Morro do Itororó, and gave classes there in theory, piano, violin, and cello, with a severity that was legendary. This is the testimony of a former student, the lutist Guido Pascoali:

> Rocchi divided his time between São Paulo and Poços de Caldas, the peaceful life and the beautiful women. A music lover, knowledgeable about many instruments, Rocchi also composed operas, which remained unpublished. His house was frequented by musicians and by children, some in search of music, others in search of adventures in its numberless rooms and parlors, always under construction.
>
> At that time, my oldest brother worked as a cabinetmaker for Rocchi and I studied violin with the maestro. For a month, I did not move from the posture he required: violin in position, a book under the arm, hand ready to finger. He was hard and demanding. After a while, he decided to go on to the next lesson: "Guido, tira l'arco." [In Italian, *tira* means "to pull," but in Portuguese it can mean "to remove."] I immediately removed the bow from the instrument and put it down on the table.[5] The maestro screamed, "Animale!" Frightened, I let go of the violin too and it fell, thus ending my career as a violinist.

When Rocchi died, some ten years before her, Teresina cried a great deal and had him buried in a lot she bought, in which she was also buried.

The Being and the "Convintions"

A Portrait in Words

She was thin, of medium height, with blondish hair that was a long time turning gray. She had blue eyes, open and round, expressing in an incredible manner the nuances of an agitated spirit. In Italy and here [in Brazil] people frequently thought she might be English, perhaps also because of the originality of her appearance, from the cut of her clothes to the unfashionable accessories, all in a good taste that was modest and personal: gloves or mittens, a black print shawl, a crocheted or lace cap, a cape of black silk, a tall old-fashioned parasol, unusual brooches, a cloth bag, and, in winter, wool gaiters. She was upright, *bien soignée*, walked with a precise and light step, very active, working alone at home, writing letters and reflections in abundance, always reading till past midnight. Then she slept tranquilly and woke late.

She lived on little, entirely from day to day, teaching knitting, Italian, and French. She helped and taught many people for nothing, gave what she had without hesitating to whoever asked or was in need, even when she had nothing herself. Tomorrow, we'll see.

The house she lived in also had an original and unusual air, full of sofas and poufs covered with cretonne prints, painted lamps (including one picturing the four seasons), ancient furniture, a kind of panoply of velvet studded with photographs and postcards, books and more books, although their number was nothing in proportion to her reading. She thought that books were made to be circulated and passed those she bought or got on to others after writing her impressions in the margins. But some she never got rid of, above all those of Leopardi, who was her greatest literary passion.

In a way, the house reflected her life, through objects which marked the passage of time: folders emblazoned with the Rocca coat of arms, autographs of friends, autographs of artists, albums of postcards, mementos of theater dressing rooms and concert halls, objects from the backland, radical manifestos, papers and magazines from every epoch. In the backyard she grew the spices for her Emilian cuisine, and many flowers: in addition to violets of many kinds, she had purple lilies, sweetpeas, and ornamental shrubs (or, as she preferred to say, *giagolli, pois de senteur, lauriers roses*). And from her there always came a vague fragrance of flowers.

Sometimes she rented one or two rooms to people with whom she established complicated relationships, generally beginning by thinking them angels and ending by throwing them out as devils, amid a web of suspicions, not uncommonly crowned by the tenant's leaving an unpaid bill behind. I once had to spend many days in Poços, a year before her death, fighting to dislodge a tenant who, alleging that he had no place to go, refused to leave. I was able to do it only by renting a small house to accommodate him and his family. But two months later she took in another, despite an agreement she had made with me not to do it any more, and the problems began all over again . . .

She gave a lot of attention to people's eyes, which served her as the basis for forming a judgment. One of the most terrible degrees in her scale of judgment was "occhi da delinquente" [delinquent's eyes], which she associated with fascism and loose morals ("a pig!" she exclaimed with respect to this feature). Conversely, when she admired someone, she supposed that they had a puritan comportment, a gift for languages, and left-wing tendencies: "He's uncorrupted; he isn't always 'in love,' he knows four or five languages, and I believe he has socialist ideas," or "I think he is an anarchist."

She always had at least one cat. She liked them very much, as she did all animals, denied indignantly that they had fleas, and attributed the most subtle purposes to them, noting them enthusiastically. "My cat is antifascist," she said one day, somewhere between seriousness and joking. "But how do you know?" She answered: "Animals are intelligent; this is a scientific assertion. Yesterday I asked him: 'Kitten, is Mussolini good?' He shook his head 'No.' Then I asked: 'Kitten, is Mussolini a scoundrel?' He shook his head 'Yes' twice!" Once a friend found in one of her drawers a package with the following note attached: "Unguini e baffini dei meiei gattini morti" [the claws and whiskers of my little dead cats].

Told in this way, these things seem picturesque and nothing more. In truth, they were the marks of an extraordinary personality, full of restlessness, ardor, and courage, vibrating with intelligence and generosity. She was egalitarian by nature and said that she was a socialist before she had any idea of political realities, because since she was small she had felt a great repugnance for the injustices of society. Perplexed by the poverty of the peasants, sad because they did not have houses like hers, and revolted by distinctions of class, she wanted to give them everything she had. In church, seeing the counts in the high pew in the front, others behind, and the little people in the rear, she asked her father or her grandmother: "But why doesn't everyone sit together?"

The sentiment of equality was visceral in her, and she probably never *felt*, personally, the differences of class among people that she *recognized* and fought against. She treated with the same naturalness the most humble of the poor and the highest class summer vacationers who came to see her out of curiosity or because of the fame of her knitting. She invited poor and rich to sit at her table, at the same time if they arrived together, offering them polenta if it was lunchtime, speaking of Russia, of music, of the news, in a fitting tone. One day someone who came to visit her found herself seated between the wife of the President of the Republic and Uncle Pete, an old, black, and extremely ugly hewer of firewood, who was lunching with her. For Teresina, there was no gulf, not the slightest gap, between the thought and the act. She was intransigent and unyielding, but filled with the inconsistencies of a passionate temperament. She went without transition from rage to tenderness, her eyes flashing or calming, cursing harshly or caressing in a tearful voice; but always crying with laughter at things that were funny. She must always have been this way, as she was to the end of her life; and when she died, at almost ninety, she had kept much of the original style of the girl of the village and the castle.

In a way, she was permanently marked by the village and the castle. Intransigent to the point of incomprehension and severity in matters of morality, she was at the same time refined and very outspoken. She knew the old parlor games, obeyed a sober and natural etiquette in personal relations, felt at home in any setting, sang parts of operas, concertos, quartets, and hymns in a refined and fragile voice, danced the minuet, the quadrille, and the waltz with the precision of a mechanical figure, curtseyed with great grace, cooked, washed, planted, sewed, went to the butcher's, quarreled with the street urchins, and chastised whoever mistreated animals in her presence.

She read indiscriminately, with a voracious hunger for the written word. We have already seen that, in literature, her favorite author was Leopardi, whom she reread constantly. But she liked others—Italian, French, Russian—classics and modern, among them Stendhal, whom she discussed with my mother in frequent conversations. Perhaps because she came from Parma she preferred *The Charterhouse of Parma*, which she reread frequently, saying cheerfully and tolerantly of Fabrício del Dongo, as if he were a living person, that he was a cunning little priest: "Quel prettino è un furbo!" [That little priest is a cunning one]. She had little discernment in painting, only a kind of sensitivity by association. For example: since she enjoyed Giacosa's play *La partita a Scacchi*, she thought a doubtful reproduction representing the final scene, which she had in her living room, beautiful. (Also, Giacosa had shown support for socialism . . .)

The quantity of poetry she knew by heart was incredible. She recited, with an old-fashioned scansion, entire poems by Leopardi, classic quotations from the *Commedia* and the *Vita Nuova*, scenes from Alfieri, pieces of Parini's *Il Giorno*, Foscolo's *I Sepolcri*, sonnets by D'Annunzio, much Carducci, Pascarella, Trilussa. And, further, some unlikely minor poets, and some who were scarcely poets at all, like the eighteenth-century Arcadian poet Luigi Fiacchi, vulgarly known as Clasio, from whom she liked to repeat to children a sententious piece that, if I remember correctly, began like this:

> Colui che nella verde età trascura
> Di lodato saper ornar la mente,
> Quand'è giunta per lui l'età matura
> D'avver perduto un sì gran ben si pente.

> [He who in his tender years neglects
> To ornament his mind with worthy knowledge
> Will regret when he is mature
> To have missed such a great treasure.]

And this does not take into account the parade of socialist and anarchist hymns, such as "Guerra alla guerra" or the "Inno dei lavoratori," with words by Filippo Turati:

> Su fratelli, su compagni,
> Su, venite in fitta schiera,
> Sulla libera bandiera
> Splende il sol dell'avvenir!
>
> [On brothers, on comrades,
> On, in solid ranks,
> On your free flag
> Shines the sun of the future.]

To Be Socialist

More than anything else, however, she was a revolutionary, cut from the same cloth as Louise Michel, Vera Zasulitch, or Rosa Luxemberg, those, that is, who belong to the category of the sainthood of the revolution.

She was not a great militant and did not leave a mark on her times, not even on the modest scale of her comrades in arms in São Paulo in the first years of the century. But she was exceptional in the way she lived her ideas at every instant, feeling and practicing in relation to her fellow man the egalitarian fraternity those ideas presupposed, which permitted her to make of life an attempt to overcome egoism, preconceptions, the taste for domination, the attachment to material goods, and the reverence for the grotesque supports of vanity.

Teresina illustrated in an admirable way what it is to "be socialist"—an apparent paradox, because, in socialism, we generally focus on thought and action, embodied in organizations or producing specifically political actions and works. This leads us to forget that there must also exist the sentiments and ethics of a socialist. She spent the greater part of her life outside party activity, living her last forty years in a small town, almost isolated politically. Perhaps this circumstance stimulated the dense precipitation of a "state of mind," according to which the revolution became an integral conception, illuminating and conditioning the details of acts and the tonality of life. In her way, she was thus a revolutionary, although the most complex one could imagine, combining fraternally the ideologies of denial, from Rousseau to Lenin. Her great strength was the coherence with which she took in all these ideas, without confusion, absorbing two centuries of liberating thought and other modalities that she reinterpreted this way.

She argued against fanaticism with Voltaire's *Mahomet*, for women's emancipation with Mary Wollstonecraft, against misery with Zola, for fraternity with Victor Hugo, against war with the Baroness von Suttner,

for worker's union with Proudhon, against capitalism with Marx, for violence with Bakunin and for cooperation with Kropotkin, against God
with Sébastian Faure, for purity of vocation with Romain Rolland. Like
the parts of a dream, there lived in her simultaneously the "principles of
89," the revolution of 1848, the Commune of Paris, the Martyrs of Chicago, the strikes, the nihilist assaults, and the Russian Revolution.

Nourished more by Proudhon, Réclus, and Kropotkin than by Marx,
she was nevertheless sensitive to the diverse arguments of Marxism;
brought up in the messianic and libertarian tradition of the Italians,
which came from Mazzini, the radical positivists, and the workers'
leagues—I believe she could be described as a kind of anarcho-socialist,
for whom ardent aspirations for the total liberation of man through economic equality and the miracles of knowledge were a livelier force than
the desire for theoretical systematization.

Perhaps she could be described, to a degree, by the characterization
made by Turati of the pioneer socialist Osvaldo Gnocchi-Viani, who

> was almost free of material necessities, alien to all mean personal vanity,
> profoundly and constitutionally optimistic, as frank as a child. . . . He had
> rejected Mazzini's religious philosophy . . . and his dominating patriotic
> preoccupations. But from Mazzinian thought he kept intact the idealistic,
> mystical, and sentimental essence, by means of which the social question,
> instead of being a peculiarly economic and historic fact, is the combination
> of all the idealistic questions that interest humanity; it is the result of
> human thought that develops slowly, and admits the existence of a cosmic
> question . . . an educational, as well as a familial and artistic, question, etc.;
> and also, among other things, an economic question and a workers' ques-
> tion, involving the relations between capital and labor; but all at the same
> level, all, we could say, linked to each other horizontally, rather than genet-
> ically. . . . As a result, the fact of economic materialism, the soul and foun-
> dation of Marxist thought, seemed to him one theory among many, a par-
> tial truth among the many truths from which the socialist cloth is woven;
> and not the key to the evolution of society.[6]

Teresina thought the anarchists were the most coherent and advanced theoretically, but doubted the viability of their ideas and judged
them too credulous, easy victims of infiltrating provocateurs. One thing,
however, distinguished her, beginning in 1917, from the anarchists and
the reformists: a constant enthusiasm for Soviet Russia, corresponding
to her great confidence in its historic role as redeemer of the world proletariat. In this respect, she liked to gloss a sentence (I don't know where
she unearthed it): "Napoleone diceva che nel secolo vinte l'Europa
sarebbe tutta russa o tutta rossa; io credo che sará russa e rossa" [Napo-
leon said that in the twentieth century Europe would be all Russian or

all red; I believe that it will be Russian *and* red]. And since she never became aware of the horrors of Stalinism, she always kept the Soviet regime in a favorable position in her ideological structure—perhaps because she had a great capacity for dreaming of the realization of ideals, as she once wrote in her notebook:

> The errors of others must indicate a better road for us to follow and . . . to dream of . . . We live better dreaming! Dreams and ideas make our life happy and prolong it, because they keep us strong and hopeful for a better future. Among them some will be unrealizable . . . utopian . . . But what does that matter? The History of Humanity says that the cult of the ideal and of the chimera is the elixir of a long life, the philosopher's stone, by virtue of which a people does not die. After us, others will see our dream realized. We will have the merit of having contributed to this realization. (January, 1935)

"Écrasons l'Infâme"

One of the ingredients that provided the mortar for this ideological structure was certainly anticlericalism. Today, with the transformation of the Church, it has become difficult to imagine what this once was and above all to evaluate its constructive force. Anticlericalism came to be considered a kind of half-comic subphilosophy of "freethinkers," of "lovers of progress with order," of rebels against nothing. But if it was that, it was also the first large movement that unmasked what the Church itself tries to overcome today: the exploitation of credulity, the reactionary pact with the dominant classes, and the neglect of justice in Christianity.

The anticlericals of the beginning of the century represented, on the one hand, a petit bourgeois movement of criticism but, on the other, brought working-class interests and demands together in many lively ways, forming a kind of international fraternity between republican, Freemason, and socialist, with a mixture here and there of the greater virulence of the anarchists. And many consecrated themselves to a true crusade, such as the campaign of lectures by Everardo Dias in the interior of Brazil, collected in the book *Delenda Roma* (1921). An example of the non-revolutionary type is the pamphlet *Os chacais* (The Jackals), by Júlio Perneta, published in Curitiba (1898).

For some, anticlericalism was combined with a strange lay religiosity, full of reverence for a Jesus interpreted as a revolutionary and Christianity itself seen as a perverted egalitarianism. But Teresina was one of those who manifested a total and disrespectful irreligiosity, based on the conviction that religion was a premeditated fraud designed to divert the heedless from the truth, which brought her to the point of denying that a priest could be honest. For her own use, she had created a slogan: "The true religion is: to have none."

With respect to these matters, there is a letter from her eldest brother, General Camilo Carini, to the other brother, Gino, the agronomist who came from Italy for a time, at the invitation of Francisco Escobar, to organize a breeding station in Poços, where he lived for some two years, from 1912 to 1914, if I am not mistaken. Gino must have commented in his letter about their sister's lack of knowledge of these matters and her antireligious invectives, since Camilo replied:

I would like Teresina, with respect to the absurdities contained in your last letter (absurdities in the moral sense), to tell me who assures her that Jesus Christ could not make a table, even though he was the son of a carpenter. But will these arguments be elevated enough, sufficient, for one of her high intellect, to combat theories so much debated by eminent theologians and philosophers? You see, Gino, while God may not always be at our disposition for everything we ask him for, observe nevertheless, and be honest in thinking about this, that he has not been so deaf to your prayers and has often helped you. . . . But Teresina has lived for so many years in an atmosphere that is skeptical, positivist, pessimistic even, having contact with people for whom everything is licit, though she herself has not lowered her standards, keeping herself clean and uncorrupted. So, for her, if it is not natural, this necessity of reaction is at least excusable. She knows only the dark side of the world and has only a vague memory of beauty and sweetness, which nevertheless she must have experienced initially in the bosom of the family; so she does not know how to humble herself to accept that God wishes her well, even though he has given her so much sorrow; and, though cultured and studious, she thinks that human existence is a simple excursion on earth. Oh, she has certainly read all the great materialist and positivist philosophers, from Spencer to Ardigò, and all the pagan and skeptical poets, from Leopardi to D'Annunzio and Arturo Graff, etc., etc.; but why doesn't she read the equally numerous philosophers and poets and the great thoughts on the other side? No, she has a preconceived idea, she doesn't want to let herself be persuaded, she has prejudices and doesn't understand, talking theoretically with that crowd of anarchist fellow travelers, that what she herself practices is, on the contrary, real virtue. But to what end? With what stimulus? . . . Ah! the conscience! . . . Here is that great word, empty and abstract, which, if it is not equivalent to that divine part that is within us, clearly differentiates us from the other animals (badly designated thus), because while we have *Soul*, they have only the vital spirit; man is endowed with progress, the other animals, no; while man knows he has a beginning and must die, the other beasts, no; while man has a thirst for light and tries to strip away the veils that surround the numerous mysteries that govern us, they only live in the present, having no need for anything else.

The letter is from 1912 and must have aroused in Teresina the steadfast will to controversy, but it seems that it went without reply, as is seen from the following note: "I still haven't answered. January 4, 1916." The general was educated and wrote poetry, and the most curious thing is that he was antimilitarist, saying that of his decorations he only esteemed the one he had received for humanitarian dedication in saving victims of the earthquake in Messina in 1908.

The letter shows, on the one hand, the primary tenor of the anticlerical arguments that Teresina made—such as the incompetence of the carpenter's son . . . On the other hand, it demonstrates the empty rhetoric of the conventional religious believers.

Teresina did indeed admire the humanistic radicalism of Roberto Ardigò, the principal Italian positivist, who influenced the theoretical orientation of socialism in his country. She always had an unsatisfied curiosity about him: the philosopher had been a priest and, so it was said, lost his faith contemplating a flower: "How could that have been? Why?" she wondered. She used to say that Ardigò wore a kind of priestly black and killed himself dramatically, at the age of ninety-two, in 1920, because he was tired of living.

Militancy and Fascism

While she was living in São Paulo she fought in political movements, but in Poços de Caldas there was little to do besides giving voice to her feelings in letters and conversations with her friends, reading incessantly, taking notes and practicing a kind of spontaneous proselytism (an expansion of her burning sincerity), in some measure picturesquely, as when, in 1919, she "baptized" the child of a coreligionist with a glass of wine; she gave him the seditious name of Spartacus. But when there was an opportunity, she acted as she always had.

Poços, a resort town, always had many hotels and, therefore, many waiters, among them socialists and anarcho-syndicalists who tried to organize political actions with other workers. Such was the case of the International Workers League (Liga Operária Internacional) founded in 1914, perhaps the first local organization of that type, perhaps inspired, who knows, by the Socialist International Center founded in São Paulo in 1902; when it was reorganized in 1914, its secretary was Fosco Pardini, proofreader for *Fanfulla*, which soon afterward moved to Poços. Then, on November 11, 1915, the League decided to honor the memory of the workers executed in Chicago in 1886, in a session to which Teresina was invited to contribute an address. Not being able to go, she sent a message revelatory of her socialism, simultaneously sentimental and pugnacious:

Honorable President of the International Workers League.
Poços:

Prevented by reasons of health from speaking at the commemoration of the Chicago Martyrs, which the Workers League has organized, I send my support, with the hope that, as much as possible, it may be worthy of the date which is commemorated today.

I am not a worker, and, even if I were, I could not belong to the League since, disgracefully, women are excluded from it; but I always was and still am sympathetic to the workers' movement, as long as it represents, as in the present case, the beginning of a civilized fight the workers carry on throughout the world for the right to existence.

I am delighted that this small city has begun to feel the necessity of a workers' organization, and I hope that it can grow and attain the ends for which it was founded.

In order to achieve that, it is necessary for every individual to understand the common goal of the organization and put aside their private interests. The example of the Martyrs we commemorate today is valuable, because they gave their lives in a holocaust in order to make their idea of social justice understandable, and they died happy, knowing that they were understood, certain that their death left an indelible memory in the hearts of the people of the entire world.

After them, thousands of others died for the same cause, a much greater one than that for which millions of proletarians die in Europe today, that is, to change the map![7]

Here, however, we don't deal with dying, but with eating and living better!

Oh, you people in misery, in rags, despised [illegible] inert, sad, starving, searching for work and not finding it and, if it is found, badly paid. These people make everything, produce everything, and yet partake of nothing, and have neither bread nor a roof!

The rich and happy pass through the streets in their splendid carriages and spend their money, unstained with sweat, on endless luxuries and pleasures. Why this disequilibrium? And who is to blame?

It is the people themselves. The obscure and nevertheless necessary mass of workers [illegible] their bodies engaged in work beyond their strength and still they cannot support their families. They are unconscious!

Those who produce everything are still prejudiced against each other, because they do not know that if they were in accord they would be better off. They do not know that the strength of organization will be the powerful lever that will lead them to the level of those who now keep them in submission.

May the workers' organization of Poços de Caldas be able to grow, develop itself, be the beginning of a great future League of Workers' Education, to obtain the legitimate ends it seeks.

Long live the working people. Long live the International Workers' League.

The affective rhetoric of this message shows the tenor of Teresina's socialism, which embraced a confidence in the power of instruction and the sense of fraternity as the "promotion" of the individual, thus defining a position of the humanitarian type, but at the same time containing the conviction that the key is in organized and unceasing struggle.

The message also shows the importance Teresina attached, for the advent of socialism, to sacrifices like those of the workers of Chicago. In this fiery intransigence lay an almost mystical conviction, as was evident in a comment she made almost twenty years later on this quotation from Balzac: "Of all the seeds scattered on the ground, the blood shed by martyrs gives the most certain crop."

And Teresina:

That is how it is and that is how it must be! I want this for my Country and for all the countries of the world, where there were and are martyrs who suffered and suffer, who died and still die in the middle of the 20th century, victims of tyrants.

At the stroke of midnight, December 31, 1935.

The message to the League further shows one of her most profound sentiments: the horror of war, which was being set loose in Europe, where it was going to cause the death of a son of her brother Camilo, Lieutenant Anacleto Carini, a healthy young man of good figure who was an officer in an elite corps and fell leading his men in a cavalry charge. Teresina never saw her nephews, but she enjoyed them very much through the correspondence they always exchanged with her, sending photographs and details of family events. This, despite feeling herself tragically isolated as the only socialist in a conservative family.

After the war there arose, as a new fact, fascism, which in the beginning bewildered many people on the left. One old Italian communist of Poços, who had been a militant socialist from his youth, said that for some time he and others thought that it was a simply a different type of radical socialism. I don't know what Teresina's reaction at that time was; when I met her in 1931 she was so violently antifascist that it never occurred to me that there could ever have been any doubt about it. Of her

5. Teresina in 1932.

brothers, the general did not join and soon retired; but the other
brother, Gino, became an enthusiastic fascist. In a letter, valuable as an
historical document, sent from his beautiful house in Salsomaggiore on
October 24, 1922, he narrated some events that were revealing about
early fascism, which though it had still not completely revealed its entire
body, had already made its truculent profile clear. It can be supposed
that a report like this helped Teresina, who reacted strongly, to appraise
its true nature:

> I don't know how the fascist movement is interpreted abroad. Just to be
> clear, I am also alderman of the district of Salso, an office that gives me a lot
> to do. From now on, bolshevism is defeated and there is no longer great
> danger, but it was an epoch in which, to be a fascist, you had to have guts,
> something I never lacked. The communists never confronted a fascist face
> to face; not even three to one, but only when there were a hundred of

them. At that time, if an isolated fascist passed they massacred him barbarously, going so far as to burn fascists alive or boil them in vats of liquid steel. Of ambushes at that time, it is better not to speak. Every thicket was a danger. It got to the point where the fascists spread groups of vigilantes who flushed out every hiding place with revolver shots. The newspapers did not tell how things were. Every party shaped the news to its own benefit and hid the corruption, which existed everywhere. When it arose, Fascism itself had to use malefactors who took the opportunity to steal, to commit illegal acts; but now the novorra[8] has been eliminated and there exist in Italy a million blackshirts. If you could see with what discipline they march and obey their leaders! The national army itself is not as well disciplined; furthermore, it is composed of elements[9] that are courageous and ready for anything, to the point of imposing themselves on the government. When these young men appear in the newsreels, then you will see and have a faint idea. *Whether people want it or not, the fascists will save Italy from bolshevism and from hunger.* Now we will see what is going to happen when they are in the government.[10] There is a certain antagonism between Mussolini and D'Annunzio, because of ambitions, but since they are two intelligent men, let us hope that they will arrive at an accord.

He then told of an elderly widowed relative, F., who got involved in a curious business, half a police matter, half political:

He has on his property a small harem that eats up everything he owns. An old man of 63 who keeps six young women with him, can you imagine . . . It's a scandal and it's ridiculous. In the past month, because he hates a young man who is courting one of his servants, do you know what he did? He sent for two bad guys who belonged to the *fascio*, armed them with rifles and set them on the boy's family, whom they attacked by night in their own house, on the pretext that they were Catholics, and against the *fascio*. . . . In fact, the boy is Catholic, and he is a fighter, so he confronted the two pseudofascists and shot one of them, wounding him in the left arm. Then the two heros, and F. as well (who had supposed the family unarmed), seeing that, on the contrary, the family had made their shots count, fled and took refuge in F.'s house. The wounded man was taken to the hospital and is going to leave his arm there. F. lost his two rifles, worth 1900 lire; he will have to pay the fascist's hospital bills and will be tried as the instigator of the crime. For political reasons, the priests paid the lawyers for the boy who defended himself in his own house.

This episode, and the opinions of the old bourgeois calmed by the *order* brought by the black shirts, reflected with zest the confused and perturbed moment from which fascism emerged, with areas of simple banditry and an intense brainwashing.

I imagine that fascism served, for Teresina, the function of unifying the field, that is, it weakened her sense of the antagonisms between various left tendencies, which she ultimately saw as a bloc, opposed to what seemed to her the incarnation of absolute evil. Further, as time went on, to the degree that age had isolated her politically in a small town, as a defense she combined these diverse, even contradictory, tendencies, still without losing the revolutionary note that was always her way of seeing and being. Though sufficiently lucid and knowledgeable to make distinctions and analyze their respective political lines, for her anarchism, communism, socialism, anticlericalism increasingly seemed branches from the same trunk, at bottom reconcilable. She divided the world into good and bad; into friends of progress, art, science—and reactionaries, clericals, the stupid. And these, finally, were embodied for her in fascism, which was long her bogeyman; in Mussolini, and then in Hitler, agents of Evil.

In a city filled with Italians and the children of Italians, who were generally in sympathy with the regime in their mother country, she was enduring, pertinacious, inflexible, and passionately antifascist, speaking out violently against the local *Fascio* (Società Stela d'Italia—Mutuo Soccorso e Depolavoro), against the sympathy for Mussolini of the bourgeoisie and the authorities, who liked to praise the advantages of "a strong government." She spoke, she scolded, she wrote, she argued for more than twenty years, until the day when the hated regime fell in its own country and, finally, she saw the horrible photographs of the Duce hanging by his feet. Delirious with joy, she celebrated with an irrational quantity of cheap wine, which she also gave to her cat. But she was old, and she never purged herself of her antifascist bitterness and the poignancy of her horror of war—as can be seen in a letter she wrote me on June 6, 1945:

> Yesterday I went out and learned some news about Poços. The first thing is that there have been some strikes, which have been successful; one in the Britador, another for the laundresses of several hotels and, it seems, also in the Quisisana! The other news is that the old headquarters of the Italian Society (excuse the expression) had a meeting of the Communist Party, and it seems that there were almost a *thousand* people there. And to think that those walls had been *drenched* with fascism! How times change. I will keep you fully informed.

Two or three years before she died she declined a little. Always lucid, she lost some of her attentiveness and her eager curiosity, disillusioned and perhaps confused by events that seemed to her, still dreaming of the optimistic models of her own nineteenth century, difficult to understand and likely to delay the coming of the social millennium. One New Year's Eve at the height of the Cold War she wrote in her notebook:

6. Around 1934 or 1935; at the airfield of Poços de Caldas, Teresina with a young friend.

7. A section of Poços de Caldas, around 1940. The headquarters of the Italian Society was, at the time, in the large white building at the upper right, whose walls, according to Teresina, were "soaked in fascism." The small house fourth from the corner on the near side of the street leading diagonally across the picture down and to the left of the Society's building, next to the white two-story building, is Teresina's.

8. Teresina in 1948.

Midnight, 1946–47!

Another year! How will it be? and what fault will the date have, if Humanity has the unique responsibility for all the bad that occurs? I am very sad at this year end, and without hope for anything better.

Or, in a bitter letter of of June 14, 1948: "I am at the end of my time on earth, during which I collected only *fiascos*. It will be better for others, won't it?"

Nevertheless, she was more or less in good shape, as she had said at the beginning of 1947 (when she was going to be eighty-four), after telling of several serious ailments: "but, seeing that my body has so far resisted such provocations, I hope to emerge victorious over this one as well, since till now I have kept my good appetite, good sleep without nightmares, and a strength of mind and memory that is truly exceptional." (In the same letter she sent congratulations to her anarchist friend Edgard Leuenroth and said that she was reading Cicero with much pleasure.) Beyond this, she never lost her strength of feeling or failed to retain her convictions (or "convintions," as she said) nor her interest in politics, as can be seen in the already cited letter of June 14, 1948, written (unusually for her) in Portuguese, or in the mixed language she used at times (the newspaper mentioned is the *Folha Socialista*, of which I was one of the editors):

I haven't received any copies of your newspaper; can it be that it doesn't come out any more? It's a pity that everything the workers need takes so much work. I still don't know what the result of the railroad workers' strike was, but I know that they arrested many and beat them in the prisons, and afterwards they speak badly of the communists! Ah! what an unjust world it is. When are you coming here? Send news of the movement and I hope that the newspaper comes out. . . . [In Italian] Pardon me for my terrible handwriting. I embrace you affectionately and hope for the realization of *our* ideals. [At the beginning of the letter she had mentioned the Brazilian Socialist Party as "our party."]

At the end of 1948, alluding to her old antireligious slogan, cited earlier, she commented in her notebook: "It is with this opinion and conviction that I record the date of passage of the year 1948–49, at exactly midnight. And I nourish the hope that it may be the last of my already very long life, whose only satisfaction was always to have thought in my own way and never to have believed in any superior being."

And on December 31, 1949:

Old, alone, sick, and poor, I put one more year behind me, without knowing if it will be, finally, the last of my life! With me will die all the dreams of a better society, of a better humanity. Scientific discoveries change, in a short time, all humanitarian ideals; and the atomic bomb becomes the preferred argument of every chief of state and the reciprocal bogeyman of the Nations. We hope that it will be, on the other hand, the reason not to cause wars . . . That is my hope. With much sadness I leave here my thoughts at half past midnight.

These stocktakings, which she did punctually at the end of each year, but also at other times (because she was always writing and annotating), were, as we have seen, very bitter, showing that these final encounters with herself only served to reveal all her frustration. But much earlier, in February of 1935, with respect to some reflections about the stages of life (of which she read in a book about the captivity of Napoleon III in Germany) she had already commented in her notebook:

Many stages were lacking in my life: childhood without a mother, tormented by relatives; another stage, youth, relying only on myself, responsible for a house and a family; another, sorrowful, the trip to the hospital with my father, leaving the house where I was born, never to return again! Another stage, a short stop, at my uncle's house, to cry and wait . . . Another: marriage, the total change of home, of city, of life . . . disillusions, disaster . . . and afterward: America. Another long stage of work, of pains, of tragedies . . . And, finally, I hope the last will be this one of twenty years in Poços de Caldas.

To understand the normal rhythm of her life, made up of equally strong emotional highs and lows, it is necessary to compare this distressed recapitulation with a euphoric note about the dream that exalts and saves, written only a month later (described earlier, in the section "Being a Socialist").

Finally, she died—on August 12, 1951, fifteen days before her eighty-eighth birthday, impatient, complaining irritatedly, imagining conspiracies by the nursing sisters that seemed obvious to her. To put it more strongly—she died fighting, because she was always a fighter. It is true that she fought on a narrow field, to which destiny had confined her. But, still, a fighter from head to toe. For that reason, a verse by Leopardi is engraved on her tombstone:

> Erta la fronte . . .
> E renitente al fato.

> [With head held high . . .
> and resisting fate.]

THE OTHERS

Visitors

Teresina had a gift for friendship, and from it she drew comfort for a life that was always hard. Extremely sociable, despite being suspicious and precipitate in her judgments, she visited and received others with pleasure, had dedicated men and women friends, whose beliefs she did not dispute on the condition that they not speak of fascism, because for that she would ban them from her house. At the end of her life, her good angel was the excellent Santina Lari, a native of Montacatini, a great virtuoso of crocheting, who gave her daily care that was loving, selfless, and happy. My mother, when she lived in Poços and when she visited there, went to see her every day after lunch, and was there at her side during her last illness; Teresina dined at our house on Thursdays, prolonging the evening until midnight. Of her other friends, I am going to mention some who I met when they came to visit her, and who had in common that they were antifascists with a political past.

During the time I knew her, that is, in her last twenty years, from 1931 to 1951, among the visitors was the vehement Adelino Tavares de Pinho, "the Professor," who had a little school in Poços for many years and who was active in workers' schools and in strikes at the beginning of the century, particularly in Campinas, where he took part in the great strike of the workers of the Companhia Paulista (Railroad Company of São Paulo), in 1906. He was Portuguese, from the north, short, stout, and explosive, had been a streetcar motorman in his youth, and was self-taught, eventually publishing several small books and writing frequently for libertarian papers.[11] A great reader of Buckle and Spencer, in addition to the classics of anarchism, he adopted an evolutionist formula mixed with a theory of "mutual support," and thought that the X in the social question was moral, and not the class struggle. He hated Stalin ("That monster with the mustache dripping with blood"), generally disliking the Communists. For this reason he lamented that "a young man as intelligent" as Astrogildo Pereira (who once criticized him in an article) had joined their side. According to the Professor, Astrogildo should have restricted himself to literature, which was his forte.

An occasional visitor, endowed with a charm and a cordiality that did not immediately reveal his combative spirit, was Edgard Leuenroth, then middle-aged, but whom she continued to describe as "a very good young man, a pure soul," Teresina said.

Piccarolo also appeared, when he occasionally came to take the waters with his family. "L'amiciza è il vincolo piú puro che puó unire due esseri umani" [Friendship is the purest link that can unite human beings], he wrote in her visitors' book on January 14, 1941. Years later, she asked me in a letter: "Do you know anything about Piccarolo? Go dig him up at home and tell him to write to me."

A welcome conversationalist, despite being a fervent Catholic, was Dr. Badalassi, "Lawyer Badalassi," who went to Poços, the land of his wife, since the climate of Italy was inhospitable for a discreet, but convinced, antifascist like him. He had been the secretary of Don Luigi Sturzo and active in the Popular Party. The war had affected his life profoundly and contributed to a hemorrhage that left him half paralyzed, as Teresina told me in a letter dated July 6, 1945: "I went to visit Mr. Badalassi: I think he is much better and in better shape than before his attack; he is in full possession of his mental faculties and remembers everything that has happened in the world . . . The cause of his paralysis was, in good part, the tragedies of war in general and in particular those concerning his birthplace, Florence, as well as the present condition of his family there."

Parallel Culture

Many of her friendships went back to the time she lived in São Paulo—the hope-filled germinating moment of socialism, as the years between the end of the century and the First World War were in Brazil. Someone should study thoroughly the militant Italian groups active at that time—socialists, anarchists, and syndicalists. It was a time filled with the founding of leagues, newspapers, and movements of women's emancipation.

Some visiting foreigners contributed a little to this process, visitors who, though invited officially or semiofficially and highly esteemed by the bourgeoisie, were also reformist socialists, thus giving some prestige to the local Left.

Such was the case of Enrico Ferri, who came in 1908, "when he was Ferri," Teresina said, alluding to his later joining the Fascists; or of Guglielmo Ferrero (of much greater integrity), who came in 1907 and whose book *Grandezza e decadenza di Roma*, was then at the height of its success. His wife Gina, daughter of Lombroso, also gave lectures here, and her feminism (much admired by Teresina, a great reader of her books) was a stimulus for women who wanted to be active in reform and in the movement of ideas.

All this contributed to a kind of culture that was, to some extent, at the margin of the dominant culture. In the socialist and anarchist world it manifested itself in picnics, concerts, lectures, song recitals, poetry readings, collaboration in small papers, and the exchange of books. It was a time in which socialism and, above all, anarchism presupposed a strong belief in the revolutionary capacity (transforming and humanizing) of knowledge and art. With respect to literature, this took place in the sense of what one could call a culture of content, entirely turned toward the explicit message of works of art, without any specific preoccupation with whether the form, even the most academic, was modern or not. It is the problem of the mixture of an advanced political goal with a backward taste, frequent in the leftist cultural universe, because the touchstones were the attack on the bourgeoisie, the description of working-class life, humanitarian sentiments, antireligious positions, solidarity with the poor, and so on—so that ideological relevance was taken as aesthetically sufficient.

It is important to remember that in a city such as São Paulo, bubbling with immigrants, with the majority of the labor force composed of foreigners, Spanish and Italian were the languages of popular struggle, while French (important among the bourgeoisie as a criterion of social distinction) was used less, and then only in reading. The activities I mentioned above were organized for the most part in Italian, by means of newspapers, some codirected by Brazilians who had become quite bilingual. It is sufficient to read the lists of recommended books in the socialist and anarchist publications to verify how the presence of militant foreigners showed itself in the scant bibliography in Portuguese, which made reading in other languages imperative.

In the documents of the time, anarchists and socialists, while fighting for a reduction in the hours of work, always mentioned the vital necessity of some minimum amount of time for the worker to be able to read, and some means of access to a more dignified human condition. This can be seen in a quotation from, among many others, the touching manifesto of the garment workers, transcribed by Edgard Carone:

> And we also want our hours of rest so that we can dedicate some time to reading, to study, because we have little education; and if this situation continues, we will always be, by our lack of consciousness, simple human machines manipulated at will by the greediest assassins and thieves.
>
> How can anyone read a book who goes to work at seven in the morning and returns home at eleven at night? Of the 24 hours we only have eight for rest, which is not enough to recover one's exhausted strength in sleep. We have no horizons or, rather, we have an horizon without light: we are born to be exploited and to die in ignorance like brutes.[12]

Obligatory readings were Victor Hugo's *Les miserables*, the Zola of *Germinal* and *The Four Gospels* (which in the end were only three). But also the brothers Réclus, Augustin Hamon, Sébastien Faure, Jean Grave, his wife Séverine, Errico Malatesta, Russians like Tolstoy and Gorky, the political novels of Blasco Ibañez, "our comrade Edmondo de Amicis" (in the words of *Avanti!* of São Paulo), and even the humanitarian fiction of the Portuguese João Grave.

There was a predilection for moralistic and sententious poetry, from which one could extract "thoughts" to transcribe in albums and cite in speeches. These socialists and anarchists liked political poets, old and new, beginning with Giuseppe Giusti and his satirical diatribes against the petty Italian tyrants protected by Austria:

> Vostra Eccellenza, che mi sta in cagnesco
> Per que'pochi scherzucci di dozzina.

They admired the enthusiastic radical republican Felice Cavalotti, his parliamentary and journalistic outbursts, his tough character, and his duels, in one of which he was killed. They recited his bad poems and read with immense pleasure his anticlerical comedy *Cantico dei cantici*, of which there were little cheap editions, and which was presented by amateurs, but also by professionals, as in a show which took place at the League for Democracy in São Paulo on August 1, 1914, the day Germany declared war on Russia, initiating the great conflagration. They adored the theatrical Mario Rapisardi, a kind of Italian Guerra Junqueiro of great activity and great ambitions; and also Guerra Junqueiro himself, from the sharp anticlericalism of his *The Old Age of Father Eternal* to the sweet-as-honey populism of *The Simpletons*. They liked the satirical and anticlerical aspects of the work of Eça de Queirós, as well as the political pronouncements and the *Modern Odes* of Antero de Quental. Ada Negri enchanted them with her social poetry and by the fact that she was, unusual for a writer, of working-class origins. And they shared with the Parnassian bourgeoisie an admiration for Lorenzo Stecchetti, who was translated and recited all over Brazil.

Teresina's friends played an important part in the political struggles and cultural currents of the time, as a kind of informal Brazilian wing of the Italian Socialist Party; and she with them.

Bertolloti and *Avanti!*

The engineer Alcibiade Bertolotti, born in Parma in 1862, and acquainted with her family, came to Brazil in 1890, the same year Teresina did, but as a political fugitive. By 1891 he was already editing the newspaper *Messaggero* in São Paulo. In 1894 he started the Italian Bookstore, which existed for a long time, and in 1900 he was among the founders of the already mentioned League for Democracy or *Italian Democratic League*, organized by republicans, socialists and anarchists in order to stimulate the workers' movement in opposition to the conservative organizations of the community. It operated in the Largo da Memória and became an active center in the promotion of festivities, shows, recitals, lectures, and instruction. Also born in 1900, and with its editorial office in the same place, was the first socialist paper of São Paulo in Italian, *Avanti!* with the same title as the daily of the Socialist Party in Italy, which had been publishing since 1896. It was a lively weekly, preoccupied with education but also with recruitment. It later merged with the International Socialist Center, which also had its offices in the League's headquarters and was the name under which the PSB [Brazilian Socialist Party], founded by Brazilians and above all by the Italians of *Avanti!* was organized.[13] The party soon disbanded, but the journal lasted for a long time. One of its objectives was to defend and organize the Italian farmworkers against the landowners, emphasizing this in the papers of the interior of the state [of São Paulo], where the Center had at one time more than twenty active nuclei. Some were in fact of appreciable size, such as the one in Ribeirão Preto and São José do Rio Pardo. In that city, the journalist Pascoal Artese, with whom Euclides da Cunha worked and shared some activities, carried on the struggle.

Bertolotti was one of the founders and principal editors of *Avanti!* writing serious articles under the initials *ab*. He was a moderate, but active, reformist, firm in his ideas and actions, to the point of fighting a duel with the journalist Umberto Falcinelli. In the initial article October 20, 1900 he said that the paper's purpose was to fight for "reforms of the social character," but, he added, those "compatible with the laws and the present organization of society." He gave frequent lectures in the capital and in the interior of São Paulo, one of them dealing with Karl Marx, whose portrait *Avanti!* offered as a premium to subscribers. (Note that there was an entrance fee for the lectures of militants and sympathizers, which was a way of obtaining funds.)

I believe that the paper ceased publication sometime after 1908, the year in which its then director, Vincenzo Vacirca, who ended up in Italy as a Fascist legislator, was imprisoned and expelled from the country. But it had a second phase in 1914 and 1915 (it would have a third and final one in 1919), with a contentious staff directed by Theodoro Monicelli (who came to Brazil in 1911), and, as well, the support of Bertolotti, the tenacious survivor of the initial group.

Bertolotti never stopped working in the engineering profession after his arrival in Brazil, retiring in the 1930s from his position as engineer of the Prefecture of São Paulo. And he maintained a firm antifascist position until his death, which occurred in 1957.

In the 1940s, when he was more than eighty, I had some contact with him and spoke with him about Teresina. He became animated, evoked their common past, and then specified that he was always in the reformist wing, led in Italy by Leonida Bissolati, commenting: "Ma, la Teresina, oh! la Teresina è sempre stata rivoluzionaria" [But, Teresina, oh! Teresina is always in a revolutionary state]. She said to me, about him, in a letter of August 2, 1946: "When you see Bertolotti again, greet him for me. I don't know why he doesn't write me any more; but the reform socialists don't look well on those who are a little revolutionary, like me. Be that as it may, we are old, I think that he is a year older than I am, and soon we will meet in hell, where we can talk about it."[14]

Piccarolo, *moderato assai*

Of a similar political tendency, but much less determined in his militancy, was Antonio Piccarolo, a Piedmontese from Alexandria, born in 1868, who came to Brazil in 1904.

Like Bertolotti, he adopted the theoretical positions of Marxism, but with a strong evolutionary flavor, of the kind favored in some of Engels's writings, as occurred among the reformists. Unlike the the anarchists and revolutionary syndicalists (who then predominated in the Left in São Paulo), he thought that socialism was not possible in Brazil in the short term, nor was it ready for struggle in the classic mold, because the necessary social conditions, that is, a bourgeoisie and an industrial proletariat, were not present (a point of view that coincided with that of Sílvio Romero, and with the ideas expounded by Ferri in his lectures in Brazil). "Natura non facit saltum" [Nature does not move by leaps], he judged. But he understood that this did not make it less urgent to fight for so-

9. Antonio Piccarolo in Poços de Caldas (1941).

cialism—at the level of the defense and organization of workers, above all rural workers, in the development of cooperatives, of teaching, and of diverse kinds of assistance. Even more, he had the merit of criticizing the imitative mentality developed by the Europeans transplanted to Brazil, calling attention to the necessity for solutions adequate to the conditions of a country based on plantation agriculture. As Edgard Carone said about one of his writings, "In contrast to the earlier documents and most of the later ones, this is one of the few that does not imitate the style and the content of the European manifestos, but tries to apply the communist philosophy to the Brazilian reality."[15]

This sense of local peculiarities differentiates him from his coreligionists and perhaps contributed to the conflicts he had with them. In fact, having been director of *Avanti!* since his arrival in 1904 until November of 1905, he quit, alleging that a comrade had acted improperly. But I don't think it impossible that the origin of this incompatibility might have been his different and more realistic vision and, who knows, perhaps his accentuated moderation as well. With a base in this vision and moderation, he founded the Paulist [that is, of São Paulo] Socialist Center, and because of them he meshed well with the Italian and Brazilian bourgeoisie of São Paulo. Perhaps these things, or envy of someone like him, whose intellectual capacity was so elevated, were what provoked an incredibly violent attack by Theodoro Monicelli in *Avanti!* (second phase), in various issues of 1915, leading the attacked to resort to judicial remedies.

Piccarolo became a socialist, above all doctrinal, for the rest of his life as a respected professor, journalist, and writer in the intellectual world of São Paulo. A friend of Freitas Valle (the symbolist poet Jacques D'Avray, his colleague on the teaching staff of of the Ginásio of the state), he frequented the literary and artistic salon of Vila Kyrial devotedly and gave various talks there. An indication of his prestige is his participation in the lecture series of the Society for Artistic Culture, which was, in the first and second decades of this century one of the principal cultural centers of the city.[16] His cordial relations with the bourgeoisie are exemplified in the fact of his having dedicated to the then president of the state, Washington Luis, the libretto of the opera based on Machado de Assis's novel *Dom Casmurro*, the music composed by João Gomes de Araújo (1922). Let us recall that he also translated the novel into Italian.

One of Piccarolo's cherished ideas was the founding of a school of humanities on the college level, conceived both as a center of research and for the training of teachers. He fought for and made attempts to accomplish this from before the First World War until, in 1931, he succeeded in getting started the Paulist Faculty of Letters and Philosophy, of which he was Secretary-General and whose director and vice-director, respectively, were Alcântara Machado and Ricardo Severo. The faculty was made up of the finest of the liberal *intelligentzia* of São Paulo, Piccarolo himself being charged with Latin Language and Literature, in addition to Comparative Literature (which was never actually taught). A private institution with some official support, it was then situated on the ground floor of the Cactano de Campos Institute of Education.[17] In a way, it was the precursor of the Faculty of Philosophy, Science, and Letters founded by the University of São Paulo in 1934. Piccarolo's school closed that year, and he later taught Latin Language and Literature in the new institution. In 1933, when the Free School of Sociology and Politics (Escola Livre de Sociologia e Política) was founded, he joined the teaching staff and arranged this motto for his coat of arms: *Scientia Robur Meus.*

He never, in the midst of all his activities, gave up his convictions, and during the thirties he seems to have had a renewal of hope, in the burst of radicalism that for a time followed the October Revolution. Examining industrial progress and the growth of small property ownership, he thought that conditions had begun to mature, at least in the Central South and the South. He began to speak again of the necessity of socialist preaching and action, following the perspective defined above; and his reformism did not keep him from analyzing, in a critical but comprehensive spirit, the political evolution of the Soviet Union.[18] Because of all this, from the twenties on, he was the constant target of the strong and aggressive Italian-language fascist press in São Paulo. After 1945 he joined, sentimentally, the Brazilian Socialist Party, to which he left his library. And he committed suicide in 1957, at the age of eighty-nine.

Rossoni: Hero (and Villain) of Two Worlds

Quite different from this half-patriarchal figure, more or less adjusted to the intellectual liberalism of the Paulist bourgeoisie, were the radical friends with whose ideas Teresina was much more in tune. They were among those who formed a kind of extreme wing of the Italian Socialist Party, which many of them had quit, especially after 1904, in order to characterize themselves clearly as revolutionary syndicalists—proponents of intensive activity in the proletariat rather than in the middle class, with the stimulus of the strikes and the hope of a significant victory against the bourgeoisie by means of the general strike. The reform socialists reacted, and dissension and polemics followed. The syndicalists finally achieved a better understanding with the anarchists, through whose movement they brought greater aggressiveness to Brazil.[19] Edmondo Rossoni was of this breed, an inflexible activist who gave incendiary lectures to workers' groups, preaching "direct action" and the expropriation of the bourgeoisie. His name is linked in São Paulo with one of the most interesting left-wing movements—the movement of the "modern school," a great enthusiasm of Teresina's, who admired its founder Francisco Ferrer, the "victim of the priests," the renowned Spanish educator put to death by reactionary and clerical repression after the riots in Catalonia in 1909.

It is a question here of a pedagogic orientation that took education as the necessary base of social transformation. It recommended a rigorously lay education, in mixed classes, without religion, with a predominance of science, appealing to the initiative of students and creating attractive conditions of learning for them, with the idea of creating independent citizens not stuffed with preconceptions. At the same time, Ferrer preached the syndicalist organization of teachers and their solidarity with the workers' movement, as a logical consequence of the assumption according to which lay scientific instruction would necessarily lead to the desire to transform society.[20]

This was called the "modern," "free," "rationalist," or "rational" school, and, according to the socialists and anarchists of Brazil, it opposed not only religious education but also education by the state, the two, according to them, linked to one another. (In the bosom of this movement was trained a graphic artist of a more or less socialist orientation, Roldão Lopes de Barros, who was later one of the fighters for the New School in the twenties and thirties and who ended his career as as occupant of the chair in Philosophy of Education at the University of São Paulo.)

Rossoni participated vigorously in the movement, having been a teacher in the Rationalist School of Água Branca (founded and supported by the workers at the Santa Marina Glass Factory), whose students he appeared among in a photograph Teresina possessed. The clerical element of São Paulo (led, according to the radical newspaper *The Lantern*, by Asdrubal de Nascimento, a Papal count and owner of the Antartica Brewery) succeeded in closing the school and getting an order of expulsion against Rossoni in 1909.

Persecuted by order of the Secretary of the Interior, Washington Luis, Rossoni went into hiding for a while in friends' houses, including that of the Rocchis, finally settling in the house of the militant anarchist Benjamin Mota, director of *The Lantern*. Seeing himself encircled, he prepared himself with romantic dignity: he dressed in good clothes (as he liked to do), put on the flowing artist's cravat *La Vallière*, blue with gold dots, donned a large felt hat and, when they ordered him to prison, came out majestically carrying a bengal stick, for jail and banishment.[21]

Returned to Italy, he fought in 1914 and 1915 for entrance into the war, as did, in general, the anarchists, syndicalists, and the radical wing of the Socialist Party, led by Mussolini, of whom he was always a friend. Having a notable capacity for action and organization, he became, after the armistice, a syndicalist leader, well known as one of the directors of the Unione Italiana del Lavoro, of a syndicalist-revolutionary orientation, the smallest of the three big workers' federations, the others being the reformist Confederazione Generale del Lavoro, and the anarchist Unione Sindacale Italiana. Joining the Fascists, he took part in atttacks and demonstrations of force during the "heroic" phase, such as the capture of Genoa and of Massa. More than that, he rendered Mussolini inestimable service in organizing Fascist labor groups, giving the new regime a base it had not had until he assured it of a solid bridgehead in the labor sector, which was afterward enlarged by force. With his syndicalist experience, he contributed to the definition of corporativism, which was organized on the foundation of the Confederazione Nazionale dei Sindacati Fascisti (of which he was president) and presented itself legally in the Carta del Lavoro.

Throughout Mussolini's regime he saw action publicly as an active doctrinaire journalist, corporatist leader, and political director. He was a senator and, from its founding to the end, a member of the Great Fascist Council, the Holy of Holies of the regime, in whose dramatic session of July 25, 1943 he voted with the majority for the motion of Grandi, which overthrew the Duce. He was also a government minister more than once, including being minister of agriculture. In this connection, it is curious to mention that Ezra Pound admired his economic ideas and compared him to Confucius for his wisdom in agricultural matters.[22]

To see in the newspapers the story of the career of an old comrade in arms and his joining with the Fascists was inexplicable for Teresina. She was astonished and, in 1926, she wrote him asking what had happened, if the news was correct. Rossoni responded with this letter:

National Confederation
  of Fascist Unions

Rome March 1927
Piazza Colonna 136

The President

Dear Madame:

I was very pleased to receive your letter. The memory of you always brings me great pleasure, and I have had it in mind even through my peregrinations and in the small moments of truce in the hard battle fought in these last years.

I have always been the prey of an enormous amount of work. The corporations are the foundation of the fascist revolution. Italy is no longer recognizable. Everything is young, vibrant, dominated by a limitless will to power. We will triumph in many ordeals. I have ordered my daily newspaper and my magazine "La Stirpe" to be sent to you.

Think of me and receive a cordial salutation from your affectionate friend Edmondo Rossoni.

With no doubt remaining in the face of this piece of orthodox fascist phraseology, Teresina sent the following letter in reply:

Rossoni
You are a dog.

Teresina Carini Rocchi

Years afterward she wrote in her notebook: "*Frangor non flector*—I break but I don't bend—That's what Rossoni said in 1909. In 1912 [sic] he was a propagandist for the war; later a fascist, and now (1932) Minister!! O what a show!"

Vacillating De Ambris

Another political comrade, whose portrait hung in her parlor, was Alceste De Ambris, born in 1874 near Massa ("a blond son of Tuscany," his Brazilian friends called him, with the affectation of that time). A fugitive in Brazil because of his socialist ideas, he had a great capacity for agitation and was for a year, from 1900 to 1901, the first managing editor of *Avanti!* But he soon left it for radicalism, alleging as a pretext the desire to have more time for indoctrination. From the beginning, in articles signed *ada* (his initials in lowercase letters), he distinguished himself from the other editor, Bertolotti, by his radical stamp. Condemning reformism, and above all Bernstein, he accentuated the revolutionary nature of socialism, about which he gave, in January of 1901, an overly lengthy lecture of three and a quarter hours in the Lega della Democrazia. On giving notice that he had left the editorship (October 12–13, 1901), he attacked Turati in passing, provoking a note of defense, probably written by Bertolotti, which showed the tension within the group, as a reflex of the internal fight between the left and right wings of the Italian Socialist Party. Soon afterward, he published an interesting socialist almanac with excerpts, portraits, caricatures, and news and notes, all oriented toward indoctrination.[23]

In 1903 he left for Italy in order to avoid being imprisoned for libel (it was a matter of a violent article against a Mattarazzo, who was not, by the way, a member of the well-known family of that name, very powerful in the economic life of São Paulo). There, in 1907, he participated in the Third Conference of Socialist Youth in Bologna, as one of the leaders of the dissident, revolutionary syndicalist left wing, and the next year he led the big strike of rural farmworkers (*braccianti*) in the region of Parma, which made it necessary for him to leave the country again, first for Switzerland and then Brazil.[24] In this second stay he lived in São Paulo and also in Rio, where, in 1910, he started a paper called *La Scure* and worked in the Havas Agency, making friends with a group of Bohemian writers, including Olavo Bilac, on whom he may have imposed the vague, sentimental socialism he displayed at times. According to the testimony of Luis Edmundo, he was credulous and half disarmed in his good faith (which may have contributed to his later ideological deviations).[25] In 1911 he was in Europe for good, more precisely in Lugano, in Switzerland, where he published a pamphlet on immigration in America and where he awaited the possibility of being admitted to his own country, in which, in 1914, he fought, like Rossoni, for Italy's entering the war, including participating in a campaign of assemblies with writers of a more or less anarchist tendency, such as were at that time Lorenzo Viani, Ceccardo Roccatagliata-Ceccardi, and Giuseppe Ungaretti, who

10. Alceste de Ambris.

alluded to his calm in the midst of the furies of the multitudes, and to his ability to control them.[26] In 1915, he went to Paris with some fellow believers to ask for support from the French comrades. He returned carrying money that Jules Guesde, then minister, had given him to deliver to Mussolini as a contribution to his pro-war campaign.

The experience of the war, in which he participated as a soldier, developed in him a nationalist component that led him to move from the extreme left to the extreme right of socialism. "In May of 1917, the right-wing "interventionist" socialists had regrouped in the Socialist Italian Union (USI), a heterogenous group of reformists, autonomous socialists, dissidents from the Socialist Party, and revolutionary syndicalists like Alceste De Ambris."[27]

His behavior after the war was a good example of the ambiguities nascent fascism could stir up in a militant leftist. He participated on the margins of the movement, as a kind of comrade, despite quarrels with Mussolini because of differences with respect to tactics and the doctrine of workers' struggle. And Mussolini presented him to D'Annunzio, whom he accompanied in the political and military adventure of Fiume, where he had an important role as head of the Cabinet of the poet in arms, trying to influence him to give a workers' dimension to the movement. Others, like the old anarchist Enrico Malatesta, acted with the same intention—such was the confusion, such were the false trails and the unexpected possibilities of that most confused moment of all in the contemporary history of Italy. De Ambris was the principal editor of the programmatic document of that short-lived government of Fiume, the *Carta del Carnaro*, which launched the idea of corporative organization, which, without its authors intending it, became Mussolini's inspiration. D'Annunzio's adventure was, further, a sort of general rehearsal for fascism, above all with respect to theatrical display and jingoism. "Fiume . . . was also a training ground for Fascism, as was, similarly, the Spanish Civil War for World War II."[28]

But the truth is that, like the beginnings of fascism themselves, this adventure seemed to contain a certain socialist potential. D'Annunzio thought it convenient to contact the Russian and Hungarian soviets, and was sensitive, in his opportunism and incoherence, to the claims of the Left, in addition to which he wanted, for tactical reasons, the support of the workers' movement. After the Italian government dislodged him from Fiume, and the spectacular adventure was over, he went to his villa at Lago de Garda while Fascism, which had supported him briefly and then took the reins with greater efficiency, grew. Many thought then that his leadership of the Left was, in a sense, worthwhile. It seems that Lenin advised an alliance with him, and it is certain that the Soviet government tried an approach through Ambassador Tchitcherine. Various Italian Communist leaders had similar thoughts, including Gramsci, who nevertheless always distrusted him and never met him, though he still thought that D'Annunzio's movement had appreciable popular support.[29]

Seeing, in 1922, the preparations that were being made, De Ambris realized what was happening and tried with other comrades to convince the poet to put himself at the head of a large movement to defeat Mussolini and prevent his taking power. But this didn't work, and, following a failed attempt to get himself elected to the legislature, he went into exile in France. He lived in Marseille, where he published the book *Mussolini: La leggenda e l'uomo* (1927) and where he died in December of 1934, after taking part in the battle of the fugitive Italian socialists against fascism, to which he himself had come very near.

It is curious that his last book, published posthumously, could be about corporativism, whose plan he reclaimed, accusing Mussolini of having stolen and deformed it. In that book he also emphasized the role

of the moral element in social revolution and made an argument for
elites not based in privilege—all defining a strange syndicalist socialism
gone astray.[30]

The Weight and the Measure

This introduction to four of Teresina's political friends in São Paulo
demonstrates something that later occurred with many other militant
leftists in Italy: while the most radical, revolutionary syndicalists and extreme socialists, became fascists or were on the point of doing so, the
moderate reformists, most of the time, did just the opposite. In 1915,
for example, Bertolotti allied himself with the group from *Avanti!* in
São Paulo (second phase), who were ardently internationalist and
against the war and were virtually aligned with Rosa Luxemburg and
Karl Liebknecht, much cited and praised in the paper. It is, without
doubt, a problem worth confronting, trying to situate it in the context
of the times.

Rossoni renounced socialism; De Ambris, almost. What could have
passed through the heads of these agitators of syndicalist socialism, tired
of the compromising gradualism of the reformists, revolted by the egoism of the Great Powers in relation to their country, looking for a solution that was innovative, revolutionary, and national? Looking at it
today, it is easy to censure them and show what the right thing would
have been. But the fact is that while fascism was quickly evaluated properly by liberals and conscious socialists (including the former Communists Gramsci, Silone, Togliatti, and Tasca), in the beginning it was
ambiguous, as has been said here, and only the assassination of Mateotti
provided the decisive argument for categorizing it as a reactionary dictatorship of the Right.

Today, that precocious opposition of many reformists is considered
a manifestation, then, of the true socialist attitude, while the adherence
of the revolutionary syndicalists to fascism is seen as an incomprehen-
sible treason. Nevertheless, if we put ourselves in the perspective of the
time, the opposition of the former perhaps owes less to socialist reason
than it does to a liberal type of reaction (a reaction characteristic of the
liberalism embedded in reformism) in the face of a kind of heterodox and half-savage socialism (as fascism might initially have seemed),
which threatened to overthrow the rules of the parliamentary routine.
With the passage of time, this opposition has gained, retrospectively, an
elevated tone of socialist coherence that it perhaps did not have in the
beginning.

On the other hand, among the revolutionary socialists, eager for
action, open to violence, suspicious of the quasi-liberal reformists, and

furthermore surrounded by the rhetoric of fascist populism that, it is important to remember, appeared to be the product of a radical socialist wing, those of a revolutionary stamp could have thought that Mussolini's movement was a plausible alternative, an unexpected way of arriving at the desired ends. As late as 1925, Il Duce seemed to have thought seriously of capturing his old coreligionists, in part because of a certain nostalgia for his origins. Thus, it can be supposed that it was perhaps because they professed an active and demanding socialism that many, paradoxically, sailed on that sinister ship.

The dividing line, and thus the definitive judgment on political conduct, must be put later, after the assassination of Mateotti. After the results of the trial and Mussolini's dictatorial hardening in 1926, with the hard line of Fascism dealing the cards, doubt was no longer possible. Those who continued with him, like Rossoni, were in fact renegades. Those who pulled back in time, like De Ambris, could recover their political dignity. That is why Teresina sent, at the right moment, that ferocious note to one and kept the portrait of the other in her living room. She knew how to evaluate correctly the highways and the dead ends of the old, Italian inspired socialism of São Paulo.

NOTES

First published as "Teresina e os seus amigos" in *Teresina etc.* (São Paulo: Editora Paz e Terra, 1980), pp. 13–73.

1. Thus, we see that Albertina was the half sister of Napoleon II and the cousin of three emperors, her mother's nephews: Pedro II of Brazil, Franz Joseph of Austria, and Maximilian of Mexico.

2. On the important frescos of Parmiggianino in the Rocca, see Enrico Bodmer, *Il Corregio e gli Emiliani* (Novara: De Agostini, 1943), p. xxvi. In the same book, p. xxviii, there is an analysis of two admirable portraits by him: a count and countess Sanvitale, now in the Prado, in Madrid.

3. After her marriage her official name was Teresa Maria Carini Rocchi. She herself always used the diminutive as a name, signing herself Teresina Carini, Teresina Rocchi or Teresina Carini Rocchi. In Brazil people called her Dona Teresa, Dona Teresina, or Dona Teresinha.

4. [The excerpts from the writings of Teresina and her relatives were translated by Antonio Candido from the Italian into Portuguese. I have translated them here from the Portuguese. HSB]

5. [This is an interlingual joke. Candido notes that the word *tirare* in Italian means to pull, in this case to pull the violin bow across the strings. In Portuguese the appropriate word would be *puxar*, since *tirar* would mean to remove it altogether. Guido misunderstood it that way. HSB]

6. Cited in Piercarlo Masini, *Eresie dell'Ottocento: Alle sorgente laiche, umaniste e libertarie della democrazia italiana* (Milan: Editoriale Nuova, 1978), p. 288.

7. Teresina refers here to the slaughter of the First World War, which was then in its second year.

8. [I asked Profesor Candido to explain *novorra*. This is what he said: "I don't know what 'novorra' is. Perhaps it was an idiom of the time, or a word in local use, which the dictionaries did not record. I imagine that it could be a neologism, formed from 'nuova Camorra,' the Camorra being the Neapolitan Mafia." HSB]

9. This refers to the million fascists.

10. When Teresina received this letter, Mussolini was already in power, having arrived there on October 31, 1922.

11. One of his articles is reproduced in Edgard Carone, *O movimento operário no Brasil (1877–1944)* (São Paulo: Difel, 1979), pp. 474–77.

12. Ibid., 471.

13. Ibid., 327.

14. On Bertolotti, see: Franco Cenni, *Italianos no Brasil: "Andiamo in 'Merica . . ."* (São Paulo: Martins, n.d.); Boris Fausto, *Trabalho urbano e conflito social (1890–1920)* (São Paulo and Rio de Janeiro: Difel, 1976); and the newspaper *Avanti!* above all in its first phase.

15. Edgard Carone, *A Republica Velha (instituições e classes sociais)*, 2nd ed. (São Paulo, Difel, 1972), p. 206. Read the document and the analysis he makes of Piccarolo's writing.

16. See, on his participation, alongside other notables of the time, Sociedade de Cultura Artística, *Conferências, 1914–1915* (São Paulo, 1916).

17. See *Boletim da Faculdade Paulista de Letras e Filosofia*, São Paulo, 1934, which was given to me by the secretary of the institution, Dr. João Guilherme de Oliveira Costa, whom I thank for this information.

18. Antonio Piccarolo, *O socialismo no Brasil: Esboço de um programa de ação socialista*, 3rd ed. (São Paulo: Piratininga, [1932], passim. For more on Piccarolo, see also: Fausto, *Trabalho*, and Cenni, *Italianos no Brasil*.

19. See the polemic article in *Avanti!* September 3, 1908, which explains the reformist positions and attacks the anarcho-syndicalists, reprinted in Edgard Carone, *Movimento operário no Brasil*, pp. 218–20.

20. See the presentation made under the pressure of events in *Un martyr des prêtres—Francisco Ferrer (10 janvier 1859–13 octobre 1909)—Sa vie, son oeuvre*, Comité de Défense des Victimes do la Répression Espagnole (Paris: Schleicher Frères, n.d.).

21. See the indignant notice in *The Lantern* volume 4, number 7, November 29, 1909, under the title: "Infamy: The expulsion of Rossoni," for the communication of which I thank Edgard Carone. The account of how he was detained was told to me many times by Teresina.

22. On Rossoni, see Jacob Penteado, *Belenzinho, 1910 (Retrato de uma época)* (São Paulo: Martins, 1962); Angelo Tasca, *Naissance du Fascisme: L'Italie de l'Armistice à la Marche sur Rome* (Paris: Gallimard, 1967); Ernst Nolte, *Three Faces of Fascism: Action Française, Italian Fascism, National Socialism* (New York: Holt, Rinehart, Winston, 1966); Ezra Pound, *Guide to Kulchur* (London: Peter Owen, 1952); Giorgio Pini e Duilio Susmel, *Mussolini: L'uomo e l'opera*, 4 vols., 2nd ed. (Florence: La Fenice, 1957).

23. *Almanacco socialista pel 1902*, Alceste De Ambrys, ed. (São Paulo, Riedel and Lemmi, 1902). When he lived in Brazil he spelled his last name with a *y*.

24. Renzo de Felice *apud* Paulo Sergio Pinheiro, and Michael M. Hall, *A classe operária no Brasil: Documentos (1889 a 1930)*, vol. 1, *O movimento operário* (São Paulo: Alfa Omega, 1979), p. 34; Paul Guichonnet, "Le socialisme italien des origines à 1914," in Jacques Droz, ed., *Histoire générale du socialisme*, 4 vols., (Paris: Presses Universitaires de France, 1972–78), v. 2, pp. 271–72.

25. Pinheiro and Hall, *op. cit.*, *loc. cit.*; Luis Edmundo, *O Rio de Janeiro do meu tempo,* 3 vols. (Rio de Janeiro: Imprensa Nacional, 1938), v. 2, pp. 659–63.

26. Leone Piccioni, *Vita di un poeta: Giuseppe Ungaretti* (Milan: Rizzoli, 1970), p. 59.

27. Paul Guichonnet, "Le socialisme italien," in Jacques Droz, ed., *Histoire générale du socialisme*, vol. 3, p. 177.

28. Sir Ivone Kirkpatrick, *Mussolini: Ensaio sobre a demagogia* (Lisbon: Morais, 1965), p. 101.

The writer and consul Afonso Lopes de Almeida, who at the time was part of the Brazilian delegation to the Peace Conference, went to Fiume to interview D'Annunzio and told of the experience in a hyperbolic book: *O gênio rebelado* (Rio de Janeiro: Anuário do Brasil, 1923). At the opposite ideological pole, Lima Barreto dealt, more clearly and with great sarcasm, with the martial adventure of the poet, whom he called Rapagnetta (which he said was his real name). See "D'Annunzio e Lenine," January 8, 1921, *Feiras e mafuás*, 2nd ed. (São Paulo: Brasiliense, 1961), pp. 202–7.

29. Salvatore Romano, *Antonio Gramsci* (Turin: UTET, 1965), pp. 453–59.

30. On De Ambris, see, in addition to the works cited the newspaper *Avanti!* in its first phase; Kirkpatrick, *op. cit.*; Nolte, *op. cit.*; Idem, *La crisi dei regimi liberali e i movimenti fascisti* (Bologna: Il Molino, 1970); Pini and Susmel, *op. cit.* Of his own work, see: *Dopo un ventennio di rivoluzione: Il corporativismo* (Bordeaux: A. Mione, 1935).

INDEX

Acevedo Díaz, Eduardo, 137
Achebe, Chinua, 123
Alegría, Ciro, 138
Alencar, José, 98–99, 100, 137, 143–144
Almeida, Manuel Antônio de, xiv, 79–103
Almeida, Pires, 127
Amado, Jorge, 130, 137, 138
Ambris, Alceste de, 187–190
Andrade, Carlos Drummond de, 131
Andrade, Mário de, 32, 79–80, 83, 87, 132, 134, 157
Andrade, Oswald de, 98, 132, 134
anthropology, xvii
Aranha, Graça, 107
Arguedas, Alcides, 138
Arguedas, José María, 137
art and society, ix-xiv
Assis, Machado de, xxi–xxii, 62, 104–118, 131–132, 139; archaicism and modernity of, 109–110; psychological interpretation of, 108; sociological interpretation of, 108–10; style of, 106–107, 109–110
Asturias, Miguel Ángel, 138
Auerbach, Erich, 150 Avanti!, 180–183
Azevedo, Aluísio, 149
Azuela, Mariano, 138

backwardness, 128–129, 135
Badalassi, Dr., 177
Balzac, Honoré de, 5, 7, 9, 10, 13, 14, 75–76, 115
Bastide, Roger, xvii, 109, 117
Baudelaire, Charles, 15
Beljame, Alexandre, 148
Bertolotti, Alcibiade, 180–181
Bonfim, Manuel, 125
Borges, Jorge Luis, 105, 131, 132
Bourdieu, Pierre, ix
bourgeoisie, xiii, 10, 86
Bourget, Paul, 106
Brazil, xiv–xvi, 85–87, 95–102; scholarly tradition of, xv-xvi
Brazilian Academy of Letters, 104–105, 135
Brierly, Captain, 37–41
Bruford, W. F., 147

Brunschvig, Henri, 147
Buarque de Holanda, Sérgio, xv
Buzatti, Dino, 53–64
Byron, Lord, 7–9

Cabrera Infante, 134
Calderón, Francisco Garcia, 128
Caldwell, Helen, 112
Camus, Albert, 105, 112
Candido, Antonio, ix–x; analytic style of, xii–xiv, childhood, xvi–xvii; political activity, xviii–xix; teaching career, xvii; university training, xvii; world writer, xx–xxii; writing style, xix–xx
Carini, Teresa Maria (Teresina), 152–193; anticlericalism, 165–167; appearance and personality, 159–163; equality, sentiment of, 161; family of, 152–154, 166–167; house of, 160; married to Guido Rocchi, 154, 157–159; militancy, 167–169; old age of, 172–176; socialism of, 163–165
Carone, Edgard, 179
Carpeaux, Otto Maria, 150
Carpentier, Alejo, 137, 140
Carvalho, Elísio de, 129
Castro Alves, 120, 126, 147
Caudwell, Christopher, 148
Cavafy, Constantine, 45–49
Chamisso, Adalbert von, 110
Chekhov, Anton, 147
choice, 113–114
Citizen Kane, 18
class, ruling, 87, 95
Classicism, 11
Conrad, Joseph, 22–44, 66, 112, 113
Cortázar, Julio, 134, 140
Costa, Cláudio Manuel da, 127
country, 120; "new," 121; "underdeveloped," 121
cowboy hero, 124
cruelty, 116
Cunha, Euclides da, xv, 109

Damasceno, Darcy, 79
D'Annunzio, Gabriele, 127, 129, 188–189

Darío, Rubén, 127, 130
death, 40–42, 53, 57–58, 61–62
dependency, 134
Dickens, Charles, xii, 13, 104, 150
disenchantment, 62
disincorporation, 59–60
documentary, 86–89, 149
Döblin, Alfred, 133
Dom Pedro II, Emperor of Brazil, 85, 125
Dostoyevsky, Fyodor, 25–26, 31, 36,
    43n.9, 76, 104, 108, 110, 114
Dumas, Alexandre, xii–xiii, 3–21, 26
Durkheim, Émile, ix

"enlightened" ideology, 125–129
Escarpit, Robert, 146
Escola Livre de Sociologia e Política (Free
    School of Sociology and Politics), 183
espionage, 66
Estève, Edmond, 147

Farrell, James, xi
Fascism, 169–172, 185–186
Faulkner, William, 105, 110, 133
Ferri, Enrico, 178
Flaubert, Gustave, 109
Fogazzaro, Antonio, 106
folklore, 83–84, 123–124
Forster, E. M., 111
fragmentation, 34, 37–39, 48–53
France, Anatole, 106, 107, 129
Frankfurt School, ix
Freire, Gilberto, xv
Freitas, Maria Theresa de, 66, 71
Freud, Sigmund, 114

Gallegos, Romula, 137
García Marquez, Gabriel, 137
Geiger, Theodor, 147
gentleman, 28–29
Gide, André, 110, 114
Gnocchi-Viani, Osvaldo, 164
Goldmann, Lucien, 150
Gomes, Alfredo, 157–158
Gonçalves de Crespo, 10
González, Pedro, 134
Gracq, Julien, 31, 65–74
Gramsci, Antonio, 21n.3, 148
Grosz, George, 138
Guillemin, A. M., 147
Guillén, Nicolás, 137
Guimaraens, Alphonsus de, 128

Guimarães Rosa, João, 137, 139, 140
Gûiraldes, Ricardo, 137

Hardy, Thomas, 136
Hawthorne, Nathaniel, 99
heights and depths; geographical, 3–6, 53;
    social, xiv, 10, 12–13, 51, 82, 90
Hennion, Antoine, xii
Hernández, José, 137
Hower, Alfred, 112
Hughes, Everett C., xiv
Hugo, Victor, 5, 13, 75
Huidobro, Vicente, 128, 132
Humanitism, 115

Icaza, Jorge, 138
identity, 110–112
Iliad, 10
illiteracy, 121–122, 125
incorporation, 53–57
individualism, 10, 19
influences (on literature), 124, 126–134;
    internal and external, 142–151
interdependency, cultural, 133–134
islands, 3
isolation, 18, 24–25, 53

Joyce, James, 26, 30, 105, 133

Kafka, Franz, xi, 30, 49–53, 76, 105, 110,
    114
Kazantzakis, Nikos, 136
Kettle, Arnold, 150
Knights, L. C., 146

labor force, 87, 95
language, xiv–xv, xxi–xxii
Lari, Santina, 176
Leavis, Q. D., 147
Leuenroth, Edgard, 174, 177
Lima, Heitor Ferreira, 147
Lima, Jorge de, 137
Lima, Lezama, 134
Lispector, Clarice, 140
Lorca, Federico García, 136
Lord Jim, xiv, 26–27, 34–42
Lukács, Georg, 143, 148, 149

malandro, 79–103
Mannheim, Karl, 147
man surprised, 24, 26–28
Manuel, Cláudío, 6

Manzoni, Alessandro, 149
Maquet, Auguste, 6
Maritain, Jacques, 34
Marlow, 23, 37, 41, 43–44n.10, 43–
    44n.12
mass culture, 123–125
Matos, Mário, 108
Maugüé, Jean, xvii
meaning, 112–113
Mello, Mário Vieira de, 119
Meol Neto, João Cabral de, 131
Mendes, Murilo, 131
metaphor, 66, 71–73
Meyer, Augusto, 108, 110, 117
Miguel-Pereira, Lúcia, 108, 113
Milliet, Sérgio, 128
Modernism (Brazilian), 131
"Modernism" (Spanish), 130–131
Monegal, Rodríguez, 134
money, 3, 17
Montello, Josué, 80
morality, 114
mother countries, relation of Latin-Ameri-
    can writers to, 127–134
Mussolini, Benito, 185, 188

Nabuco, Joaquim, 127
Napoleon, 4, 75, 164
nature, 120

Obligado, Rafael, 120
occasion, 24–26
order and disorder, 89–96
Orientalism, 8, 48, 65
"Outpost of Progress, An," 28–29, 33

Paes, José Paulo, 47
Park, Robert E., xv
Peirara, Astrojildo, 109
Peixoto, Afránio, 129
Petri, Elio, 77–78
picaresque genre, 12, 80–83
Picasso, Pablo, 30
Piccarolo, Antonio, 177, 181–184
Pirandello, Luigi, 31, 108
Poços de Caldas, 158–159, 167–169
police, 68, 75–78, 93
Prince Roman, 29–30
prolixity of style, 7, 9
Proust, Marcel, 4, 26, 36, 104, 105, 110,
    112, 133
Providence, 9–10

publics, 122–123
Pujol, Alfredo, 107

Queirós, Eça de, 106

Ramos, Graciliano, 32, 130, 137, 139
realism, 86–89, 95–96, 112
reflection theory, x–xi, 147
regionalism, 135–140
Rego, José Lins de, 130, 138
Reyles, Carlos, 137
Richardson, Dorothy, 133
Roa Bastos, Augusto, 137
Rocchi, Guido, 155–157
Romanticism, 4–6, 11, 13–14, 16–19, 46,
    71, 119–120, 130, 132, 139
Romero, Silvio, 146
Rossoni, Edmondo, 184–186
Rulfo, Juan, 140

samurai, 124
San Martín, Juan Zorilla de, 128
São Paulo, 177–180; University of, 109
Sartre, Jean-Paul, 112
Schücking, Lewin, 147
sea, 6, 22, 68
"Secret Sharer, The," 31–33
self, 31–34
Senghor, Léopold Sendar, 123
serial music, 30
sertanejismo, 137
slaves, 87
socialism, 177–191; in Brazil, 177–180
sociology, xvii–xviii, 145–151
Sousa, Inglês de, 136
Stendhal, xi, 4, 7, 9, 10
Sterne, Laurence, 109
Sutherland, J. H., xii

Taine, Hippolyte Adolphe, ix, 146, 147
Tavares de Pinho, Adelino, 176–177
Thackeray, William Makepeace, xii
Thompson, George, 148
torture, 19, 116
Toscanini, Arturo, 155–156

Unamuno, Miguel, 26
underdevelopment, 119–141
Ureña, Pedro Henríquez, 119

Valera, Juan, 130
Valéry, 131

Vargas Llosa, Mario, 133, 136, 140
vengeance, 11–18
Venice, 66, 75
Verdi, Giuseppe, 93
Verga, Giovanni, 136
Veríssimo, José, 79, 136
Viana, Javier de, 137
Vieira, Antônio, 119
Vigny, Alfred de, 15, 18, 78
Vittorini, Elio, 136
Volpe, Galvano della, 148

Voltaire, 109

Warner, W. Lloyd, xi
Weber, Alfred, 126
Weber, J. P., 149
Weber, Max, ix, xi
Wilde, Oscar, 129
Wilson, Edmund, xxi
Woolf, Virginia, 133

Zola, Emile, xii, 106, 109, 115